THE VERMONT PAPERS

THE VERMONT PAPERS

Recreating Democracy on a Human Scale

Frank Bryan
John McClaughry

Chelsea Green Publishing Company
Chelsea, Vermont 05038

Printed in the United States of America
First printing, March 1989

Library of Congress Cataloging-in-Publication Data

Bryan, Frank M.
    The Vermont papers : recreating democracy on a human scale /
by Frank Bryan & John McClaughry.
        p.   cm.
    Bibliography: p.
    Includes index.
    ISBN 0-930031-19-9 (alk. paper) : $18.95
    1. Vermont – Politics and government.   2. Political participation – Vermont.
    3. Democracy.   I. McClaughry, John.   II. Title.
JK3095.B79   1989
320.9743 – dc19   89-569
                                                        CIP

Dedication

This book is dedicated to the memory of Ethan Allen and all those hardscrabble Vermonters who, in his tradition, and through their cussedness and liberal vision, have worked to preserve real democracy in Vermont for over two hundred years.

Acknowledgments

We wish to thank the following people for their help. Some read parts of the manuscript, others helped us with their encouragement and counsel: Susan Achenbach, Ian and Margo Baldwin, Albert W. Barney, Hamilton Davis, Wayne Dyer, Daniel Elazar, Fritz Gaenslen, Robert B. Hawkins Jr., Warren Johnson, Bill Paine, and Bob Taylor. I (John McClaughry) would like to thank the John M. Olin Foundation for its financial support. I (Frank Bryan) would like to thank the students in my graduate seminar in state administration and the undergraduate honors seminar in the Department of Political Science at the University of Vermont for their helpful comments and criticisms. Both of us are deeply indebted to Melissa Bryan, who did all the typing through three drafts and the editing. She also suffered through the complications that only those who have shepherded a manuscript through to completion can fully appreciate.

"If the spirit of liberty should vanish in other parts of the union and support of our institutions should languish, it could all be replenished from the generous store held by the people of this brave little state of Vermont."

Calvin Coolidge

"There is no more Yankee than Polynesian in me, but when I go to Vermont, I feel like I am traveling toward my own place."

Bernard DeVoto

CONTENTS

Chapter 1

VIEWING THE PASTURE SPRING

You cannot run away from a weakness
You must some time fight it out or perish
And if that be so, why not now?
And where you stand?

        —Robert Louis Stevenson

F OR all its inspiring success, the American dream still lies beyond our reach.

America stands as a beacon to liberty, democracy, and community. But that tradition is under challenge from the forces of centralized power. Those forces have never wholly succeeded, but neither have they been decisively repelled. That task still lies ahead. The little green-clad state of Vermont may well become the place to show America how liberty, democracy, and community can be restored.

We live on dirt roads in the back country of northern New England. As this book goes to print, the shadows of November's sun lie flat on the face of the land. Birds gather against the sky, and the orange needles of the tamaracks fall silently onto the forest floor. None of this has changed in two hundred years. Vermonters have treated this land with relative care. True, like others, we have slashed and hacked and gouged and spilled and spewed. Yet here the planet still breathes as it spins through the galaxy. So far at least Mother Earth has pardoned our sins. So far she has repaired herself. You sense that watching a chickadee sass the cold at twenty below.

There is no such forgiveness in human affairs. There is no self-repair. Like dawn through a drizzle a vision is forming across the political horizon – the specter of a government that no longer works. Senator Daniel Moynihan said it succinctly in his book on Lyndon Johnson's "War on Poverty," *Maximum Feasible Misunderstanding*, published twenty years ago. "The government," he said, "did not know what it was doing." Things have gotten worse since then. Much worse.

Presidential elections have become empty and even disgusting spectacles avoided by those best prepared to lead. National election campaigns today are an issueless soap opera feasting on scandals and trivia. Their language is the language of horse races or of sports commentators awaiting the next play. The news media have become enamored of campaign tactics and bored with substance. They hype the process month after month, insulting the people with their inflated speculations, usually couched in terms of intrigue and deceit – anything to keep the viewer's fingers off the remote-control button.

Meanwhile the voters, dismayed, are opting out. If the Gross National Product had fallen the way voter turnout has since 1960, there would be panic in the streets. The most poignant bumper sticker of 1984 was gallows humor: VOTE FOR MONDALE. AT LEAST YOU'LL LIVE TO REGRET IT. Curtis B. Gans of the Committee of the American Electorate wrote in 1987 in *Public Opinion*: "The central and perhaps greatest single problem of the American polity is . . . the degree to which the vital underpinnings of American democracy are being eroded . . . the level of political participation is now sinking and the decline seems irreversible." A year later in 1988, the percentage of eligible voters in America that went to the polls to vote for president (and the thousands of other national, state, and local offices up for election) barely reached 50 percent, the lowest since 1928.

Back at the grass roots the people have barricaded themselves in interest groups as insurance against defeat in the one or two areas where government action is most important to them. Political parties, once healthy, decentralized, and citizen-based, have become too weak to provide coherence and direction. Congress stumbles along, deferring decisions right and left to the courts and the bureaucracy. The president faces incessant attack by the electronic media, which are more interested in scoring points than in informing the public on key matters of governance. Washington seems more and more remote and irrelevant. The danger is that it is remote but *not* irrelevant.

National political leaders seem to have a sense that something is amiss, but they lack the understanding to identify the solution or do anything about it if they could identify it. For the solution must push up from below, like wild violets through the dark earth in springtime.

Historian Barry D. Karl puts our condition in brilliant perspective. Centralism may have been necessary at a point in our history, he concedes, but now it has "severed our contacts with the more familiar state and local governments" and has "threatened our sense of ourselves as citizens." No one has better expressed the paradox of politics in the post-modern period: "At a moment in history when the technology of communications is improving by quantum leaps, our suspicions of the truth of what we are told and what we know are greater than they have ever been. These suspicions have their source in our oldest and most profound need: our need to govern ourselves."

The collapse of the American center is a manifestation of a vanishing democracy in the heartland. Jefferson, as Hannah Arendt pointed out, had a "foreboding of how dangerous it might be to allow a people a share in public power without providing them at the same time with more public space than the ballot box and more opportunity to make their own voice heard in public than election day." Jefferson's fears were justified. As the watersheds of community democracy are sucked dry, the rivers of citizenship that fed our great national institutions grow ever more shallow, and the American republic is withering away.

In short the republic cannot survive without representative bodies that are credible and competent. Representation is founded on citizenship. But citizens cannot be factory-built or found in electronic villages. They must be raised at home. That rearing takes place in real polities: places where community and politics meet, where individuals learn the *habit* of democracy face to face, where decision making takes place in the context of communal interdependence.

This then is the great American challenge of the twenty-first century: saving the center by shoring up its parts, preserving union by emphasizing disunion, making cosmopolitanism possible by making parochialism necessary, restoring the representative republic by rebuilding direct democracy, strengthening the national character through a rebirth of local citizenship.

Over the past quarter-century there have been many recommendations to save American politics, but they have been mainly cosmetic and superficial, like giving smelling salts to a fighter whose legs have gone. We propose to return to where the roots of democracy are still firmly established and nourish them into new life. We propose to focus on a place where citizenship still lives, where a small pastureland of liberty and community of the kind America so desperately needs still lies intact. There we propose to build a new, resurgent twenty-first-century politics of human scale. As that promising place which will inspire all America, we suggest Vermont.

A Pasture Spring

Vermont is physically in the past and technologically in the future. It leapfrogged America's urban-industrial period and landed smack in the Information Age. It is still green. Unfettered by the baggage of urban-industrialism and free of the problems associated with it, Vermont nevertheless is among the leading states on measure after measure of technological maturity. On every side those that live here are struck by the fusion of past and future. We can touch the ingenuity of our ancestors. We can imagine the merging of old values and new technologies.

Vermont is an ideal setting, too, because it is still a governable place. With half a million people scattered over a granite wedge of field and forest about twice the size of Connecticut, it is small enough to meet the concept of a manageable polity. Vermont can't save the world, but it can save itself and by its example show America how to get its democracy back. Working things out in a small place first is far preferable to banging one's head against the wall in a larger system. Vermont matters most *because* it is small, not in spite of it.

Moreover today there is no other place in America where the battle for liberty, lost elsewhere, is still as fiercely waged as in Vermont. Vermont democracy is under attack from the same forces that have undercut democracy throughout the nation. But they are far less formidable here, in part because they are far more visible. The juxtaposition of freedom and authority in Vermont is always striking. For Vermont, with its tiny state capital (still the smallest in America with 8,241 people), with its town meetings, its citizen legislature, its two-year term for governor, has preserved the institutions and traditions of liberty and community. Because of its unique historical circumstances Vermont has a rare opportunity to breathe new life into its democracy.

The Vermont Papers is a call for rediscovering homeland, for turning about. It is an exhortation to think grandly on a small scale, to have faith in little things, to pause and explore a modern place of human dimensions. A former poet laureate of Vermont, Robert Frost, caught the sense of this faith when he wrote as the preface to his first and

4

most famous volume of poems, *North of Boston*:

> I'm going out to clean the pasture spring;
> I'll only stop to rake the leaves away
> (And wait to watch the water clear, I may):
> I shan't be gone long. – You come too.

America still has a pasture spring in Vermont, a place where it is possible to rake the leaves away and wait to watch the water clear. This is our invitation.

Where We Stand

This is a book about how Vermont can save its democracy and in so doing demonstrate how the rest of America might learn to recreate its own. It calls for radical change – the most complete restructuring of an American state in two hundred years. Democracy is too precious, and the forces aligned against it too powerful, for timid measures. In the words of Ernest Callenbach, "If democracy is such a good idea, the time has come to try it." It is, and we shall. We take democracy seriously.

Liberty and democracy are the stars that guide us. New advances in information technology are the ship we sail. The wind at our back is a faith in the common person. Norman Cousins had it right when, after cataloging the lessons he had learned in a long life exploring the human condition, he wrote in *Human Options*, "The most important single lesson I have learned, therefore, is that human capacity is what it has to be." We have the capacity to renew America, and it is time to begin.

Who are we to try it now? One of us is a writer who has served in Vermont's House of Representatives, worked as Senior Policy Advisor in the Reagan White House, and was recently elected to the Vermont Senate. He claims as his proudest political achievement twenty-two elections as moderator of the town of Kirby (population 282), in Vermont's Northeast Kingdom. The other is a professor who teaches political science at the University of Vermont and has written two books about Vermont politics. He lives in a converted deer camp on Big Hollow Road in Starksboro, a mountain town of 1,336 people.

Our values are libertarian in the face of authority, decentralist in the face of giantism, and communal among our townspeople. We were country when country wasn't cool. We were serious about town meet-

5

ing democracy when town meetings were considered anachronisms. Most of all we want to bring power home from centralized institutions and distribute it widely among the people. In 1983 one of us wrote: "What is wrong is the creation of great concentrations of power that can manipulate government for their special advantage – an advantage that frequently benefits the privileged few who control those interests at the expense of the rank and file in whose name the influence is wielded."

Good Fences Make Good Neighbors

Lest our neighbor's pines work their way into our orchard, our first chore is to clear up a few problems of language.

You Can't Get There from Here

First of all we believe the liberal/conservative definition is a black hole in the universe of ideas. Liberals and conservatives agree that mega-bureaucracy is fundamentally dehumanizing and destructive of civilization. Earlier the Left correctly abhorred it in the private sector, and the Right correctly abhorred it in the public sector. Now both the Left and the Right are beginning to realize that the evil of large, centralized bureaucracy transcends the sector that theoretically controls it. Harry Boyte (*The Backyard Revolution*, 1980) writes: ". . . the strong theme throughout [the new citizen's movement] is to challenge public bureaucracy as directly as it challenges corporate plunder."

The new movement afoot in America is neither Left nor Right, liberal nor conservative, Democratic nor Republican. It is an ideological bridge to a new future. On this bridge one will find people whose politics have differed – many of them combatants in the past – who now seek together a global society of just, peaceful, and dutiful human communities. The story is told in Vermont of the stranger who stops a Vermonter to ask directions to Burlington and is told, after a thoughtful interlude during which several alternative routes are considered and then rejected, "If I were going to Burlington, I wouldn't start from here." If those who seek a new commonwealth of liberty and virtue insist on packing themselves into the same old ideological vehicles, we have a similar response for them.

Loving Comes from Hoeing

A second conceptual trap that needs avoiding is the one set by the term "environmentalist." We want desperately to keep the planet clean, but we are *not* interested in the color people paint their houses, how many junk cars they have in the front yard, or whether their kid is trying to raise twenty Rhode Island Reds in the back. If the term "environmentalist" triggers visions of movie stars protecting baby seals or romantics extolling the virtues of noble savages or rural gentry protecting the hinterland for their own exclusive recreation, then we urge a redefinition. Humans are not just another species. As Carl Becker has said: "The significance of man is that he is insignificant and is aware of it." Thus we see the human race at the center of our world with responsibility for its care. In large part we are followers of the poet Wendell Berry; we are environmentalists of use. One small farmer whose subsistence depends on his plowed fields is worth a thousand armchair protectionists proclaiming concern about the problems of soil erosion. Work, discipline, intelligence, and commitment are what is needed. Berry puts it this way:

> I am talking about the idea that as many as possible should share in the ownership of the land and thus be bound to it by economic enterprise, by investment of love and work, by family loyalty, by memory and tradition. . . . It [this idea] proposes an economy of necessities rather than an economy based on anxiety, fantasy, luxury, and idle wishing. It proposes the independent, free standing citizenry that Jefferson thought to be the surest safeguard of democratic liberty. And perhaps most important of all, it proposes an agriculture based upon intensive work, local energies, care, and long-living communities.

Our environmentalism features work not dreams. When the counterculture movement hit Vermont in the late 1960s, we can remember commune dwellers happily planting corn in the spring and settling back to love it and let Nature take its course. They did and Nature did. By fall the corn was nowhere to be seen – nor were the people who planted it. They were long on vision and short on character. In protecting one's garden plot as with protecting the planet, loving follows hoeing.

Technopeasants and Technolords

Technology is to our era what machines were to the industrial period. Today's technology processes information just as the machines of yesteryear processed raw materials. And just as advancing industrial technology gave rise to thinkers who deplored technology itself, and as information technology becomes more and more important, a predictable reaction has developed against it. Authors and others who see technology as an uncontrollable tail wagging the body of society we call "technophobes."

Many technophobes have been concerned not so much with technology as with who controls it. They warn of the clustering of technology in the hands of "technolords," and they call for the democratization of information technology.

Meanwhile a profoundly important event has taken place. Third-generation computer technology, driven by the integrated-circuit chip, has heralded a new technological revolution. The micro-computer is both a metaphor and an indispensable tool for a new and immensely hopeful movement toward a decentralized polity. The pathways to the old centralized "computer centers" in universities all over America have become choked with weeds. More important, that undergrad in the tee-shirt and dirty jeans, that quintessential technolord who ran the "input-output" room, is gone forever. He has been replaced by briefcase computers blinking out regression equations in one's lap 30,000 feet over the Rockies. Throughout America's industrial revolution decentralism gave way to centralism. In the revolution brought on by computers and information technology decentralism is ascendant.

All this is fairly well known around the campfires of futurists, but the notion that decentralists and environmentalists (and we count ourselves both) are caught up in the technophobes' crusade to bring back the horse and buggy days still dominates popular culture in America. We pose it as the third conceptual trap to sidestep if one is to avoid precluding options for the future.

Getting Down to Business

The Vermont Papers is an unusual book in several ways. First of all in its setting: it treats one of the states instead of a town, city, or neighborhood. Most books on political reform in America concentrate on a single community. Secondly in its method: this is not merely a theoretical model. It is as well both a plan and an appeal for action, and begs the reader's involvement as such. In the jargon of the computer this is a "real-time" book. Thirdly in its aspiration: we have written it with the question in mind, "How will the new Vermont really work, and how will we defend the outcome when it is set in place?" Finally our book is different in its ambition: this is not a book about legislatures, or parties, or governors, or public policy. It is a book that proposes nothing less than a wholly redesigned structure of government. We see a threat to our liberty, and to combat it we seek fundamental reform – real change – in the *architecture* of politics.

The first part of the book places our plan in context. In Part I we explain the philosophical underpinnings of our position ("The Gods of the Hills"). This is followed by a chapter which shows how Vermont fostered and maintained democratic values and how Vermont's history predicts a future of human-scale democracy (Chapter 3: "The Leapfrog Theory"). The next chapter treats the nature of the social virus threatening Vermont now, the same virus that has brought most of American democracy to its knees; it is called "The Promise of Democracy Denied." Chapter 5 outlines the trends in Vermont that can restore the promise of democracy.

Part II of the book puts our plan in place and defends it. Chapters 6, 7, and 8 are called "The Shires: Government with a Human Face," "The Shires: Architecture for a New Democracy," and "Celebrating Shire Identity." Chapter 9 outlines the role the state government will play after the shires have been created.

Part III treats five specific policy areas (finance, education, welfare, land, and agriculture) in the context of Vermont's new federation of shires. "No State Is an Island" deals with the relationships between a new, truly democratic Vermont and the other American states, regions of the country, the federal government, and the rest of the planet. The last chapter ("Getting from Here to There") presents the political framework in which the transformation to a federation of shires can occur.

As we Vermonters restore our liberty, community, and democracy, perhaps others will learn from us. Our dream is that Vermont will meet its own challenge and thereby provide the nation with the hope it now so desperately needs. We must summon our will and genius to answer an incandescent question for America: If democracy cannot succeed in Vermont, where can it?

Part I
Vermont: Cradle
for a
New Democracy

Chapter 2

THE GODS OF
THE HILLS

*The Genius of Vermont was fruitful in
resources; even in the gulph of difficulties
and on the verge of ruin she waxed strong,
extended her wings, and made herself
known among the nations of the earth.*
— Ira Allen

THE year was 1770 — to the men who had hoped to settle in
the inviting lands of the Green Mountains, a year of dark
foreboding. They had land grants from the governor of New
Hampshire, Benning Wentworth. But Wentworth was far away, the
right of New Hampshire to grant the lands was not at all certain, and
those in control of the government of the Colony of New York were
determined that the New Hampshire Grants, comprising much of what
is modern-day Vermont, belonged to New York, and could be settled
only by men bearing New York title.

Josiah Carpenter, a New Hampshire grantee in the town of Shaftsbury, had been served with ejectment papers by a Yorker sheriff and
was summoned to Albany to stand trial. Justice, Yorker style, was swift.
Carpenter, the court summarily found, had no right or title to his farm.
He was told to get off or be thrown in jail. It was obvious that Albany's
legal profession, its judges, its sheriffs, and its great landowners were
working smoothly together to make sure that Vermont farmers would
pay their price — or be driven away.

Assisting Carpenter's defense counsel in the trial at Albany was
that magnificent, brawling, boozing, blasphemous giant, Ethan Allen,
recently arrived in the grants. The Yorker land barons rightly had some

12

apprehensions about what angry farmers led by such a man might do to disrupt the King's peace. They recalled, for instance, that when their Yorker sheriff arrived two years earlier to dispossess a New Hampshire Grants farmer named John Breakenridge, a large number of the victim's neighbors had rather ominously appeared "to help him harvest his corn." The neighbors, curiously, had brought long rifles to help in the harvest process, and when called upon to disperse in the name of the King and the Colony of New York, they had shown a marked reluctance to comply. In fact they sat on tree stumps, spit on the ground, and made some rather truculent conjectures about the future health of the New York visitors. Breakenridge's last remark to the Yorkers, before they packed up and retreated empty-handed to the west, was also ominous: "I hope you will not try to take any advantage of us, for our people do not understand law."

To forestall just such trouble, two of the most accomplished Albany land jobbers, Attorney General John Tabor Kempe and James Duane, a prominent lawyer, decided to seek out this Green Mountain rustic and try to enlist his influence on their side of the matter. They came to Allen at his tavern as he was preparing to return to report to the Hampshire Grants landowners assembled in Bennington.

At first the Yorkers were suave and considerate. They told Allen that all this conflict was really unnecessary. If only someone held in high repute by the "Bennington Mob" – himself, for instance – were to go back and counsel the New Hampshire claimants correctly, all might be worked out agreeably to the rightful owners in Albany without undue disturbance. He who accomplished this, they made it clear, would be in the way of receiving a large land grant for his services in the cause of peace and harmony. But if things went on as they were going, Kempe and Duane observed darkly, the rightful owners, with might as well as right on their side, would find it necessary to eject the squatters by force.

Ethan Allen may have been unlettered in the law. He was certainly, as the historian Walter Crockett later observed, "not distinguished for modesty or refinement." But he knew at once what was being proposed to him. He looked Kempe in the eye and replied with the cryptic but compelling line that has echoed down through two centuries of Vermont history: "Sir, the gods of the hills are not the gods of the valleys." Historian Richard Carlson, referring to Allen's reference to the "gods of the hills," put it simply and well: "If every society needs to possess a mythical moment of creation, this is Vermont's."

13

No, the gods of the Vermont hills are not the gods of the Hudson Valley, or of the flatlands and the cities to the south. For Vermont, from its unique circumstances and from the character of its early leaders, developed a unique set of values. Those values, both social and political, have come down to us through history, even as the economics and culture of the state have experienced drastic change. They exist in that dim region just below our consciousness, unrecognized and unseen but always living. They are there, flowing through the centuries, as the subterranean waters have coursed since time began through the limestones of Danby and Proctor. On rare occasions they bubble up, like Cold Boiling Spring at the foot of Wheeler Mountain in Westmore, to shape our perceptions and influence the choices that Vermonters make about their society's future.

One such occasion occurred more than a century and a half after the Allen-Yorker faceoff. In 1935, in the depths of the Great Depression, Vermont's most famous statesman, George Aiken, issued his own version of the gods of the hills. The situation was the same. A great central government was trying to con and bully Vermont into swapping liberty for gold.

Short of stature, mild of manner, and soft of tone, Aiken, then lieutenant governor and soon to become governor, was in many ways the antithesis of Ethan Allen. He made his mark raising wildflowers, not applying floggings to Albany sheriffs. But on one dimension they were exactly alike: they both understood the code. Allen acted to save Vermont from the Colony of New York. Aiken acted to save Vermont from the government of the United States. Allen spoke his words in a bar in Albany; Aiken wrote his in a book, *Speaking from Vermont.*

In the summer of 1934 agents of Washington moved into Vermont with the intention of buying up "submarginal land" and transferring the people on this land down into the valley towns where they would be given federal loans to get started on new farms. How much of Vermont did they try to buy? Fifty-five percent!

The agents from Washington hit a snag almost immediately: the mountain people didn't want to sell. Aiken: ". . . then the boys from Washington resorted to other means by which to get options on the land. They told them that if they did not sell to the government, schools and roads in these areas would be given up and they would be left in isolation." Threats and lies: the muskets of twentieth century tyranny, the way the big control the small, the rich the poor, the cities the country.

14

With individual land purchases not going well, officers of the Resettlement Administration came to the Vermont legislature in Montpelier in the winter of 1935 to try for a package deal. Aiken: "Such a display of flattery—attorneys, theorists, scientists, doctors of all degrees—converged on us. We should have been honored. This was February, and usually federal officials arrange to do their work in Vermont between June and October."

The argument of the federal administrators was old and, one must imagine, tiresome for the Vermonters in Montpelier. Worse, it was couched in insult. It was an insult Ethan Allen would have recognized. Aiken: "They placed before the members of the Legislature the astonishing story that, not only were these people in certain areas of the State very unhappy because of their condition, but that the State itself was very unhappy because such people existed in such areas. Vermont was very, very sick. It would continue to be sick until fifty-five percent of its area had been transferred to Federal control; What of the fact that the people in the areas concerned did not care to be moved from their homes? Well, possibly these people weren't of high enough mental capacity to understand that they really were unhappy."

Aiken and his colleagues kept their humor. A committee was appointed to confer with the federal officials. Aiken notes irony in the fact that he himself, who lived on a very submarginal farm, was named to the committee. He continues: "There was a bit more irony in this legislative action in making the Speaker of the House a member of the board, for the legislators knew that the Speaker lived comfortably in an area which was rated as a hundred percent submarginal for twenty miles in all directions from his home." What the federal authorities didn't realize, of course, is that a majority of Vermont's House of Representatives lived in submarginal areas and so evidently were not of sufficient "mental capacity" to understand how unhappy they were. That is why "The Vermont legislators exchanged strange looks on hearing the story from Washington. Some of them indulged in sly grins. Others maintained poker faces. The majority kept tongues in their cheeks. But all listened courteously."

The final offer worked out by the federal government was that Vermont would turn over half the state to it. Recreation and forest areas would be created. And more. Aiken: "Miles of road would be abandoned, relieving the State and towns of the necessity of keeping them repaired. Schools could be abandoned, saving more expense." The federal government would then turn its 55 percent of Vermont back to the state on a long-term lease, retaining all rights over minerals and other natural products. Aiken: "All the state had to do to take advantage of the munificent offer was to agree that it would maintain and operate these areas in such manner as the Federal authorities might direct and pay the expenses of maintenance forever." Then Aiken adds: "And also that we would never again permit any of this land to be occupied as homes." He then pauses to begin a new paragraph—a short, blunt, one-line paragraph: "The Federal government did not buy any submarginal land in Vermont."

Aiken understood what was meant by "the gods of the hills are not the gods of the valleys." He summed up:

> Why do folks live in the hills? Why do they persist in clinging to steep, rocky slopes and in living under conditions which modern humanitarianism says can only produce unhappiness for them, when some of them, at least, have the means to move out and go elsewhere and go in debt all over just like other folks? The reason is that some folks just naturally love the mountains, and like to live up among them where freedom of thought and action is logical and inherent.
>
> I look off to the east and see Mount Monadnock rearing its peak through the clouds. Tonight the lights of the neighbors' houses twinkle in friendliness and neighborliness from a dozen locations. Some of these neighboring houses are better than mine, some of them not quite so good. None of us would willingly move away.

These are the words of a man who accepts the covenant established by Ethan Allen: freedom in the context of neighborliness; liberty *and* community—the gods of the hills.

Two decades after the Resettlement Administration imbroglio, when McCarthyism was at white heat in the valleys of America, things were calm up in the hills of Vermont. Nevertheless a former congressman, Charles Plumley, got the anticommunist jitters. He convinced a neighbor to introduce a bill in the Vermont legislature creating a state board to ensure that school books were free of subversive intent.

Vermont's House of Representatives at the time had a legislator from each town. There were 246 of them, representing less than 400,000 people—about 1,500 men, women, and children per member. When the bill got to the floor—that infamous bastion of "conservatives" representing what the progressives of the time were calling "rotten boroughs"—it faced the judgment of 84 farmers, 35 housewives, and 20 blue-collar workers (among others). Over half the members had been born in the nineteenth century. Less than 40 percent had a college education. Only 25 of the 246 called themselves Democrats. More important, only about a quarter of them were out-of-staters. If ever there was a legislature which, according to the urban-based elite in America, would exhibit the reactionary pathologies they assumed were festering in the rural backwaters of the nation, this was it. Yet when the time for voting came, the roll call was: McCarthy 11, Hillbillies 202. There would be no censorship committee established to review textbooks. And that was that. The gods of the hills had spoken.

Another twenty-five years passed. Once again federal officials visited Vermont in search of land, and again there was bubbling in the deep waters of Vermont's consciousness. This time the feds were looking only for a small parcel for a very specific purpose – a nuclear-waste dump. At Blue Mountain High School in the town of Newbury (population 1,699) two thousand people came down from the hills and jammed themselves into the auditorium for a public hearing. The federal officials were very, very kind and understanding. No, the chances were slim that a dump would be located in Vermont and, yes, they understood how Vermonters felt about the issue.

After a prolonged period of give and take, questions and answers, there came a point when the visitors had been pushed ever so gently against a wall of argumentation which, quite irrationally of course, went as follows: "We don't care what you say, just keep the hell out of Vermont." One federal representative, with great care and patience, explained the notion of national sovereignty and then suggested, with an I'm-sorry-to-have-to-remind-you smile, that if Washington wanted the land and Vermont didn't cooperate, the federal government could, after all, simply, well . . . take it.

There followed a moment of dead silence, the packed audience of two thousand was seemingly checkmated. Then, from deep in the bleachers a commoner's hoarse cry crashed toward the podium. "Hey, have you guys ever heard of Ethan Allen and the Green Mountain Boys?" The roar (half laughter, half defiance) that followed originated deep in centuries past. Every soul in the gymnasium understood at once. They were Vermonters, and when push comes to shove the gods of the hills, still, were not the gods of the valleys. The covenant holds. (The dump ended up in Nevada.)

Specifically, what are the values of the covenant? Perhaps it was George Aiken who provided the best summary. "The first ideal that prompted the settlement of Vermont was the love of liberty," said the governor in 1938. "And it is this love of liberty that today prompts Vermont to revolt against the approach toward that type of centralized government which history has so often proven undesirable." Their love of liberty, coupled with their belief in self-reliance, thrift, and genuine liberalism, said Aiken, "have inspired Vermonters to the greatest, most satisfying of all ideals – self respect."

The values that shaped Vermont's covenant with democracy, although unique in many ways, did not lack antecedents. To fully understand the world view of the men and women who came north and west into the wilderness of the New Hampshire Grants around the time of the American Revolution, it is necessary to go back half a millennium and more, to the field at Runnymede where in 1215 the imperious King John was forced to grant rights to freeborn Englishmen.

To be sure, the Englishmen who forced John to sign the Magna Carta were not what one would call ordinary citizens. They were barons, ranking just below the king in the feudal order. They did not see themselves as spokesmen for their villeins, franklins, and serfs. And yet the concessions they wrung out of their sovereign laid the framework for the development of the English scheme of ordered liberty which is that "scepter'd isle's" grandest contribution to human civilization.

From that historic encounter came the affirmation of ideals which in our time became the security of the freeman's liberty and property against invasion by the government and affirmed his right to trial before an impartial judge, with a verdict given by a jury of his peers. In the Magna Carta, too, are found the seeds of the principles that there may be no tax levied but by the consent of the people, and that no ruler may stand above the law.

Other long-forgotten provisions of the Magna Carta related to administration of the forest laws. The descendants of William the Conqueror had a nasty habit of claiming large tracts – at one point, one third of all England – as the king's personal forest, and woe unto the honest yeoman who went thither in pursuit of a wounded hart or lost swine. The Magna Carta forced John to relinquish claim to all forests taken by him since the time of Henry II, twenty-five years earlier, and repealed the "bad customs" which excluded the people from common lands that were rightfully theirs and not the Crown's.

The spirit of Saxon liberty, which began to flourish within the *tunscipes* (townships) and shires before the Norman Conquest, grew fitfully after the Magna Carta, flamed bright in the seventeenth-century resistance to Stuart despotism, and glowed from the pages of Locke and Harrington and the English Bill of Rights. That spirit came with Englishmen to the New World, and it was highly concentrated among those who were to become Vermonters. These people had come from Connecticut, Massachusetts, and New Hampshire, where they had learned the virtues of liberty and self-government in the town meetings and justice courts of those colonies. They well knew the dangers of centralized power and resented the Crown's infringement upon the rights of freeborn Englishmen. And they believed that one developed to one's fullest not only when one's enterprise was given full scope to prosper, but when one actively took part in the public life of the community.

Because the early Vermonters were willing to pack up and leave more comfortable places to civilize a wilderness, they also had the values and virtues of pioneers everywhere. Jealous regard for their liberties. A willingness to fight if necessary to defend their right of private property ownership. Rugged independence of thought and action. Self-reliance tempered with the willingness to come to the aid of the common good.

Such people, clawing out a toehold on a wild frontier, did not spend their evenings poring over Locke's theory of the social contract, but in their hearts, placed there by a tradition stretching back over centuries of English heritage, was a deep understanding of the essentials of republican liberty. The foundation of this heritage was in the sanctity of freehold property. Every man was to be an owner of his own property, from which he provided the sustenance of his own family, property which could not be invaded by others without his consent nor taken from him but through due process of law, and then only with just compensation. Every man was to be a citizen, in the fullest sense of the word: not only a voter, but an active and responsible participant in the public life of his community, as selectman, constable, juror, or fence viewer. And every citizen was to be a defender of the independence of the town meeting, the descendant of the *mark-moot* and *shire-moot*, "the chief council of the ancient nation who possessed the district in independence" in the Saxon England of a thousand years before.

Unknown to all but the most scholarly of the early Vermonters, this way of thinking about life, rights, duties, and the public good had been given eloquent expression in the seminal work of James

Harrington, whose masterpiece, *The Commonwealth of Oceana*, appeared in 1656 in England. *Oceana* gave force and illustration to an Anglo-American form of what historians of ideas call "classical republicanism" or "civic humanism."

Civic humanism is the affirmation that the good and virtuous society is one in which all individuals have the opportunity to develop their powers and talents toward a self-fulfillment which benefits all. It is called "humanism" not because it scorns religious values, but because it is concerned with the growth and development of men and women in the here and now, and not with their preparation for eternity. It is called "civic" because it looks to the civic arena – beginning with the neighborhood, the precinct, the polis, and in our instance the town – as the locus of virtuous activity.

To one with this habit of mind, it is essential that each individual, to be truly human and lead a life of virtue, must take part in public life as a fully autonomous being. Autonomy, and thus virtue, rests upon a material foundation. Each person should possess and control the means of his sustenance, a principle which underlies the institution of privately owned property. The ideal Harringtonian form of property is the self-sufficient freehold estate in land.

But "property," in the language of civic humanism, had a somewhat different meaning from what the term implies today. To Harrington, and to Thomas Jefferson after him, property had a moral connotation. It implied the personal and moral supervision of a responsible freeholder. Obviously the kind of property that lends itself to this description is not a portfolio of stock certificates, but land – productive land, homestead land, the "mean and sure estate." The concept carried with it a sense of place, of continuity, of preservation, of improvement, of personal sovereignty, of sufficiency without excess. The idea of a huge estate existing amid the hovels of hundreds of poverty-stricken peasants denied access to land and sustenance was a horror to the civic humanist.

Of equal horror, however, was the incubus of feudalism, land not held in fee simple, but held with the permission of a superior. Feudal tenures constricted autonomy. They bound each vassal to the will of a superior lord – effective perhaps, for public administration and the raising of armies, but wholly destructive of the flourishing of virtue. Hence, Jefferson's and Madison's determined and successful fight to abolish the feudal remnants of primogeniture and entail in Virginia, and Jefferson's unsuccessful proposal to endow each white male turning twenty-one with fifty acres of the state's public domain.

The civic-humanist view of the virtuous society cast the individual not only as freeholder but as warrior. The model was the legionary of the Roman republic – the yeoman farmer who, like Cincinnatus, set aside his plow for the sword when his country was in peril. The civic humanist expected the landholder to defend his republic. This implied universal service, at least of freeholding males, a militia of the sort created in the earliest days of New England and built upon the idea of the ancient Saxon *fyrd*.

But lest anyone leap to the conclusion that the civic humanist favored universal conscription, it should be pointed out that there is a world of difference between a people's army, in which service is a duty freely accepted along with citizenship, and a professional standing army, which uses the power of the state to force hapless youths to serve or go to jail. The civic humanists viewed this latter force as no more than a tool of tyranny, supporting itself by plunder and, as the instrument of rapacious kings, threatening the liberties of the people of its own country.

A strong local militia, on the modern Swiss model, is fully compatible with the civic-humanist ideal, but the mass conscript armies of a Napoleon, a Stalin, even a Westmoreland, would be viewed as contrary to the spirit of a free society and dangerous to its liberties. Witness Article 16th of the Vermont Constitution: "The people have a right to bear arms for the defense of themselves and the State – and as standing armies in time of peace are dangerous to liberty, they ought not to be kept up; and that the military should be kept under strict subordination to and governed by the civil power."

There is a final ingredient to this civic-humanist vision of the immortal republic: the proposition that human virtue cannot be attained without participation in civic life. This communalist spirit and the morality associated with it separates the traditional liberal interpretation of American political thought and the civic-humanist model. In a great nation only a relative few can participate in the councils of state – holding public office and sharing in the administration of justice, to use Aristotle's criteria for participation. Therefore, if virtue is to pervade the society, as many public decisions as possible must be made by the broadest range of citizens possible, and they must be made at a level as close as possible to citizens' daily experience. To Aristotle, the precursor of civic humanism (and for that matter, to Lao Tzu), the ideal place to do the work of public life was the small city or polis. To Jefferson it was the ward republic. As Hannah Arendt has observed, Jefferson constantly feared the corruption of the American revolutionary experiment by a government guilty of "generalizing and concentrating all cares and powers into one body," rather than dispersing them throughout the polity.

The goal of the republic, Jefferson wrote, was "to make each person feel that he is a participator in the government of affairs, not merely at an election one day in the year, but every day; when there shall not be a man in the state who will not be a member of some one of its councils, great or small, he will let his heart be torn out of his body sooner than his power wrested from him by a Caesar or a Bonaparte."

This civic-humanist view of the virtuous society, built around the growing, enterprising, achieving, contributing individual as freeholder, warrior, and citizen, carried with it, though implicitly, a strong bias toward preserving the life of the small community and cooperating with fellow citizens at the local level to create workable, human-scale institutions of civic betterment. A young Massachusetts congressman named John F. Kennedy, long before he rose to national fame, perfectly expressed the civic-humanist ideal when he told the Italian American Club of Boston that "only by doing the work ourselves, only by giving generously out of our own pockets, can we hope in the long run to maintain the authority of the people over the state, to ensure that the people remain the master, the state the servant. Every time we try to lift a problem from our own shoulders, and shift that problem to the hands of the government, to the same extent we are sacrificing the liberties of our people."

It is worth briefly considering what the civic humanist viewed as the ultimate horror: a state characterized by the opposite of virtue – corruption. To the civic humanist corruption meant more than the existence of venal public officials. It meant a society where individuals were denied the opportunity to develop their talents toward self-fulfillment and the public good.

In the corrupt state political rule is held and controlled by a few. Decisions are made by an elite, in elite councils. The leaders give the citizens – or rather, the subjects – all necessary instructions, which must be obeyed. The state, or a few individuals virtually synonymous with the state, have supreme control of property, as in feudal times. Wealth and thus power are concentrated, not dispersed. Heavy taxation burdens the artisan, mechanic, farmer, and honest working man. Everyone is subservient to the central power, in whatever form it might take.

22

The powerful few use the state, as Marx charged, to create privilege for themselves. The state manipulates debt, legitimizes monopoly, systematically debases the currency, and stifles the activity
of a free people. Such a state can be expected to engage in foreign
adventures, paid for with the blood and treasure of a populace which
desires only peace and the fruits of industry. A powerful military and
police apparatus – composed of persons wholly dependent upon the
state that employs them – keeps that populace in line. Giantism is the
rule in such a society, and with the rule of giantism, the dream of the
civic humanist must perish.

In our time, interestingly enough, no more powerful attack on this
corrupt giantism has been voiced than that of the pre-presidential
Ronald Reagan. Said he, in a major Chicago address in 1975:

> I am calling for an end to giantism, for a return to the human
> scale – the scale that human beings can understand and cope with;
> the scale of the local fraternal lodge, the church congregation, the
> block club, the farm bureau. It is the locally owned factory, the small
> businessman who personally deals with his customers and stands
> behind his product, the farm and consumer cooperative, the town
> or neighborhood bank that invests in the community, the union
> local. In government, the human scale is the town council, the board
> of selectmen, and the precinct captain.
>
> It is this activity on a small human scale that creates the fabric
> of community, a framework for the creation of abundance and
> liberty. The human scale nurtures standards of right behavior,
> a prevailing ethic of what is right and wrong, acceptable and
> unacceptable.

It is tempting to inquire whatever became of the fellow who said those
words, after he became president of the United States.

The theoreticians of civic humanism, from Aristotle and Polybius
on, feared that the balanced, free republic would inevitably become
unbalanced and degenerate into monarchy, aristocracy, or anar-
chy. "The best instituted governments," wrote Lord Bolingbroke in
eighteenth-century England, "like the best constituted animal bodies,
carry in them the seeds of their dissolution. . . . All that can be done,
therefore, to prolong the duration of good government is to draw it
back, on every favorable occasion, to the first good principles on which
it was founded."

If this language sounds familiar to some Vermonters, it is because
it so strongly resembles Article 18th of the Vermont Constitution of

1777: "Frequent recurrence to fundamental principles, and a firm adherence to justice, moderation, temperance, industry and frugality, are absolutely necessary to preserve the blessings of liberty, and keep government free." Indeed, the Vermont Constitution, particularly Chapter I, reads today like a textbook of civic-humanist, Jeffersonian-republican principles.

The American civic humanists, like their British forebears of the 1600s, constantly feared the onset of civic corruption, which would doom their proud and hopeful American experiment. In the first decade of the new nation they constantly viewed with alarm many features of the evolving Federalist system, particularly the vices exhibited by both Alexander Hamilton and John Adams. The Federalists were quick to confer titles on public officials, a practice smacking of a new nobility. They showed little interest in the problem of inequality of wealth and viewed with scarcely concealed gloating (particularly in the case of Hamilton) every trend toward a nation where a few owned the bulk of the wealth and the dispossessed did their bidding. The Federalists wanted a standing army. They created Hamilton's Bank of the United States to unite the monied commercial interests with the government. They accepted the national debt not as an unfortunate legacy to be erased as soon as possible, but as a device for the profitable manipulation of "paper wealth" by what the Republicans of that era called "the stock-jobbing crowd." They were constantly devising new taxes to burden the farmer and craftsman of the hinterlands—the whiskey excise being the most notorious.

Nowhere were Federalist policies viewed with more horror than in the Green Mountains of Vermont. Though the mention of "civic humanism" might have drawn blank looks, the early Vermonters instinctively held civic-humanist values and abhorred their corruption. They were in a new land, and they had a magnificent opportunity to create a new, clean republic that just might be able to avoid the corruption that had destroyed so many earlier experiments.

And so the values of this political tradition, reaching back to Saxon England even before the Magna Carta, flowered once again amid the Green Mountains. Over the years of Vermont's existence they have persisted. Vermonters' abiding love of their own hillsides and valleys, their reverence for the land as the anchor for their spiritual existence, their disdain for the haughty and dishonest, their respect for diversity of opinion and eccentricity of behavior, their willingness to defend their God-given liberties, their hostility to the central power, whatever it may be, their attachment to their towns and schools and local communities, their dedication to common enterprise for the common good – all these have been among the most cherished Vermont traits, the subject of countless eulogies of Vermont tradition over the years.

The question today, however, is not whether we should once again celebrate these ancient values – of course we should. Our celebration, however, must be more than an empty exercise, like an atheist's singing hymns. The question is whether there is hope for recreating the Jeffersonian civic-humanist republic of Vermont in an age when the forces of centralism and giantism seem to be so strongly ascendant. Will Vermont become little more than a distant rural suburb of urban, mass-media America? Or can it remain something unique – a civic society which has consciously determined to reshape its traditional values even as its people participate in a twenty-first-century economy and society?

We believe that the Vermont tradition still runs strong and deep. We believe, further, that unlike old traditions which deserve to disappear, like leeching to cure a fever, the historic Vermont tradition does offer us a useful guide for shaping our future, even in an era radically different from that in which it first took root. The applications of Vermont's historic principles may change, indeed, must change; but the principles themselves live on undimmed. Our forebears chose well when they chose the gods of the hills. We cannot, we should not, sell out our principles and values to the successors to the Yorker land grabbers of 1770. To do so, to kneel at the altar of the gods of the valleys, would be more than treason to a great cause. It would be treason to all America, whose future successes may well depend upon emulating the kind of Vermont we have it within our power to shape and build.

Chapter 3

THE LEAPFROG
THEORY

Two roads diverged in a wood, and I—
I took the one less traveled by,
And that has made all the difference.
  —Robert Frost

V ERMONT never had what most Americans are longing to
    be rid of. Over its bedrock of civic humanism has developed
    a unique set of historical circumstances that pivot around
one critical event: Vermont leapfrogged urban-industrialism, ignoring the astounding transformation of American society that took place
in the years between 1840 and 1940. The result is a state that is already
free and clear of the twentieth century.

When historian Arnold Toynbee said Vermont was above the
"optimum climatic area of the United States," he identified the key
to the threshold on which the state now finds itself. Because Vermont
endured the later nineteenth and early twentieth centuries as a great
"dark age" (as it is called by historians), its task now is one of preserving a society of human scale. In that part of America where the vast
majority of the people live, by contrast, the task is to rebuild a society
of little places where people can see themselves in their government
and their government in them.

Turning the key to Vermont's future, however, requires a second
understanding, one less appreciated: while sitting out the urban-
industrial revolution, Vermont remained in the mainstream of America's technological advancement. Indeed, as historians of science are

now discovering, technology has never been limited to cities in America. Hard living in the cold encourages the habit of "working smart" that Vermonters have always known. The perception that they worked hard is true. But the perception that they didn't *need* to and did so only because they rejected modernism or were prisoners of the Protestant Ethic is a mistake. Vermonters adopted new technologies as fast as circumstances allowed and created their own at a rate far faster than their tiny population would predict.

In short Vermont combines state-of-the-art technological development with an environment not fashioned after urban-industrialism. The result is a society with a far more progressive potential than those primarily concerned with struggling to overcome the burdens left over from the earlier period. By way of illustration, this little, cold, rural state, perceived in the national consciousness as backward, conservative, and populated by weather-beaten Yankees with an eye on the hereafter, has over the last decade scored among the top five states on two interesting statistics: the percentage of its work force employed in high-tech industries and the average SAT scores of its high-school graduates.

Vermont's story is best told in four episodes, each making its own contribution to the thesis of a regenerative democracy. A traumatic birth under fire and the emergence of the independent Republic of Vermont (1763–91) established a profound sense of polity which will give Vermont the ability to act as it must in the coming years. A dynamic half-century of growth, radicalism, and innovation (1791–1840) established Vermont's progressive traditions so evident today: entrepreneurialism, a tolerance of eccentricity, a deep-seated commitment to human rights, and faith in technology.

Then came a century or so of massive out-migration (1840–1950). Vermont stood aside as the rest of America rushed headlong into the urban-industrial revolution. Yet under the cover of this great dark age, we preserved our liberalism and our democratic institutions. Only recently, of course, has it been possible to suggest that such a period of no growth could be a contribution in itself. The recent historical period (1950 to the present) has contributed both a new wave of settlement (which has revitalized rural Vermont) and a new high-tech infrastructure, the latter supported not only by the newcomer but also by Vermont's own disposition.

The result of Vermont's peculiar history is a state relatively free of the baggage of the old urban-industrial condition and advanced in those areas critical to post-modern society. This confounds the current wisdom that metro-industralism is a *precondition* of technological progress. What can happen in Vermont if we pay attention to the opportunity history offers is no less than revolutionary.

Born Free

In its first quarter-century, Vermont conducted armed skirmishes against New York, battled the British, independently negotiated with them (well before Yorktown ended the war), absconded with a tier of New Hampshire's western border towns, gave them back, annexed part of New York, and reclaimed some of New Hampshire. Finally in 1791 Vermont joined the Union as the fourteenth state.

Sort of. Vermont writer Vrest Orton in a letter to Judson Hale of *Yankee* magazine explained it this way: "You must remember that Vermont was *never* a colony of Great Britain." In 1777 Vermont declared itself "to be an independent, sovereign Republic or Commonwealth. Then, when we entered the Federal Union (a colossal mistake) in 1791, we became the 14th state." One of the most important points Orton makes has been often overlooked by historians. "All five of the other New England states had a period of aristocratic oligarchy. We didn't. All Vermonters were middle-class, hard-working, and young! No other state was like that."

Historian Frederic F. Van De Water: "The land also taught its people democracy. . . . Vermonters established an almost casteless society based on rigors commonly shared." In effect the settlement of Vermont had in its relationship to the colonies many of the qualities that the settlement of the colonies had in their relationship to Britain. As America's *first frontier*, Vermont combined the egalitarianism associated with the nineteenth-century westward movement with the brash ideological radicalism of the late eighteenth century. It was a mix of geographical and intellectual influences not found elsewhere in American development.

Vermont was slapped into life during a thunderstorm. The delegates to Vermont's constitutional convention at Windsor were actually proceeding with the last reading of the document on July 8, 1777, when word came that Ticonderoga, the most important fort on America's northern frontier, had fallen, and western Vermont lay exposed to General Burgoyne and his Indians. Pandemonium broke loose. The convention was about to dissolve when the storm struck. In the few moments it took for the deluge to abate, the final reading was completed, the Vermont Constitution was accepted, and the Republic of Vermont was born. Then, as historian Earle Newton puts it, "The delegates from over the mountains . . . dashed off to the westward." They left behind a fundamental law for Vermont unequaled in its liberalism by the constitution of any other American state.

Throughout this period Vermont created its folk hero, Ethan Allen, the most underrated revolutionary in American history, who once wrote the president of the Continental Congress (during the time Vermont was an independent republic): "I am as resolutely determined to defend the independence of Vermont as Congress are that of the United States, and rather than fail will retire with the hardy Green Mountain Boys into the desolate caverns of the mountains and wage war with human nature at large." Allen's statue now stands by the doorway to the statehouse in Montpelier as well as in the halls of the United States Congress. He is Vermont's George Washington; the person who, more than any other, helped create our image of ourselves and our concept of Vermont as a unique polity.

Ethan Allen may not have possessed the fighting skill of a Robert Rogers, but he came close. There is no doubt he was a hard-drinking rascal. Given the tenor of the times Allen might be termed "nonviolent," since no one was ever killed by him or his Green Mountain Boys, even though at their hands property was destroyed, floggings were amply applied, and people were regularly run out of town. Allen distinguished himself in the Revolution by capturing the largest British fort in North America (the same Ticonderoga), with about seventy men. It was the first major offensive action against the Crown by the colonists.

Allen also had an original mind. His book *Reason: The Only Oracle of Man* was a substantial work, and as a pamphleteer he had great influence throughout New England. Herman Melville writes of Allen in a sketch entitled *Samson among the Philistines* as "a man of Patagonian stature . . . whose defiant head overshadowed theirs, as St. Paul's dome, its inferior steeples." There was, said George Washington of Ethan Allen, "an original something in him that commands admiration."

Why our preoccupation with Ethan Allen? Because Vermont has been preoccupied by Ethan Allen. Vermont can be a twenty-first-century model for the nation because it has what Daniel Elazar calls a "civic culture" of shared norms and self-consciousness. It has a special history. It has heroes like Ethan Allen. This is the stuff on which communities thrive. Our history is a backdrop against which we can act, not just talk. Ethan (real Vermonters still call him by his first name) was the prime mover in our living history. We were an independent republic. We did coin our own money. We did establish our own post office. We did conduct foreign policy. We did elect our own president, Thomas Chittenden. We did adopt and still have in force the first constitution to outlaw slavery, provide for universal manhood suffrage, and require just compensation when private property is taken for public use. We are the only state of the fifty that can point to armed involvement in the Revolutionary War as a free and independent nation. Vermont was never a colony of an empire, never a territory of a central power, never a province of some distant authority. We were born free, and we lived free, and when we finally did join the United States we did it surrounded by options, with our eyes open and our hearts full of joy.

Outwardly the Vermont republic seemed hellbent for liberty at any cost. Inwardly it agonized over the question of freedom (we liked being independent) and unity (we liked the idea of union with our brethren in the colonies). Our constitution was copied after Pennsylvania's, and our first name was New Connecticut. In the end Vermonters balanced the notions of freedom and union by deferment, a trick nature teaches. They decided to "live with it" much as they would a boulder in the middle of the plowed ground. They even flaunted it. This puzzling contradiction became the state motto: "Freedom and Unity."

Vermont's wild beginning, its intellectual traditions following the radicals Paine, Franklin, and Young, and most of all its posture as the renegade republic of the north (coveting and then annexing its neighbors' towns, thumbing its nose at the Congress, negotiating a separate peace with Canada) set in place a self-portrait of individualism that no other state (save, perhaps, Texas) can match.

Yet the imperatives of Vermont's geography then as now are equally important to its identity. For Vermont is a place of ups and downs. Its land seems to cluster people in little communities by nature. The winters are cold, the coldest in New England. The snow comes early and lasts and lasts and lasts. The soil is rocky, the living tough. Vermont's geography contained a dual imperative: it cradled settlements and it made living difficult.

So Vermonters, harkening to humankind's basic need for cooperation, came to huddle together like the Swiss in small communities, mountain towns and villages. They sought the safety of unity, of Congregationalism, of neighbor, church, and town. Their spirits craved liberty, but the land compelled union. That is why Vermont's ethic does not mesh well with the rolling, big-sky libertarianism of the High Plains West.

Vermonters have kept an eye on liberty by maintaining a seemingly irrational proliferation of neighborhood and community. If others were going to tell them what to do, at least those others would be close enough to be called by their first name or grabbed by the scruff of the neck. Thus the twin forces of history and geography created a felicitous blend of liberty and community where citizens can thoroughly know a good portion of the people with whom they share common, thus public, interests.

Vermont's civic identity, outlined above, was more or less settled by the end of the eighteenth century. The towns were in place, statehood had been achieved, and the tension between liberty and community had been reconciled. The most important outcome of the "seed time" of the Vermont republic was the emergence of polity, that self-conscious identity of a people with its past – its heroes, its villains, its accomplishments and failures. Vermonters must now harken back to that time and act as boldly and freely as they did then. If there never had been a Republic of Vermont, it is doubtful what this book proposes could even be considered.

Wilderness Cosmopolitanism (1791–1840)

Vermont's population nearly doubled in the decade following its entrance into the Union. Between 1790 and 1830 growth averaged 37 percent each decade. The people followed the waters north up the Lake Champlain and Connecticut River valleys. Then they traveled east and west, along the rivers and streams and then up the tributaries that fed them. They dug. They hauled. They burned. They chopped and they hacked. As they did they piled stone into a million meandering walls soaked in sweat which today mark both the contours of the land and an expenditure of human energy that is fundamentally incomprehensible to the modern mind.

These were hard years to be sure, as is the life on any frontier. Hunger, drought, flood, and sweeping disease were a part of everyday life. And yet it was, by and large, a good season, that first half-century that ended in 1840. Everywhere the atmosphere was optimistic. Perhaps that is why, despite a preoccupation with home building and survival, Vermonters found time to establish fundamental dispositions toward life that were preserved throughout the following century and emerged to become a sturdy foundation for the post-modern period.

Vermont was settled by a peculiar breed of farmers. Mostly self-sufficient, they yet produced a wide variety of goods, such as lumber, livestock, potash, wheat, flour, pork, butter, and cheese, that were hauled or herded to the cities of southern New England or north into Canada. In 1808, it is estimated, Vermonters drove 12,000 to 15,000 head of beef to market. During the War of 1812 Vermont cattle helped feed the British army in Canada. (We were still not absolutely certain we were not even then an independent republic.)

The important thing about Vermont's early farming was not that it produced enough to become big agriculture, but that it was *small* enough to promote subsistence capitalism and technological innovation. One of Vermont's creators, Ira Allen, Ethan's brother and the founder of the University of Vermont, noted this in his history of the state. "They are all farmers and again every farmer is a mechanic in some line or other as inclination or necessity requires. The hand that guides the plow frequently constructs it." He continued, "the labor of the axe and plane often evince a degree of genius and dexterity that would really amaze you."* American agriculture in general and Vermont's in particular were never peasant-traditional. Both have always been modern and rationalistic.

In Vermont the very forces that seemed to condemn us to an historical backwater – distance from markets, inhospitable topography, and a cruel climate – did not *allow* farming to become static. Vermonters could not wait for some other "sector" to produce the technology that would improve their lives. The division of labor that was already cooling innovation elsewhere was impossible to maintain in Vermont. The isolation of parts of production one from the other that modern management is even now desperately trying to overcome was never an *option* here. Vermont's agriculture was an incubator for the technological ethic.

Symbolic of Vermont's capacity to lead America in technology is the first patent granted by the United States government, which went to Samuel Hopkins of Burlington. Signed by George Washington and Thomas Jefferson, it approved a process for making potash. Yet the

---

*Allen was indeed prophetic. For it was a Vermonter named Deere who, later in the nineteenth century, produced the first steel plow.

most significant point is that Vermont's development was *geared to technological progress, not industrial growth*. It featured breakthroughs in measurement, energy, transportation, and communication.

In measurement Silas Howe of Shaftsbury invented the first steel square in 1817. Later Lemuel Hedge followed with the carpenter's two-foot rule. In 1810 James Wilson produced the first American globes in Bradford. In 1830 Thaddeus Fairbanks of St. Johnsbury invented the platform scale, a device that triggered a revolution in trade and merchandizing throughout America. The impetus behind Fairbanks' breakthrough was the need to weigh cartloads of hemp—an agricultural product. The rotary pump, the turret lathe, and the use of interchangeable parts in the manufacturing of guns are other examples of Vermonters' technical genius. One of the few small industries that Vermont developed was the machine-tool industry, which is principally involved with the business of helping others build things better. When Wilson Bentley produced the first photomicrographs of snow crystals using homemade equipment, his primary occupation was milking Jersey cows in Jericho.

In transportation and communication Samuel Morey of Fairlee propelled a paddle-wheel steamboat up the Connecticut River in 1793. He then shared his findings with Robert Fulton, who "invented" the steamboat in 1807. It was in Vermont that the first charter to build a canal in the United States was issued. Alvin Adams began the first American express rail service between Windsor and Woodstock in the 1820s. It later merged with Railway Express. After Thomas Davenport invented an electric telegraph in Brandon, Vermont, he shared his findings with Samuel Morse who, with Davenport's help and that of others, received a patent in 1837. By 1853 four-fifths of all horses employed on New York's Sixth Avenue Railroad were Morgan horses, the product of one of America's first major breakthroughs in animal husbandry. In energy transformation Morey had already built the first internal-combustion engine equipped with a carburetor in 1826. Charles Duryea, builder of the first road-worthy car, called Morse's innovation "epoch making."

Vermont's greatest contribution to the industrial revolution, however, was reported in the *New York Herald* in 1837 as a "most extraordinary discovery, probably the greatest of ancient and modern times, the greatest the world has ever seen, the greatest the world will ever see." An exaggeration, no doubt. But one of the most respected scientists of the time, Yale professor Benjamin Silliman, said of the electric motor:

"Science has most unexpectedly placed in our hands a new power of great but unknown energy. . . . Nothing since the discovery of the structure of the celestial system is so wonderful as the power evolved by 'galvinism.'" Thomas Davenport, a blacksmith, was held to be in pretty good company with his invention, which would, decades later, replace steam as the principal power source for an industrialized world.

The list goes on, and we need not belabor it. Its importance lies in the *kinds* of things Vermonters invented. Historian Earle Newton says of the Windsor–Springfield area of Vermont: "Here in this quiet Vermont valley, through the manufacture of interchangeable parts and precision tools like the Fellows Gear Shaper . . . began the American system of mass production." Fellow historian Charles Morrissey: "These mechanical wizards seemed to specialize in products which sprung from a compulsion to serve the New England ethic of efficiency, thoroughness, and exactness. Thus they found ways to fireproof a safe, to punch a time clock, to wring a wet mop, to refrigerate a railroad car, and in the case of Thaddeus Fairbanks, to make scales which were incredibly precise."

This period of Vermont's history tells us something profoundly counterintuitive about the relationship between America's coldest, toughest-terrained, most rural state and the industrial revolution: Vermont was part of it, even a leader, but our role was *technological* rather than mechanical. We contributed a portion – an important portion – of the brains of the movement. We provided precious little of its bulk.

Vermont politics of this time were innovative too. Often they matched the exuberance of the economic sector. Above all they contained a heavy dose of radicalism. Vermonter Matthew Lyon, publisher of *The Scourge of Aristocracy*, was elected to Congress where in 1798, armed with fireplace tongs, he engaged in violent hostilities with a colleague on the very floor of the House. Jailed under the Sedition Acts, Lyon was actually behind bars in Vergennes when he was re-elected with just one vote less than the total received by all four of his opponents on the ballot.

With its radicalism Vermont has always distrusted secretive, closed societies. Voters elected an anti-Masonic congressman and governor, and in 1832 Vermont became the only state to vote for the anti-Masonic candidate for president. Throughout this period Vermont continually backed other radical causes. When the Patriots of southern Canada rose up in rebellion against Great Britain in 1837, Vermonters gave enthusiastic support. Vermont historians Muller and Duffy refer to the episode as a "raucous din." It was part, they said, of an "anxious ardor for a host of other movements that swept the state. . . ."

Vermont's passion for openness spawned free thinking in religion as well. The Pilgrims of South Woodstock, the Perfectionists of Putney, the Swedenborgians of Cambridge, the Dorrelites and, most importantly, the Mormons (Joseph Smith and Brigham Young were Vermonters) found sympathy in Vermont. Freewheeling in religion ran so rampant that visitors to the state spoke of a "reign of infidelity." Churches emphasizing salvation through good works grew rapidly. Circuit-riding Methodists promoted their gospel of the common man. Revivalism (especially the "new-measure" code of Reverend Jedediah Burchard) and evangelical fervor were matched by a vociferous temperance movement.

The state's experiences with radical religions in the midnineteenth century are a metaphor for the tension between liberty and community that has always prevailed in Vermont. Many of the unconventional religious groups were driven out of town when patience ran thin. It isn't that Vermonters were free of prejudice. What is important is that they tried to be. Vermonters tended to abide nonconformity far more than others until radical groups began to make *public* nuisance. This kind of libertarianism (do your own thing, but don't bother me with it) is also linked to history. As Frederic F. Van De Water put it in 1941, "No people to this day are more liberal, more philosophical in their attitudes toward the wrong doer. It may be that because in her formative years Vermont and all her works were so thoroughly denounced by propriety, she cherished then and still maintains in her heart a sympathy for the erring."

The most lingering symbol of Vermont's love affair with freedom in the first half of the nineteenth century was its fierce antislavery sentiment. In 1828 William Lloyd Garrison began to publish his Abolitionist *Journal of the Times* from Bennington. In 1834 was organized America's first state chapter of the American Anti-Slavery Society. William Slade was sent to Congress and became a leading Whig Abolitionist in Washington. He was then elected Vermont's governor. In 1849 the Vermont legislature passed a resolution calling slavery a "crime against humanity." Vermonter Stephen Douglas, more tolerant of slavery, after completing what historians call a "triumphant" tour of the state, was defeated four-to-one for president in Vermont by a flatlander from Illinois in 1860. Vermonter Thaddeus Stevens learned to love freedom growing up in the hills at the gateway of

Vermont's Northeast Kingdom. His career as a United States congressman rippled with the cause of liberty. When Stevens died, he was buried – as he commanded – in a cemetery which included blacks.

When the Civil War came, no state contributed as much for its size in blood and money. Those who, like Toynbee, deride Vermont's contribution to American history would have found little sympathy among Confederate General Pickett's few brave men who struggled to the very top of Cemetery Ridge in a little Pennsylvania town, only to be surprised by a withering crossfire from a Vermont regiment under General George J. Stannard of St. Albans. It was Union General John Sedgwick who said, in that same battle, "put the Vermonters in front and keep the column well closed up." After the battle the *New York Times* reported: "A Vermont brigade held the key of the position at Gettysburg and did more than any other body of men to gain the triumph which decided the fate of the Rebellion."

Exuberance, inventiveness, political experimentation, economic growth, liberalism – these are the enduring images of Vermont's first half-century. There followed what was called by Harold Fisher Wilson in his classic, *Hill Country of Northern New England*, a "protracted autumn [and] severe winter." A cold dark age settled over Vermont that was to last for a hundred years.

The Dark Age of Making Do (1840–1950)

Two great population movements define Vermont's history between 1840 and 1950. One was outward; people began leaving the state in droves. Their places remained untaken. The other was inward; people came down from the hills, into the valleys. In 1850 Vermont's population was 314,120. In 1950 it was 377,747, an increase of barely 20 percent and a compound annual increase of less than a fifth of a percent per year. By contrast the nation's population grew 560 percent in the same century. In 1850 only 2 percent of Vermont's people lived in towns of more than 2,500 people. In 1950 39 percent did. While so much of the country was clearing the land, industrializing, and building a patchwork of gray city, clipped suburb, and groomed countryside, Vermont was reverting to forest.

By 1850 75 percent of Vermont's land had been cleared. Hill and dale, gully and riverside were treeless. Only the high mountains and deep swamps were spared. Wildlife disappeared with the trees. Beavers, fisher cats, and wild turkeys were gone by 1850. Worst of all the quintessential symbol of northland wildlife, the white-tailed deer, had been almost completely wiped out. In 1878 seventeen had to be imported from New York to prevent their total extinction.

But over the next century this pattern of clearing was completely reversed. In 1960 Vermont was 75 percent forested and only 25 percent cleared. It had the thickest deer density of any state in the Union, one for every three people. These deer lived under the curtain of trees that had been drawn over the landscape – the second growth of thousands of abandoned farmsteads. Meadows vanished, fences crumbled, stone walls disappeared under sumac and thorn apple.* Roads were abandoned. Buildings rotted and fell. Cellar holes grew to burdock. Only wild lilacs marked the places where bedroom windows once stood open to the fragrance of June. Gone were the cries of children, the lowing of cattle, the curses of men struggling against nature and their own incapacities. The lights from the windows of thousands of hill farms flickered out.

The reasons why are straightforward. The land had been opened up by sheep. When sheep farming failed due to competition from the West made possible by the railroads, the hill farms went to dairy. But dairy demands cultivation, and it is difficult to plow stone, especially on a mountainside. In addition milk as a cash crop needs to be sold quickly. To supply the Boston milkshed, which developed after the turn of the twentieth century, farmers had to carry milk to distribution points. This put a premium on being close to good roads and depots – in other words, being near a valley town. By 1880 Jerseys had replaced nearly all the sheep in the hills, and by 1950 white-tailed deer had just about replaced the Jerseys.

Some of the people who left the hill towns came down into the valley towns, but many, many others went west. Vermont became a place for leaving, a great reservoir of human talent trained to work hard and expect little in return – good stock with which to settle the moving frontier. By 1850, 145,000 Vermonters had emigrated. Half of the 35,000 who served in the Union army never reestablished permanent residence in their home state. By 1880 54 percent of all Ver-

---

*Writing in the *Atlantic Monthly* in 1879, A. F. Sanborn tells of stone walls. They were "immutable relics of the hill country. . . . Built with ceaseless energy – work comparable only to the building of the pyramids – these walls extend through a field now become the forest, as silent memories of a dead race."

monters were living somewhere else. Vermont led the nation in "getting out."

It was a Vermonter, Horace Greeley, who said "Go West, young man, go West." As Charles Morrissey points out: "He said it to another Vermonter, Joseph B. Grinnell, of New Haven, Vermont, who went to Iowa, founded the famous college town which bears his name, was elected to Congress and became Iowa's best and most famous publicist." Charles Spooner Forbes reported in 1900 that in the last half of the nineteenth century eighteen other states were represented in Congress by emigrants from Vermont. "Vermont enjoys the distinction," he said, "of furnishing more of her sons to other states for Senators and Congressmen than any other state in the Union."

Some scholars, notably Wilson, argue that the early years of the present century (1900–30) could be called a "spring" in comparison to the "winter" period of 1850–1900 and the "summer" of 1790–1850. If so, it was a true Vermont spring, i.e., hard to detect, well camouflaged by snow, wind, and freezing rain, and very high water.* Even Wilson admits that his model "may seem over optimistic."

Economic benefits were occurring, however, notably through the recreation and tourist industries. The granite and marble industries also flourished, and there was a significant machine-tool industry in the southeast quadrant of the state. Yet neither of these two industries was a large producer of employment, and both were closer to artisanship than industrialism. Vermont had some woolen mills, especially on the Black and Winooski Rivers, but they were in decline by 1930.

The dairy industry did well in Vermont in the first half of the century. But even here Wilson's caution seeps through to dampen his "springtime" thesis: "Under these circumstances, the future seems to offer [farmers] some assurance of a fair livelihood." Hardly an exuberant prognosis. And rightly so. For while milk *production* has continued to increase throughout the twentieth century in Vermont, the number of cows, farmers, and farms has continued to drop markedly. Vermont geographer Harold Meeks reports that "In 1920, the peak year for cows," there were 290,000 cows producing 122 million gallons of milk. "By 1963, 251 million gallons were produced by 51,000 fewer animals. . . ." More significantly, the number of dairy *herds* has constantly dropped. Between 1953 and 1966 the number of herds in Vermont was cut in half. The herd is key to the association between human

---

*The flood of 1927 was the greatest natural disaster in the state's history.

activity and notions of production, pride, and longevity. Thought of as a statistic contributing to Vermont's economic base, dairying was indeed in a springtime between 1900 and 1950. Thought of in human terms, it was in late autumn. Farms and farmers were dropping like leaves from a red oak – stubbornly, defiantly, holding off until December, but falling nevertheless.

From the late 1840s to 1950 the balance between open space and forest tipped drastically in favor of forest. Vermont was once *covered* with small farms; by 1950 it was *dotted* with small farms. Yet over this long period of nondevelopment, many of the scars that accompanied the deforestation of Vermont's environment in the first half of the nineteenth century were healed, especially the erosion and flooding caused by overgrazing. By 1950 the farmland-to-forestland balance was more in sync with carrying capacity. In terms of the variety of landscape, surely Vermont was a more beautiful state in 1950 than in 1850.

The most significant point about Vermont's "dark age," however, is that it is called a dark age primarily because Vermont didn't *grow*. Example: Urban America tittered when Vermont rejected the growth and "progress" promised by the federal government's offer to build a superhighway down the crestline of the Green Mountains. (Vermonters voted it down in a statewide town meeting referendum in 1936.) But at the same time, led by George Aiken, we were pushing hard for federal funds for rural electrification. Technology, yes. Growth, no.

The period 1840–1950 is called a dark age, too, because of an expectation denied: Vermont, which in 1830 seemed poised to leap into industrialism with the rest of America, didn't. The years 1840–1950 are called a dark age, finally, because they saw the loss of Vermont's dominant culture – the homestead hill farm. Viewed in terms of different values, and in terms of Vermont's own topography, however, this dark age lightens up considerably.* If the dominant value system is *not* growth at any cost, and if the loss of a goodly portion of our hill farms is seen in the light of its achieving a balanced ecosystem of small farms, forests, and towns rather than one of small-farm domination, Vermont entered the 1950s looking very hale indeed.

---

*Hal S. Barron's account of life in Chelsea, a small Vermont hill town, is typical of the revisionist thinking on this point. See: Hal S. Barron, *Those Who Stayed Behind* (New York: Cambridge University Press, 1984).

Green Shoots and No Concrete:
Thesis and Antithesis (1950–Present)

After World War II Vermont was seen as a green jewel on America's northern border. Clean. Open. Still conducting its local business in town meetings. Still governed by a parliament of common persons. Still tolerant. Still operating from a strong infrastructure of schools, roads, and public welfare. It was an oasis in a desert, a refuge from the darker side of urbanism: crime, pollution, congestion, and the neurosis of the fast lane. Vermont had escaped the basic social and political characteristics of the urban-industrial period – concentration and hierarchy – and seemed to be as suited to those qualities of life that fit the post-modern period – deconcentration and democracy – as it had seemed ill suited to the earlier pattern.

Suddenly people began coming back. Between 1960 and 1970 Vermont's population grew by 14 percent, the greatest single jump in 140 years. For the first time since the early decades of its existence, Vermont's population growth rate exceeded the nation's. This increase was sustained during the next decade. Between 1970 and 1980 the increase in population was 15 percent.

The newcomers were not interested in big-town life. They wanted to live in the hills, and that is precisely where they went. Thus both patterns of the dark age were reversed. Instead of a steady emigration, Vermont experienced a steady immigration. Instead of a flow of people out of the hill towns to the bigger places, Vermont experienced a new rural renaissance. All over the outback lights flickered on again in the dusk of summer and the deep blue of winter's afternoons.

When one understands that this migration was not the result of an economic "push" by poor people seeking new opportunity but rather an influx of status-secure people being "pulled" by concerns for their quality of life, the dimensions of the compliment being paid Vermont become clear. The new settlers saw a promise in Vermont. They saw an opportunity to establish a place to be, one final attempt to live close to the earth again, one last chance to live the hope that marks the human race – we are each other's keepers. Vermont's second great wave of immigrants came for all the right reasons. Indeed their motives may have been far purer than those of the immigrants who arrived two hundred years ago with Ethan Allen. They came to slow down, taste life, understand the planet, sink roots, and manage their own lives. More than anything else, they were drawn by an anticipation left undefined: they came to live democratically.

Along with this cadre of enthusiastic, educated, and essentially democratic newcomers, the post-war period has made a second contribution to the potential for a continuing democracy in Vermont: the growth of a high-tech economic structure. Here is the most rural state in America listed among the top half-dozen states on the percentage of its work force engaged in high-tech enterprises. On many measures Vermont's technological orientation ranks higher than that. Data compiled by the Bureau of Labor Statistics show Vermont placed fourth, sixth, and ninth on three indicators of high-technology employment by the mid-1980s. These rankings would be higher still if farmers were included in the high-tech cohort, as, of course, they should be.

This current fusion of newcomers and high technology offers a tremendous promise for Vermont and by example for the nation. It is a promise spelled out by L. S. Stavrianos in his *The Promise of the Coming Dark Age*. Stavrianos looked at America in the 1970s and observed what he called the "wreckage of contemporary civilization," in four manifestations: (1) economic imperialism; (2) ecological degradation; (3) bureaucratic ossification; and (4) a flight from reason. Yet he sees in this dark age a new hope for the advanced societies. He urges us to focus on the "green shoots" that are growing everywhere, bursting through the concrete of the American dark age. These green shoots, Stavrianos explains, are called "demo-technology," "participatory democracy," and "self actualization."

In Vermont the green shoots are not covered by the cement of the urban-industrialism period. We have a head start, a long one. By 1950 we had *already fought through* our dark age, and in so doing we poured precious little pavement. We *lived* green and paid the price. The point is this: the metaphor used to describe the birth pains of the new humanistic, decentralist order is inappropriate to Vermont because in Vermont, so far at least, the grass (human capacity for self-management) has never been killed by concrete (dehumanizing imperatives of mega-bureaucracies).

As Murray Bookchin explains the hypothesis, American society is gripped by the disintegration of the bourgeois city: metropolitanism has run amok. The solution, outlined in his *The Limits of the City*, demands that the megalopolis be "replaced by new decentralized ecocommunities, each carefully tailored to the natural ecosystem in which it is located." These new structures should "possess the best features of the *polis* and medieval commune, supported by rounded ecotechnologies that rescale the most advanced elements of modern technology – including such energy sources as solar and wind power – to local dimensions." What will emerge, Bookchin continues, is an "equilibrium between town and country . . . not as a sprawling suburb that mistakes a lawn or patch of strategically placed trees for nature, but as an interactive functional ecocommunity that unites industry with agriculture, mental work with physical, individuality with community."

Bookchin uses the words "restore," "dissolve," "replace." He is arguing that there is a massive overload to be dealt with before the new condition may be framed. Our claim is that Vermont contains few of the negative elements that Bookchin says need replacing elsewhere and that it already has ample supplies of the desired new elements.* It never gave them up. The Vermont of the past rejected what now are fast becoming the old ways: the ethic of growth at any cost, the creation of giant bureaucracies, the dehumanization associated with both, and with it an insatiable thirst for perfection, symmetry, order, sameness, compromise, and obedience to routine. Vermont simply wasn't *made* for them. Vermont is made for the future. Its culture is green, and its technological base advanced. It can carry its democracy with it into the twenty-first century. This is the promise offered in the fourth phase of its development.

But Vermont's historic promise is now confronted by a powerful antithesis which is driven by an appealing, yet fundamentally inaccurate and conservative assumption held by a good number of Vermonters and newcomers alike: the view that metropolitanism and its attendant characteristics – centralism, hierarchy, and authority – are *preconditions* to the future. Vermonters have been told this for decades, and the newcomers (who came here to escape the twentieth century) are plagued by a subconscious incapacity to shake their longing for the old ways. Both have been instructed that "urbanization" and "progress" are synonyms. Modernization is believed to be "doing things the way they do them in the cities." Thus many Vermonters and newcomers have learned to kowtow to the imperialism of a dialectic that demands servitude to a preordained future. This future includes "passing through" a period which features the end of democracy.

Vermonters are equally at fault with newcomers for accepting the

---

*This may be one of the reasons that Bookchin is now living in Vermont.

pernicious assumptions of this false modernism. But the great discouragement is that many newcomers (who had the advantage of seeing what has happened elsewhere) have not been able to lead in the proper direction. These "flatlanders" (as they are called by the native "woodchucks") came from places where they watched their fields turn to asphalt, their friendships snapped by family mobility, their neighborhoods disappear under the rubble (the often very *tasteful* rubble, mind you) of growth at any cost. Worst of all they saw their values assaulted and insulted by an uprooting relativity that eats away at the dearest of all human longings: the hope that somewhere, somehow there is a life that promises peace and happiness. Turning away from all that, they came to live among the Vermonters.

There is one word for that, and only one.

Good.

But the newcomers' hopes often turned to confusion, and their confusion sometimes to despair, even bitterness. They were different, and the real Vermont is stranger to a resident of Fairfield County, Connecticut, than say, Massachusetts was to the Pilgrims. They were amateurs. Slowly many have begun to do what comes naturally to anyone caught alone in a new land: they have reverted to habit, sought security in the familiar and the understandable. In value and action they are gravitating toward the same destructive urban culture they cast aside. Aided by Vermonters who have always longed to "catch up" with America, they are cross-wiring the two great contributions (themselves and technology) of Vermont's modern period by using technology to destroy rather than build the society of human scale they sought in the first place. These newcomers do not want to build cities, mind you. They know what they want Vermont to *look like*. But they are confused as to what Vermont should *be*.

Nor do they have the advantage of a statewide political leadership in Vermont to help them resist these temptations. Instead Vermont's leadership (native and newcomer alike) is caught up in the second-wave, urban-industrial mindset. Most of our political leaders were trained by professors who defined rural as backward and urban as modern. And so the great potential these newcomers represent is actually dysfunctional. In part because they are so influential, Vermont itself teeters on the cliff face of self-denial. It seems ready to sigh and give up, to accept the fact that modernism and democracy cannot endure together, to cease to try to live its dreams, to abandon the promise.

43

There is one word for that, and only one.

Bad.

In short many of the new settlers who arrived in Vermont after 1950 came with hope and enthusiasm and immediately ran afoul of reality. They brought with them a vision of the good life absolutely compatible with the one to which Vermonters had always claimed allegiance. It detracts not one whit from the wisdom of their decision and the glory of their dream to cry warning: they are helping to kill the thing they love. We turn now to a discussion of that gloomy possibility.

Chapter 4

THE PROMISE OF DEMOCRACY DENIED

Men fight for liberty and win it with hard knocks. Their children, brought up easy, let it slip away again, poor fools. And their children are once more slaves.

—D. H. Lawrence

VERMONT stands at a crossroads. It may fashion a future after the metro-industrial model that its historical isolation earlier denied it. Or it may preserve and enhance the decentralized, communal environment it has been fortunate to have retained. The first road leads back through familiar urban terrain. It is seen, wrongly, as a passage to the post-modern world that must be taken if Vermont is to "catch up." The second road leads straight ahead, carrying Vermont as it is into a position well in advance of the rest of America.

The first way involves the misuse of technology—the establishment of buffers between individuals and between each person and the planet. This was the way of urbanism, the way of David Riesman's "lonely crowd." It results in routine, symmetry, and depersonalization. Technology is matched to systems rather than to human beings. Jacques Ellul describes the ethic accompanying the shift in technology from a means to an end as *la technique*—the urge to be perfect for the sake of perfection. The massive concentrations of people needed to build and staff the metropolis were *made possible* by a technological infrastructure geared to hierarchy and authority, not community and democracy.

The second way involves technology correctly applied—to bring people together and reassociate them with the world they live in. It perfects the capacity for human interaction, not estrangement. Most important, it expands human options, generates a healthy chaos of activity, and empowers individuals to actually *offend* systems. Concentration is replaced by diffusion, hierarchy by networks, authority by democracy, rigidity by adaptability, conservatism by innovation, and symmetry by variety. While technology in service of what we call the "systems axiom" forces the individual to accept the "one best way"—even to the point of servitude, technology in service of the "community axiom" frees individuals to choose ways which best serve human need.

What follows is an examination of misplaced metro-technology, of the systems axiom that justifies it, and of what both can do to Vermont. It is a look down the wrong road. This is the road that destroys community, cosmeticizes the landscape, precludes environmental ethics, and poisons the atmosphere of human interaction. *Society* and *governance* are equally at risk. For technology as a tool of the systems axiom separates democracy from governance in the same way it separates humanity from society. Thus our town meetings, citizen legislature, and human-scale educational systems are threatened by techno-centralism in the same way the hill farm, the small town, and the joining of neighbors in enterprises of mutual aid are threatened. To be blunt, what follows is the damnation of a trend—an abominable set of events that is leading Vermont away from its roots, away from its strength, away from its character, and, most lamentably, away from a future of promise toward a future of despair.

The Lonely Villagers: The Darker Side of Development

A fundamental misconception has beclouded the resettlement of Vermont. It is that rural places are "good" by nature. By nature, of course, they are not. When this reality sets in, two things generally happen, both of them bad. Rural places are made to *look* simple and good. Then they are reshaped to provide urban amenities. This process destroys the countryside for everyone, especially for the people who love it for what it is, country.

•

Witness: Jack and Sally (from Manhattan) thought they were doing it right. According to a story in *The Burlington Free Press* they "found an old farmhouse 15 miles out of Burlington, bought an English setter and a truck, started a large garden. . . ." They even put down wide-plank wood floors in their house, which was 150 years old. Tom and Sue tried the country life, too. Their house was "a sleek split-level with solar panels and a large redwood deck on a grassy knoll surrounded by 13 acres of woods." There "is a view of Camel's Hump [the best-known peak in the Green Mountains] and no other houses."

Enter country life. Jack and Sally carpet their wide-plank floor to cut down on utility costs. The pond freezes over, and the dog kills their ducks. Then comes the boredom. Evidently Sue did not find watching Camel's Hump particularly rewarding. She did, however, "find the isolation overwhelming." The restriction to location is also bothersome. Another pair of newcomers, Mary and Phil said, "living in the country you find yourself restricted to the immediate area because it is a major chore to go to the store or take the children to swimming lessons." Tom and Sue complained that their children "learned how to ride bikes and then had nowhere to ride, for only hilly dirt roads surround them." Nowhere roads, inconvenience, nothing to do – the scenario is etched again and again in the souls of urban people gone "up country."

Throughout these accounts is evidence of an impatience with country life, even a basic distaste for things rural. Tom, for instance, who works at the University of Vermont, returned from a sabbatical in Bloomington, Indiana, saying, "We did more in one year there than we did in ten years in Vermont." Accordingly Tom's family moved from its grassy knoll into downtown Burlington, where "we will attend more concerts and plays and take the children swimming every Friday night." Sue adds, "We realize the family needs can be met more easily in the city. That's what is important to us, not 13 acres and a view of Camel's Hump."

Which family needs is Sue talking about, one might ask? About the same time the Sue and Tom moved into Burlington, the city began a program to provide chains with whistles on them for citizens to wear around their necks in case of an attack. Swimming every Friday night? Where? In the University's heated pool, which is maintained so a teensy portion of Vermont's population may splash about in happiness while outside the trees snap under a white moon at twenty-five degrees below zero. Anyone who has walked back from the barn on creaking snow knows that country living does not include the option of swimming after dark in February. Are hilly dirt roads nowhere roads? Must kids be taught by strangers to swim in groups? Is country life unpalatable without plays and concerts?

The point is, of course, a very simple one. City life and rural life are different. There are fully as many options in the country as in the city. But they are different options. They are options dependent on the very things so many city people dislike: isolation, dirt, stillness. They are options that demand an awareness of and an appreciation for the complexities of nature. They are options that involve knowing a few people very well instead of many people on the periphery. They are options that cannot always be planned or organized. Building a picture window so one may sit and watch a rain cloud cover a mountain top is not the same as glancing up from a shovel and catching a glimpse of that same mountain in the sweat of an August afternoon. Country life means being with the mountains – becoming a *part* of the view.

Nor is country life "better" than city life. Watching a white-tailed deer emerge from a cedar swamp is no better than sitting at a sidewalk cafe and watching the people go by. But they are different. You can see white-tailed deer in the zoos of the cities, and you can sit on a porch in the country, watching for someone to walk down the road. Both will leave you wanting. Trying to make the experiences the same will destroy both.

•

Exploiting Rural Life

Some of Vermont's newcomers tired of the country and moved to cluster housing in the larger towns. Like Tom and Sue they are not the problem. Metro-imperialists who stay in the outback and do their best to make it conducive to urban living – who apply the technologies (social and physical) of the city to the country – are.

They have found rural life more difficult and complex than expected and have reverted to the urban principle of the division of labor. It is not a simple thing to cut down a tree with a chain saw. It is both physically and intellectually demanding. The human-scale life calls upon you to do it yourself anyway. The metro option is to spend your time organizing others to do it for you. This leads to the successive steps: hiring the organizers themselves, the adoption of the principles of concentration and hierarchy, the loss of human choices, and the myopia of special-interest decision making.

The new exploiters tire of driving thirty miles an hour on country roads, so they have them straightened and drive forty. They came to grow their own vegetables, discovered that weeds pull hard, and now demand a new grocery store on the village green. Or they support paving of still more roads so they can drive to a shopping center in the next town ten minutes quicker without the dust. They ferry their children here and there in an everlasting attempt to orchestrate an agenda of urban options for them – team sports, harp lessons, and play schools. These are the people who believed the Dogpatch stereotype of the rural dweller and who, from either ignorance or arrogance, came to the country and expected to know at once how to live there competently and happily, forgetting that water freezes in the winter and dogs like to kill ducks.

It is hard to watch the end of the hill farm, the passing of neighborhood, the closing of school house and grange hall – in short the conquest of the small, the understandable, and the personal by the big, the obscure, and the systematized forces of megamarkets and marketed megavalues – and not be drawn to the words of the poet Wendell Berry, and his brilliant analysis of such exploitation in *The Unsettling of America*:

> Let me outline as briefly as I can what seem to me the characteristics of these opposite kinds of mind. I conceive a strip-miner to be a model exploiter, and as a model nurturer I take the old-fashioned idea or ideal of a farmer. The exploiter is a specialist, an expert; the nurturer is not. The standard of the exploiter is efficiency; the standard of the nurturer is care. The exploiter's goal is money, profit; the nurturer's goal is health – his land's health, his own, his family's, his community's, his country's. . . . The exploiter wishes to earn as much as possible by as little work as possible; the nurturer expects, certainly, to have a decent living from his work, but his characteristic wish is to work *as well* as possible. The competence of the exploiter is in organization; that of the nurturer is in order – a human order, that is, that accommodates itself both to other order and to mystery. The exploiter typically serves an institution or organization; the nurturer serves land, household, community, place. The exploiter thinks in terms of numbers, quantities, "hard facts"; the nurturer in terms of character, condition, quality, kind.

Many who came to Vermont to resettle the outback "unsettled" it. The unsettlers didn't come here to strip mine coal (as in Montana) or to ax forests (as in Oregon or Mississippi) or to plow up prairies (as in Iowa). They came to feed, instead, on our beauty, our solitude, our communities, and our democracy. They exploited the very culture itself. They mined it for its ambience.

Just as a great corporation uses up the metals of the soil and destroys the very resource that attracted it in the first place, so the new unsettlers in Vermont are turning Vermont into an artificial, systematized, techno-suburbia at the cost of the human-scale community life which beckoned them originally. The final indignity is the unsettlers' "quainting" (as one reporter put it recently) the landscape to cover their tracks, by the building of postcard villages and the creation of artificial scenic vistas. Meanwhile the native population is moved onto reservations (called trailer parks) or is otherwise zoned away from the places where the urban unsettlers might want to be. What has made all this possible? Metro-technology, epitomized by the highway, the power line, and the bulldozer. But most critical is the systems mindset, which features a faith in the centrist social technology of the urban-industrial revolution.

Those That Labor in the Earth

Another misunderstanding of rural life is the belief that rural people are somehow morally better than urban people, that Jefferson was right when he said "those who labor in the earth are the chosen people of God." There *is* something about the relationship with the earth and the seasons engendered by farming that provokes an appreciation and respect for the life forces of the universe. But the first great sin took place in a garden, and the degree to which urban people are quicker to condemn mischief practiced in the countryside, where it "ought not to be," is a constant source of amazement and amusement for rural people, who have been sinning with great lust and enthusiasm ever since the beginning.

Many fail to see that the neighborly mutual aid which is often the source of the countryside's assumed moral superiority is not always freely given – although it is no less beneficial for that reason. The reason why a passerby is more likely to stop to give aid in the country has as much to do with assumed reciprocity as it has with divine goodness. It also has something to do with the expectation that both helper and helped may meet face to face at a gas station the next day. Playwright Jonathan Miller points out that for a relationship to be human it must be both complicated and dutiful. A sense of duty is stimulated by proximity. You cannot ignore the plight of those you meet on the street every day, those with whom your family intermingles, those with whom you work and play. One acquires a *habit* of mutual aid.

When your choices of friends and acquaintances are limited by place, they become more complicated. You have to deal with people on many levels: social, economic, political. Patience with a friend's weaknesses becomes obligatory. Thus friendships in the country are deep and long lasting. They are more complicated, and they are more human. What is often missed, however, is that this quality comes from life in small, narrowly bounded communities and not from the spirit-elevating experience of looking at mountains through a living-room window. In those few urban places where neighborhoods still exist, the same kind of virtue is apt to prevail.

Rural life is based on sociability, not estrangement – togetherness, not distance. Living in the country may mean giving up the perfect tennis partner. It may mean that your kids have playmates they, or you, don't particularly like. It may mean listening to jackasses sound off at town meeting. Rural life breeds a patience with the human condition that is fundamental to a successful democracy.

When people fail to recognize that rural goodness is linked to the spatial nature of population arrangements, and worse, when they fail to recognize that this goodness is further generated by long-lasting and complicated interactions of people rather than by their separation (remember Tom and Sue originally felt a view of Camel's Hump was more important than a view of another house), they are encouraged to abandon the most important element of Vermont's personality – small-town life. When this happens the hope for a human-scale future is severely endangered.

Behind this threat to small-town life is the mentality of the systems axiom, which leads to the creation of administrative systems rather than human communities, to slicing up neighborhoods and estranging neighbors, and to making friendships conform to functional criteria. Systems life means you live in one town, work in another. You shop here, join a health club there. You politic in one place and send the kids to school somewhere else. Relationships are parceled out – one to work with, another to play with, a third to sell to, a fourth to buy from, a fifth to educate the children, a sixth to argue with. To make all this possible we employ bulldozers and learn to welcome the smell of hot tar. We fear our schools are too small. We make them bigger.

51

Our roads are too slow. We make them faster. Our democracies are too clumsy. We made them efficient.

We conceal the steady advance of the systems axiom in rural America with Currier and Ives postcard images of pastoral simplicity. We put barn boards on houses and build split-rail fences around pastures where there is no stock. More and more people are living in Vermont in spite of Vermont. They are spinning technological cocoons to protect ways of life more appropriately practiced elsewhere. They don't want to *be* Vermonters as much as they want to *look like* Vermonters.

Case in point. Several years ago the state legislature passed what was called the "junk-yard law." Many people living in the country, especially poor people, keep old cars lying around their property. These affront the sensibilities of those who like the front yards of poor people to look like the front yards of country yeomen. A rooster walking around is perfect. Sheep behind the barn is even better. Junk cars are ugly. The law reads that you may have three junks in the yard, but the fourth has to go.

Yet junk cars are a classic example of recycling. For many they are a source of economic security. They are used for spare parts for the car that does run. They also make useful outbuildings in which to store tools and equipment and other stuff that someday you might need. They are good for sitting on in the evening while talking to a neighbor. They make handy chicken coops. They protect grain bags from the rain. They are great for kids to play around – perfect for hide-and-seek.

The only thing wrong with junk cars is that they don't look nice. So the state legislature began, in effect, to banish them. This is the kind of mentality that accompanies the systems axiom. Junk cars don't fit the image that the systems axiom favors. They hurt the tourist business. They expose a glitch in the system of stylized rural life called poverty. The junk-yard law exposes the new class of rural dwellers who care most of all about crafting the Vermont countryside to the specifications of a rustic painting – forgetting that the old paintings of country life reflected living culture. Holders of the systems axiom dominate state-wide decision making, and they are fabricating an environment of chic by design.

Democracy vs. the Systems Imperative

If there is one thing techno-systems cannot abide, it is variety. And

yet the drive to arrange perfectly and predict completely often transcends the ends for which particular technologies are devised. Thus
the state government in Vermont for years urged the towns to adopt
uniform auditing procedures. It became apparent that having each
town's audit done in exactly the same way became an end in itself—
that state officials were more interested in the means of centralized
auditing than they were in the ends for which towns audit their books.
Symmetry became more important than substance. For those who hold
the systems axiom, variety causes complexity, complexity breeds
uncertainty, and uncertainty leads to anxiety. Administrators strive
to lessen the anxiety in their lives by minimizing the chance that anything out of the ordinary will ever happen. Authority cannot permit
variety. Democracy, on the other hand, cannot exist where variety and
the complexity it causes are precluded.

This drive for symmetry is reinforced by bureaucratization and
credentialism. Some years ago Vermont state government did a wise
thing. It encouraged citizens to hold on to their forestland instead of
developing it by giving them a property-tax break to reduce the pressure to sell. All landowners had to do was draw up a forestry "management plan" for their parcels. But soon after the program encountered
the professional foresters in the state bureaucracy, the criteria for the
management plan began to grow more and more complicated. It wasn't
long before the ordinary citizen became discouraged with the application procedure.

No problem. The state could give you the addresses of professional
"consulting foresters" (many of them former state employees) who
could plan your forest for you. This was the proper way to go, it was
hinted darkly, because if you got the plan wrong—for instance you
underestimated the per-acre DBH (diameter at breast height) of your
trees—you will be in noncompliance and might be in a "penalty situation."

Large lumber companies could afford to hire consulting foresters
—most are staffed by foresters anyway. But the citizen landowner who
is willing to defer his right to develop for a cut in his taxes, and who
would learn something about his land by developing his own plan,
may abandon that activity because paying for a consulting forester
could wipe out a large percentage of his tax break. This would destroy
the program for the common person, while the big companies continue
to use it. Sound familiar?

Consider town meeting. In every possible way it is anathema to the systems axiom. At the same time it is central to the aspirations of every true democrat. Town meeting government asserts the fundamental wisdom of the common person, sanctifies openness, abhors secrecy, holds the human spirit in the highest esteem, and is grounded in a fundamental trust that the truth will out in any free debate of citizens assembled. Town meetings must have been in the mind of E. B. White when he conceived his classic definition of democracy: "the recurrent suspicion that more than half the people are right more than half of the time." Jefferson said it was the wisest instrument of self-governance ever devised by the wit of man. Lewis Mumford, one of the twentieth century's leading scholars of the urban place, has lamented the passing of town meeting in most of America, calling its loss one of the great tragedies of the post-colonial period. *Every citizen a legislator*: the town meeting is based on principles which for 2,500 years have been in the dreams of those who have sought to build democratic governments.

Town meeting's oxygen is the capacity of townspeople to do what they damn well please. It does not need pure oxygen. But when the flow of decision-making power has been turned down to a whisper, town meeting will drift off to sleep and die. Since town meeting generates variety, a propensity for doing things different ways, for doing things that were not expected to be done, and in some cases for doing nothing, it cannot be condoned by the systems approach to governance.

It is difficult to kill democracy quickly. That is why the systems elites in Vermont are doing their best to bleed it to death. By the mid-1980s the local town meeting had become frightfully weak. The cause-and-effect sequence is not perfectly clear, but it is the case that the most serious erosion of town power in Vermont came with the second great migration into Vermont (1960 to the present) and the systems approach to politics which accompanied it.

Town meeting took a heavy blow when the "bigger-is-better" revolution in education (more on this in Chapter 11) that was in vogue in the 1950s came to dominate the education lobby and to be entrenched at the highest levels of state government. The state then bullied and blackmailed the small towns into school consolidations. Funding and running their schools, a critical political issue, was removed from the towns and the town meetings. Equally significant was the loss of the dominant social touchstone in the community – the local high school, with its sports teams, its senior play and holiday concerts, its junior prom, and its graduation ceremony. The great majority of Vermont's towns no longer have their own high schools. Many are losing their grade schools as well.

Welfare, education, highways, financial management, and taxation, once under the control of town meeting, have been the constant object of the state's grasp. There has never been a blatant grab for power. The state takes it a bit at a time, here and there, now and then. How the state took away the right of the people to elect their road commissioners is a perfect example of the loss of liberty through attrition.

Traditionally townspeople elected their road commissioners at their town meetings every single year. That didn't fit the prescriptions of the systems axiom. What if the people threw out a perfectly good road commissioner and elected a bad one? Besides, the systems axiom held, fixing roads was fast becoming a tricky business. It took an expert. The people were not to be trusted to make judgments that involved expertise. The selectmen should appoint the road commissioner. Lacking the courage to mandate this, the state passed a law requiring that each year each town would vote on the question of whether to elect or appoint a road commissioner.

The people handled that subtlety well enough. Often the question of election or appointment sparked long and heated debate. Many times the move to appoint was a maneuver to secure the position of road commissioner for a friend or neighbor. Fair enough. Skulduggery is not unexpected in the politics of real people. Often when this question was being debated, one was reminded of Jefferson's most telling praise of town meeting. "It is," he said, "a school for citizenship."

The state was unhappy. Not enough towns gave up their right to elect their road commissioner. In the 1970s a law was passed denying the towns the right to elect the road commissioner. The uproar that followed taught the state a lesson. It had not been underhanded enough. So the state turned the question around and established appointment, not election, as the status quo by providing that the commissioner would be elected *only if* the town voted to do so. Worse. Even if there was an election, the new statutory provisions deftly depoliticized the office of road commissioner by reducing the position to foreman of the road crew, directly responsible to the selectmen. The result? Debate over the post of road commissioner is heard less and less. Another classroom in Jefferson's school of citizenship has been closed.

•

Witness: As late as the early 1970s the question of whether or not heifers (young cows that have not yet calved and are not producing milk) should be taxed as property along with a farmer's other cows and real estate was still debated at town meeting. The farmers' argument was that since heifers did not produce income as milking cows did, they should not be taxed. Others, especially wage earners and renters, were not sympathetic with the plight of the farmer, who paid almost no income tax and seemed to get enough breaks as it was. The debate on this issue often carried overtones of village vs. the outback or development vs. saving the family farm.

In 1971 a young man came into the town meeting of a small Vermont community where one of the authors (as a former resident returned to gather data on town meeting) was scribbling notes as he sat in the balcony at the back of the town hall. Call the young man Pete. Most Vermonters would recognize Pete. He quit school after the eighth grade to work in the woods. In those days (the late 1950s) there were no lightweight chain saws, and Pete quickly developed the physique that went with the heavy, dangerous kind. Today he drove a pickup with a bumper sticker that said IF GUNS ARE OUTLAWED ONLY OUTLAWS WILL HAVE GUNS. Pete's gun was on the rack in the back window of the cab. From May until deer season in mid-November Pete worked on construction. The rest of the year he drew unemployment, earned a little at odd jobs, and raised heifers behind his trailer on the side.

Pete's Dad had farmed the land near where Pete's trailer now stood. The people who had bought the family place looked askance at men like Pete, wishing his trailer didn't clutter their view the way it did. Pete was bitter about that, even though the folks who bought the home place would never credit him for that much emotion. He had grown up on that farm, knew every nook and cranny of it, knew things about the land that the newcomers would never learn – ledges to stand under when it rained, easy paths around the slash that still lay entangled from the hurricane of 1938. Special places, his places. The new folks had never told him they wished he'd move his trailer from where it stood, surrounded by the paraphernalia of a big family with a thin wallet. But Pete knew.

Pete lived on the outskirts of town, and on the outskirts of the life of the community. When he came to town meeting it was because he liked to sit in the town hall parking lot in his truck and have a few beers with friends. That day he happened to wander into the meeting itself just about the time the debate on exempting heifers from taxation got underway. Pete began to listen, and he began to understand the connection between the debate and his tax bill. His derisive whispers (he sat beside the author, an old friend and a friend still) on the subject of "big shots" and "know-it-alls" slowly ended. Pete nodded appreciation and shook his head with exasperation. It took some doing, but when the time came he got up to vote on the issue.

The process of voting entailed walking to the front of the town hall, having your named checked off, and dropping your homemade ballot (the clerk provided squares of blank paper if you needed them) in a box. Pete was nervous, but he'd gone out to the parking lot and brought in a half-dozen of his friends–more for moral support than anything else, one suspects. But not only for moral support. Pete knew that if the article to exempt heifers passed he would save a considerable sum on his heifers. Watching Pete and his friends shuffle to the front amid the chaos of two hundred people voting in no particular order–a hunting license pinned to a cap, an Arctic Cat jacket, a beer bottle not too well hidden in the back pocket of great wool work pants–the author was reminded of a line from *The Great Gatsby*: "You're worth the whole damn bunch put together."

The notes taken from that particular town meeting indicate that it was pretty lively. Just before dinner the people had decided to elect their own road commissioner by a vote of 131 to 47. Orange County Mental Health Services lost its try for an appropriation from the budget, 131 to 50. Harley Kaiser's new house was exempted from taxes. (His old house had burned down.) Signa Carbee, former star of the girl's basketball team (and daughter of the road commissioner), had been defeated for the position of town moderator. That doesn't happen very often. The vote was 93 to 70. But the key vote that day was on childless cows. The town decided not to tax them, voting 109 to 103. Pete had brought in six extra votes. He only needed one, since his vote alone would have produced a tie. He looked up from the floor of the town hall to where the author sat. His grin was not smooth. But it was triumphant.

Pete still isn't a model citizen. But after that day he began to go to town meeting from time to time, and not just to sit out in his truck and bitch. Pete had been to a school of citizenship and seen the link between input and output right before his eyes. A working man made a difference–a big difference. Political scientists like to discuss the term "efficacy," the belief that you can have an impact on the political process. Millions are spent every election telling us to vote because "it really matters." The people that attend town meetings in small communities don't have to be told this. They can see democracy, and they can hear it. Most of all, they can feel it.

The state of Vermont soon removed the towns' right to decide the heifer issue. Twelve years after the vote that revealed democracy to Pete, in the summer of 1983, the author sat with him watching an ox draw at a local fair. The lines were deeper on his face. The winds strike hard in a Vermont wood lot in January, and twelve Januaries tacked onto the life of a woodsman in his twenties make a lot of difference. He'd warmed his innards with a hefty amount of beer in those days, and that showed too. The conversation (there is plenty of time to visit at an ox draw) covered the usual: deer hunting, old friends then and now, local women who had gone astray or might be convinced to. When asked if he'd been to town meeting that year, he said he hadn't. "Not much goes on up there any more," Pete said.

•

When Push Comes to Shove

You could count on it in the spring like sap in a hard maple: Vermont's press would contain stories about the debate over kindergartens. They were usually little stories – a few lines here, a paragraph there. They were little stories about the give and take of communities debating something that counts; debating in real time, in the open. They were little stories that reflected the stupidity and the intelligence, the passion and the apathy, the pride and the prejudice of real people. They were little stories about democracy – winners and losers, bitterness and happiness, satisfaction and despair. That's what happens when real people practice real democracy.

Over the years the great majority of the towns in Vermont (most think in their wisdom) had adopted kindergartens. They raised taxes and provided what they thought was an essential service. Even though, remember, it was not in the immediate self-interest of the majority of voters in any given town to do so. No one told them to do this. They did it on their own. Freely. Democratically. By 1985 the trend indicated that in ten or fifteen years all towns in the state would have public kindergartens.

Yet despite all this the state legislature mandated kindergartens. As usual it covered its tracks with language. The governor took credit for providing kindergartens for all of Vermont's children. Wrong. Kindergartens had already been provided for the great majority of Vermont's children, by the towns. For the communities that remained kindergartenless, usually the poorer rural ones, the new law gave no money to pay the bill, although it did offer loans. The politics of reason was dismissed, and the politics of brute force invoked. Fast-lane politics had replaced deliberation. Town meeting lost again.

One of us wrote the following response:

> It would be far better to have our children raised where there is a healthy, boisterous town government and no kindergarten than where the town hall is silent in March and there is one. Better to bring up our future voters in a community of free people where liberty is the fundamental principle of concern, where politics fairly oozes from the rafters of the town, where conflict and debate and "rules of order" and petitions and public outcry are part of a child's early recollections.

Perhaps the true measure of democracy, we suggest, is a human one – one of scale. Would any of the supporters of mandating kindergarten go to a town meeting, listen to and participate in the debate on the kindergarten proposal (making their best case for it), walk to the front along with the others to cast their vote – and then after hearing the moderator say, "Listen to the results of your vote: 158 yea, 172 nay. Article number seven to provide for a kindergarten in this town has been defeated," rise from his seat and proclaim: "Because I care more about your children than you do and because I am a wiser and more informed citizen than the majority, and because I understand the workings of a world where kindergarten is a necessity, I hereby decree that the vote shall be reversed."

If the governor of Vermont or any of the legislators who voted to mandate kindergartens ever tried a trick like that, they would be hooted out of the town hall immediately, and the hooting would come from voters on both sides of the issue. Let those who would execute democracy do it in person. Pulling the switch on the democratic process is easy from the state capitol. You don't have to look anyone in the eye.

Soon after the state's mandating of kindergartens passed, one of the authors was on a talk show syndicated on several radio stations around Vermont. A woman from the town of Woodstock called in with supportive comments on the thesis of the program, which was the preservation of town meeting. When the example of the kindergarten vote came up, however, she reneged. Town meetings were wonderful, she thought, but they should not deal with something as important as education. Her reason? Because every child *must* have the opportunity to attend a kindergarten. Push had come to shove. The particular good at stake – the immediate opportunity for every child in Vermont to attend a kindergarten – was matched against the good of town meeting, and the systems axiom prevailed.

For holders of the systems axiom town meeting is the hill farm of our governance. Like the hill farm, it is nice to look at and to have around, but you wouldn't want to operate one yourself. The systems axiom allows that democracy works when advice is all that is required. When the going gets tough, however, when the stakes are higher, when decisions must be made, assemblies of neighbors are not to be trusted. Better let cadres of distant elites rule. It is our premise that such thinking is akin to the kind of substance one is apt to find between one's toes after walking barefoot through a barnyard on a moonless midnight.

Key to the thesis of this book is that when division-of-labor thinking controls politics, democracy is impossible. Division of labor is a fundamental component of the systems axiom. One is, for instance, a lawyer or an architect. There is no time to be woodcutter, a swimming instructor, a gardener, a merchant, or even, in fact, a citizen.

This is not a new concept. Toulmin Smith, author of *The Parish* and other works on local self-government in midnineteenth-century England, marks the tie between the division-of-labor mentality and the eclipse of democracy that we see occurring in Vermont in an essay entitled "Local Self Government Un-Mystified":

> If the principle of Division of Labor is a sound reason why Local Self Government is not as well carried out now as formerly, and why, therefore, Centralism must be introduced, it follows, that the actual principles of human progress are, *Oligarchy* and *Despotism*; that as, in our enlightened age of Progress, one man grinds corn, and another makes bread, so all the governing must be done, and must go on to be more and more exclusively done, by some few who are Brahminically set apart for the purpose.

Genius. It is true today, well over a century hence. The people are judged not capable of deciding what shall or shall not be taxed – there are tax experts in the government to do this. They are not allowed to choose their road commissioner – there are people who understand this function better who will do it for them. They are not to be trusted to audit their own books or fashion a plan for their own wood lots.

The division of labor is accompanied by the division of friend-ships and other social relationships which in turn supports the division of politics and citizenship that will lead to the end of liberty.* All this is fed by the drive for "the one best way," condemning each person to a lifelong journey down an increasingly narrow track. This is the promise of the systems axiom. It has killed democracy throughout America. In Vermont it was held at bay by historical circumstances and the ideals of a free people. Now the systems axiom threatens to run amok even here, trashing our institutions of human scale. It is doubly dangerous because its advance is concealed by the honeyed phrases of Vermont's centrist politicians, who continue to proclaim that Vermont is one of the last places where it isn't so.

---

*See Murray Bookchin's dazzling discussion of this subject in his *Limits of the City*.

Chapter 5

THE PROMISE OF
DEMOCRACY RESTORED

*Democracy must begin at home, and
its home is the small community.*
—John Dewey

APPILY the systems axiom is not alone in Vermont. There is a countervailing paradigm: inch by inch we are moving toward the reacquaintance of work place and living place. Community and economy are becoming as one again. If governance can be included in the equation, the clash of thesis (community and democracy) and antithesis (system and oligarchy) will end in victory for democracy.

Here is why. The systems view is powerful among Vermont elites, but it is not popular among the people. While many newcomers have accepted it, a good many others have not. While an alarming number of native Vermonters have bowed to the supposed inevitability of system and oligarchy, most continue to resist. Finally, while the systems axiom finds support in the halls of state government, it is bucking fundamental currents in the flow of history.

Unlike other states in which system and democracy contest, Vermont's playing field is level. Our bypassing urban-industrialism has meant that systems forces must confront a healthy community infrastructure. Yet post-modern economic institutions, which are advanced in Vermont, favor localism as much as urban-industrial economies favored centralization. Most important, the new technology—information technology, which is especially compatible with Vermont— is also especially conducive to democracy. There you have it: community, economy, and democracy.

Technology properly handled leads not only to what John Naisbitt calls "high tech/high touch" (referring to the observation that the more we use technology, the more we strive for human interaction), it also provides the time and space for community growth. While high tech/high touch is part of the seawall against the systems axiom in human relations, technology's capacity to decentralize the *settings* for personal interaction helps us regroup our collective lives once again around work, play, eating, sleeping, learning. In a word it allows us to preserve and enhance community.

A Legacy of Communities

In Vermont community still lives. There is no agreement, of course, on what is actually meant by community, but some characteristics appear so invariably in the debate that a suitable definition can be attained by induction. A good beginning is Robert Nisbet's formula: "Community is the product of people working together on problems, of autonomous and collective fulfillment of internal objectives, and of the experience of living under codes of authority which have been set in large degree by the persons involved." Community is a bond between the past and present which extends into the future. Community is people who interact at a personal level, have a shared identity, values, and traditions, sense an organic bond to each other, possess the power to make many of the decisions about their common lives, and feel a responsibility for extending mutual aid to their fellows in need. Community, in its geographic sense, requires human scale, a scale that human beings can understand and cope with. As Aristotle observed, the scale of a state should not be so great that its inhabitants cannot know each other's characters.

A small, intimate community is essential to the flowering of the civic-humanist ideal. It gives meaning and richness to human life. Its landmarks, its landscape, its uniqueness as place afford a sense of belonging and identity. A real community becomes a place of repair and solace, a scrapbook of shared memories, a gratifying niche in history.

Most important, the preservation of community requires that decisions about things that matter be made by the people affected.

Writes Nisbet: "Where power is external or centralized, where it relieves groups of persons of the trouble of making important decisions, where it is penetrating and minute, there, no matter how wise and good it may be in principle, it is difficult for a true community to develop. Community thrives on self-help (and a little disorder), either corporate or individual, and everything that removes a group from the performance of or involvement in its own government can hardly help but weaken the sense of community."

In our time in Vermont the idea of community has reeled under the hammer blows of centralization, mobility, massification, and social disintegration outlined in the previous chapter. But even with all this, Vermont remains the first place in America one would go if one sought to preserve community. The hills are still alive with the sound of town and village, neighborhood, corner, and place.

Vermont is communal from the ground up. The great glacier that visited twelve thousand years ago rolled massive boulders between ice and soil and gouged out hundreds of nesting places for community. Vermont does not show the ruralism of the heartland – flat townships checkerboarded on an endless horizon. It is not like the great West – people enclaved in small cities at the junctures of rivers or where mountain passes meet the plains. Up and down, hill and dale, that is Vermont: a continuing patchwork of little rivers, small mountains, hollows, ridges, slopes, and bends – perfect places for small settlements. Community life in Vermont is naturally integrated into the landscape.

There is also a profound historical impulse for human-scale community in Vermont, one that can be traced to the forests of Germany at the time of Tacitus, where in the *civitas* or *Volkerschaft* decisions were made in an open council of freemen. Today, with space stations circling the planet, Vermonters meet regularly to carry on their business in similar face-to-face gatherings. And as in bygone days, extra town meetings are called when and if the citizens, even a small number of citizens, so desire. The principal differences that separate the ancient town meetings from the modern are that Vermonters attend town meeting unarmed and indoors, while the warriors of the *Volkerschaft* met under the sky, carrying weapons.

The *Volkerschaft* was brought to England, where it became the shire. With the Norman Conquest the shire began to be called a "county" after the French name. Soon it fell under the influence of centralization. The *tun* or "town," which had also crossed the English

Channel from the Continent, also fought for survival. Until the Conquest, the people of the towns met in the *tungemot* or "town meeting." When the Normans replaced the town with the manor, local self-government migrated to the parish.

It was the towns that survived the Atlantic crossing to the New World. They sprang up in New England, huddling first along the coast. Then they appeared on the banks of the Connecticut River, which splits New England in halves from Canada to Long Island Sound. The towns seemed to fit the terrain. There was no need for counties, since jurisdictions that stretched wide over the land were precluded by its natural ruggedness. The memory of the parish also gave the New England town religious sanction in size and historical precedent: the town was a social approximation of the congregation. It was the godly arm of community that fashioned early New England.

From time to time small congregations of freemen worked their way into the hill country of northern New England. Soon the towns they established covered even the remotest of places. For all intents and purposes they were the only local government in New England. Well into the 1800s many of those towns, especially those in Vermont, still flirted with sovereignty. Over the past half-century their political powers have been severely eroded, yet the communities defiantly survive because their people love them and see in them the means of their democratic fulfillment.

The strength of geography as cocoon and history as memory is readily apparent. Consider Newbury, a typical valley town on the upper Connecticut. In 1980 Newbury had a population of 1,699. It also has a two-volume town history, over a thousand pages in hard cover. Without a high school for two decades (the state forced its consolidation into a larger union district) Newbury still draws over two hundred alumni to an annual alumni banquet every spring even though there has been no graduating class since 1967 – this when the average size of Newbury High's graduating class for thirty years before that time was under fifteen! It has a vibrant small grade school (K–6) of 180 students. It has ten social organizations including the Home Demonstration Club, the 4-H Club, the Pulaski Homemakers, the Women's Club, and the Wells River Study Club. Every summer the townspeople hold a two-day "Cracker Barrel Bazaar" on the village green to raise money for town services. Newbury also has an historical society actively preserving its heritage.

This town of less than two thousand men, women, and children maintains over one hundred miles of highways winding over sixty-five square miles of rugged hill country. Most of the roads have names printed only on the memories of the people. The North Road, the Scotch Hollow Road, the Swamp Road, the Leighton Hill Road. There is one road, called the New Road, that was built nearly a century ago. There is a monument to a local Revolutionary War hero on the green. There are six different country cemeteries, each an historical trail sign of the life and death of an enduring community. This little town has three fire stations and two rescue squads staffed by volunteers. It has ten churches, two libraries, and a radio station.

Every citizen of Newbury is a legislator and can make policy in person at town meeting. The town of Newbury also includes two incorporated villages, Newbury Village (population 425) and Wells River Village (population 396), where residents may also vote at annual village meetings. It takes forty citizens to fill the town's public offices. Dozens of others serve as volunteers in a myriad of other activities. It is a truth that anyone who wants to serve the public weal in Newbury, Vermont, can do so. People do not look for democracy in this town. Democracy looks for them.*

Newbury is not unique. It is representative of the deep bedrock of community life in Vermont today. Arlington, Chelsea, Athens, Walden, Craftsbury, Roxbury, Lunenburg, Richford, Jericho, Goshen. There are over two hundred of them. Towns like Newbury have survived the union-school movement that took away their high schools and the interstate-highway system that helped further separate work place from living place. True, they are weaker now than before, but they continue to resist the elements that would destroy them. They provide a solid breastwork against the systems axiom and a hopeful cradle for the new democracy we are proposing.

An Appropriate Economics

A vast network of American communities with similar advantages, however, was not able to hold the line during the urban-industrial revolution. Even in Vermont it is doubtful the towns could have survived

---

*In her important work on democracy, Jane Mansbridge included a Vermont town as one of three case studies of participatory democracy. She found that ". . . more than half the families that had lived in town more than ten years had had at least one member pressed into service as a town officer."

66

similar pressures. Yet what really matters is that Vermont escaped such a confrontation and did not lose its small-town culture. Now the economic winds have shifted. The imperative of the coming century is *toward* decentralism and away from concentration. The future is community-seeking.

One part of the movement for economic decentralization is driven by the potentials of "high tech" and finds expression in works of the *Megatrends* and *In Search of Excellence* genre. It is given ideological form by the appropriate-scale economics most notably advanced by E. F. Schumacher, founder of a modern version of "economics as if people mattered." This scholarship is especially well brought together in the volume entitled *The Living Economy*, which puts forth the views of TOES, The Other Economic Summit. Although there are elements of contention between high-tech proponents and human-scalers, their futures are inexorably related, and the influence is two-way – for they need each other. In the post-modern world high tech without human scale would be a horror, and human scale without high tech would be impossible.

To envision what decentralist or human-scale economics can mean for community and thus for democracy, consider the technological innovation which has done the most to *destroy* community in this century, the automobile. It destroyed community by separating work place from living place. There are those who claim, we think with great insight, that the mass production of cars has had more impact on social structures in America than any other single development. Yet its impact is now being replaced by the cable and the satellite dish. Money is no longer carried from one place to another but is transferred electronically. More and more, people are working, if not at home, then nearer home. Our task is to imagine the impact the telecommunications revolution will have on politics and society in the same way we may wish our grandparents had imagined the impact of the automobile.

Even when work place is still separated from living place and commuting to work is necessary, the living place is taking on more of the functions of society: entertainment, shopping, banking, medical services, and education. First the trolley, then the automobile, made it possible to leave the work place (the city) and move to a new living place (suburbia). But suburbia became more a sleeping place than a living place. Then as technology advanced, a person's sleeping and living places were reunited. Now both are being joined to the work place.

Vermont's economy of the future promises to go hand-in-glove with this new decentralism. Our state already has twice as many self-employed workers as the national average, and by 1980 it ranked in the top ten states in percentage of population with college degrees. Vermont consistently ranks in the top ten states on the amount of "value added" to a product by employees in relation to the amount of payroll that goes into making it. Vermont's economy is far more dominated by small business than that of the average state, and a much higher percent of its work force is employed in small firms. (In Vermont the small-business survival rate is higher than the nation's.) We make no claim that Vermont can house enough small companies controlled at the community level to support the state in the near future. But we do claim that local entrepreneurialism is made more possible every day by technological advancements. In the meantime what is needed, and what Vermont can provide, is opportunities to work and live in the same community, even though the companies for which one works may be controlled from afar.

In *Megatrends* John Naisbitt describes a society like Vermont when he says: "The mechanical blueprint of industrial society required enormous centralization – in labor, materials, capital, and plant." But, he continues, "agricultural and information societies are decentralized societies. Farmers could grow crops wherever the right field was; today you can start an information business with a telephone and a typewriter. . . ." It almost seems as though Naisbitt had Vermont in mind, for Vermont's economy features the two critical tracks of Naisbitt's model: agriculture (if we can keep it), and high-tech, decentralized industry. This fact bears especially sweet fruit in our defense of the claim that community and economic structure in Vermont (to use a Naisbitt word picture) are riding the same horse "in the direction the horse is going."

The quintessential work place/home place is, of course, the family farm. Furthermore, in Vermont as elsewhere in America, the farm is the most high tech of work places. It provides a compelling metaphor for Vermont's future. At the end of World War II Vermont had over twenty-five thousand operating farms. It now has about twenty-five hundred, mostly dairy. But the number need not go seriously lower. The prevailing myth about Vermont dairy farming is that the soil is too rocky and the hills too steep to employ modern agricultural technology. Yet the farms that have survived are situated on prime dairy land, mostly flat and rock-free. Moreover Vermont is still in a highly advantageous agricultural-sales situation, only half a day from the huge Boston and southern New England markets. Finally Vermont's weather, cool and moist, is highly suited to dairying. Cows *like* Vermont.

Yet there is no better example of the danger of nondiversification in economics than Vermont and its dairy farms. A biological comparison is appropriate. When all trees except the maples are culled from a sugar bush, the maples are more susceptible to disease: ecological systems need variety to survive. So do human systems. If Vermont is to maintain its agricultural sector in the predominance it deserves as a component of a complete society, it must diversify. We became almost totally dependent on dairying. Dairy must lead. It must not dominate.

As agriculture must diversify, so too must the entire economic system of Vermont. That is why it is not altogether bad that agriculture ranks third in Vermont's economy. Today manufacturing ranks first, with the major firms relative newcomers: IBM, Digital, Simmonds Precision, even foreign-owned companies like EHV Weidmann, Tsubaki, and Van Houten. Tourism has become the second leading income producer for the state, notably in the development of the East's most famous ski areas like Stowe, Killington, and Mt. Snow.

Vermont is also beginning to develop wholly new industries that depend on the application of brain power to intangible products (software, management, information processing, marketing, financial services, education); the application of high skills to produce high-value-added products (fine furniture, computer chips, high-tech machinery, robotics, avionics, cheeses); the provision of recreational opportunities (skiing, vacationing); and, of course, meeting its own consumer needs in areas where replacing imported with local goods makes sense (wood-chip energy, produce, meat, and recycled materials). This is the very kind of economic structure that is most conducive to decentralized activity – the kind of activity that helps community flourish and democracy grow.

A good example of a "post-industrial" organization is the Lewis Galoob Toy Company, with headquarters in South San Francisco. By traditional standards this is hardly a manufacturing company at all. Galoob contracts with independent designers to design and engineer new toys and with manufacturing brokers in Hong Kong to make the toys, who in turn pass on the labor-intensive work to factories in China. When the products arrive in the United States, they are routed to commissioned manufacturers' representatives. Galoob's accounts are collected by Commercial Credit Corporation on commission.

What Galoob's management does is mastermind this flexible world-spanning operation. In 1985 it had sales of $58 million – and only 115 employees. Obviously the Galoob management team could bring virtually any consumer product to market, not just toys. It can shift rapidly from one kind of product to another as markets change. Finally, and most significantly, there is no particular reason why the company has to be located in any particular place. So long as it has access to modern telecommunications, it could be located in Florida or Alaska or Vermont. In fact, the Mary Meyer Toy Company, in Townshend, Vermont, is evolving on the Galoob pattern. It no longer makes toys. Like its competitor Galoob, Mary Meyer has redefined itself to capitalize on its ability to conceive, communicate, plan, manage, and market products made halfway around the world. Several small Vermont publishing firms approximate the same model.

Another example of a firm independent of location is FEL Computing, which develops computer software in an old farmhouse at the end of a road in East Dover, Vermont. Since its products can be transmitted through telecommunications or by express service, the firm's employees can enjoy living in attractive surroundings in Vermont instead of fighting traffic jams on Route 128 around Boston to get to their high-priced, highly taxed homes. Other less sophisticated home business and cottage industries are springing up throughout Vermont and rural areas across the country.

But a more humane, community-level capitalism will not occur automatically, even though Vermont is trending is that direction. To create a favorable climate for the kind of enterprise that promises economic prosperity for a wide range of Vermonters, to build a life-sustaining economy consistent with human-scale values, and to encourage the continued decentralization of Vermont's economic sector to the community level, there are a number of goals that should be kept in sight.

Beyond the basic need to promote diversification, there needs to be, first, a realization that economic growth and progress spring from a creative energizing principle. That principle is a unique combination of an individual's perception, energy, willingness to innovate and to take risks, and resiliency. All these in turn spring from a culture that offers rewards for achievement and a legal framework that encourages it.

While it is difficult to itemize all the ingredients that go into the energizing principle described above, it is relatively easy to identify the conditions which stifle it. Societal control of opportunity. Status as a paramount determinant of success or failure. Advancement through privilege instead of merit or effort. Resignation to custom and tradition. Salvation through faith alone. Reinforced pessimism about the human condition. Confiscation of the fruits of enterprise through overburdensome taxation or expropriation. Oppressive, arbitrary government regulation. Rigid hierarchical government which issues instructions from the top. The abundant, sustaining Vermont economy of the future must avoid all of these pitfalls.

Secondly, Vermont must return to its roots of self-reliance – not to the point of foolish autarky, where Vermonters grow $5 avocadoes in electrically heated greenhouses, but to the end that a self-reliant Vermont economy shall produce as many of the essentials of daily life as it realistically can. Jane Jacobs, in her seminal work *Cities and the Wealth of Nations*, shows how rising local economies start by finding ways to replace imports. Tokyo's bicycle industry is a good example. At first Tokyo imported all its bicycles. Then a small industry began to repair bicycles by cannibalizing junked bicycles. There followed the *manufacture* of the most demanded repair parts. Finally came the domestic manufacture of whole bicycles and the exporting of those bicycles to other cities. That same process is at work in Vermont even now, where cars are being remanufactured from salvageable wrecks and beverage containers are increasingly recycled to create an income-producing item from what was originally a consumption item.

Jacobs believes that this process can only take place in cities – or, more precisely, that any place where this process occurs becomes a city. Historically that may have been true. In an age of widespread technical education, instant communication, decentralized knowledge dissemination and storage, and efficient transportation, however, it is not true. It is possible to imagine a network of small towns which, taken together, have the economic attributes needed to create the same economic conditions that were once possible only where large numbers of people were concentrated in urban places.

A localized entrepreneurial economy will be characterized also by a widespread distribution of productive private-property ownership. Private ownership is key to the linkages between community, democracy, and economy. That ownership can take many forms: proprietorships, shares in corporations, partnership interests, cooperative memberships, employee stock ownerships or profit-sharing trusts. America's Founding Fathers clearly recognized that a free republic could not long endure unless the institution of private property were widely shared among its people. The chance for ordinary people to acquire, use and exchange property is the sine qua non of a competitive free-enterprise system, which in turn is a necessary concomitant to a stable democracy.

Thomas Jefferson recognized this when he wrote to James Madison from France in 1785 to express his disgust with the French concentration of economic power. His conclusion was that "legislators cannot invent too many devices for subdividing property, only taking care to let their subdivisions go hand in hand with the natural affections of the human mind." One of these devices for subdividing property is communal ownership at the small-town level. In communities of human scale the distinctions between private ownership and public ownership grow dim. Clearly if a small town decides to "own" a cable-television network, that ownership fits the model of "private" co-operatives – but only if the scale is small. That is why true communal liberty stills the waters of conflict between left and right on the question of ownership.

Finally, the network of local economies that is emerging in Vermont will help to reinforce community by creating once again a sense of public approval and honor for the enterprising souls who create wealth, jobs, profits, and philanthropy. Too often, in modern Vermont and in much of America generally, the entrepreneur is viewed as a Captain Hook thirsting to pillage the community and exploit its innocent people, a scoundrel who fully deserves the contempt in which he is held and the overregulation to which his efforts are subjected. In this view anyone who earns a profit is stealing from the poor. Such a societal attitude is a sure-fire way to, at best, drive the entrepreneur away to more congenial places (like New Hampshire), or, at worst, turn him into the very creature of evil just described.

This hostile attitude was virtually unknown in the Vermont of 150 years ago. Consider the case of the Fairbanks brothers and their sons of St. Johnsbury. Because they created the platform-scale industry, made lots of money, and brought about prosperity for their workers and their town, they were honored by the people of St. Johnsbury. And in return the Fairbanks family used its wealth to line St. Johnsbury's Main Street with an academy, the Athenaeum and Art Gallery, the Fairbanks Museum of Natural Science, and two great Congregational churches. Brother Erastus and son Horace Fairbanks were elected governor. Today such men might well be looked upon as robber barons, which is doubtless one reason why there are not so many of them any more.

These principles of economic diversity, self-reliance, and private ownership are conducive to a life-affirming economy, and are essential to productive enterprise appropriate to Vermont's landscape, traditions, and, especially, to its community needs. They tend to undermine the systems axiom and serve the notions of diversity, variety, and adaptation. Ultimately this constellation of values will provide the kind of underpinning community life must have to endure, and this in turn will make it possible for democracy to flourish.

Technology in the Service of Democracy

The third component of Vermont's promise for a human-scale society is the fusion of democracy and technology. A heritage of community life and the potential for a new decentralized economic structure are necessary but not sufficient causes for the maintenance of democracy in the post-modern period. The unfolding promise for a regenerative democracy in America rests squarely on our willingness to put technology to political use – in the citizenry and in the government. Vermont can provide an early example of how to make this happen.

We have made the point that Vermont has maintained its democratic institutions, and we will not belabor it here. But its broad dimensions need brief amplification. Vermont is one of only three states to keep the two-year term for governor, even though systems thinkers have consistently proposed the four-year term. The legislature is large and nonprofessional. Less than 10 percent of its members are lawyers, one of the lowest ratios in America. The Vermont House of Representatives contains 150 members – one for every 2,200 eligible voters. There are 30 senators, one for every 11,000 voters. The Vermont judiciary has maintained its tradition of including citizen "side judges" on the bench.

The most important institution of Vermont's democracy, however, is town government. There is no county government to speak of in Vermont. Two hundred and thirty-six of Vermont's 246 units of government are towns in which the executive is a three- or five-member board of selectmen and the legislative branch is a town meeting. (One

73

Vermont town, Brattleboro, has a representative town meeting.) If you live in Vermont, you live in one of 237 towns or one of nine cities. If you live in a town, you are automatically a legislator. But even the cities are democratically based. In Burlington, Vermont's largest, there is no city manager; politics are focused on an elected executive, the mayor. Burlington's board of aldermen has thirteen members, each representing about 1,800 registered voters.

We do not say that all is well in Vermont's system of local government; in fact this book is about changing it. But we do claim with absolute certitude that if you wanted to live in the state that had preserved its democratic institutions most carefully, you would want to live in Vermont.

Although democracy in Vermont is being threatened by the forces that trashed human-scale politics throughout America over the last century, it has managed to hold on long enough for the telecommunications revolution to come to its aid. We see this happening both in the enhancement of the democratic process and in the increasing capacity of little governments to do the work of democracy.

•

Witness: A single headlight pushed the darkness back from the center of Pleasant Valley Road. Carried on a wind that rattled the hood of the old truck, freezing November rain cut down from the great shoulders of Mt. Mansfield, Vermont's highest mountain. With his truck's engine idling roughly, the driver watched the trooper approach in his rear-view mirror, great arcs of blue light pulsing through the night over his head, a long flashlight weaving in and out of the glow from the cruiser's headlights. It was 10:30 P.M. on a weekday, and nothing else moved on Pleasant Valley Road.

Hovering over a clipboard, the officer peered through the open window. "Here's a warning on that headlight," he said. "And from now on please carry your registration with you." There came a series of questions. "This is a 1964? You bought it in 1976? You live in Starksboro?" And there were more questions, all answered affirmatively.

"How do you know all this?" the driver asked at last.

"I radioed in to headquarters," said the officer. "I know all about you, Mr. Bryan. It's in our computer. Drive carefully." He walked away into the dark.

Deep in the outback of the country's most rural state, in the middle of the night, with the worst of New England's winter weather blasting down from the north, a government employee had consulted a computer at the state capital fifty miles and two good-sized mountain ranges away. From the front seat of a car he had assembled an array of information, made a decision, issued a directive, and recorded the transaction. In that event is an essential truth that grounds this book. Information technology can help local people do the work of government themselves.

About that same time a minister named Gabe L. Campbell bought a strange device into his First Congregational Church in Stamford, Connecticut. It was a computer system called a Consensor. Each user is given a miniterminal small enough to fit in the palm of the hand. In the words of its inventor, William W. Simmons, the Consensor "enables any participant in a discussion to cast his 'secret ballot' on the subject at hand." Reverend Campbell used the system to obtain reactions to his sermons and to "assess the feelings of the congregation as a whole regarding certain fundamental questions of belief."

One of the great technical dilemmas of Vermont's town-meeting democracy has always been the time constraints of secret ballots. Depending on the size of the meeting, the voting itself (marking a "ballot" – usually a slip of paper – walking to the front of the hall, putting it in a box, and sitting down again) can take from fifteen minutes to a half an hour. Then there is a wait while the votes are counted. Technology of the kind the Consensor represents, applied to town meeting, would strengthen that institution. The nation's last remaining vestige of direct democracy – the New England town meeting – could become America's first new example of twenty-first century decision making.

      •

Battle royal rages in academe over the question of democracy in the world of futuristic communications. It has ebbed and flowed from pessimism in such books as Nigel Calder's *Technopolis* and A. E. Miller's *The Assault on Privacy* to the almost giddy optimism of Amitai Etzioni and his colleagues:

> The form of democracy found in the ancient Greek city-state, the Israeli kibbutz and the New England town meeting, which gave every citizen the opportunity to directly participate in the political process, has become impractical in America's mass society. But this need not be the case. The technological means exist through which millions of people can enter into dialogue with one another and with their representatives and can form the authentic consensus essential for democracy.

The meaning of technology for future democracies circles back to less optimistic, and some downright negative analyses, such as Michael Malbin's "Teledemocracy and Its Discontents," published in *Public Opinion* in 1982, and David Burnham's *The Rise of the Computer State*. At the same time we have had moderately optimistic attempts to integrate teledemocracy into the larger framework of democratic practice, such as Benjamin Barber's important *Strong Democracy*. We also have highly useful analytical works that focus on specific case studies. The best of these is Arterton's *Teledemocracy: Can Technology Protect Democracy?*

Since it is a central concept of this book that communications technology must be employed on behalf of democracy, it behooves us to deal with the most powerful attack on this proposition. We find this in Langdon Winner's *The Whale and the Reactor*, a maddening book because it jerks us back and forth between euphoric agreement and dejected disagreement.

Winner's attack is on the one hand a general one. In a chapter entitled "A Better Mousetrap," he claims that the new faith in teledemocracy is a "strange mania" reflecting "dreams of instant liberation from centralized social control [that] have accompanied virtually every important new technological system introduced in the past century and a half." We are not so naive. Yet we note that even sober scholars like Harvey Brooks, who question many of the presumed benefits of "appropriate technology" (which is what we hold computers can be in their relationship to democracy), conclude: "Cheap and sophisticated information technology, characterized by rapidly declining costs per unit function, makes possible flexibility and *individualized control of existing technologies* [our italics]."

The position that technology's impetus is centralizing would be more appealing had the one supportive example Winner used been more convincing. Electricity, he says, has been a centralizing agent, not a decentralizing one: "... the centralism of the age of steam would seem modest compared to corresponding patterns developed in the age of electricity." Yet the dominant centralist movement in American history, the growth of our great cities, peaked at about the same time electricity became *generally* available. Electricity was coincidental with the beginnings of the decentralization of the urban place and is more associated with *sub*-urban expansion than with urban concentration. Winner's final argument, that electricity *itself* has become more centralized, we can only agree with, but that is partially a function of political decisions which we have the capacity to do something about. There still is room for will.

His assault on information technology as such is focused and compelling. Winner is right when he says that "computer romantics" who believe that the new technology will *automatically* end hierarchy and promote democracy are foolish. But the answer to his charge is simple: It is our task as citizens to make sure our technology promotes democracy. His point that the evidence (as of the mid-1980s) indicates that telecommunications technology has enhanced the already powerful is on balance true, even though Dan Rather and the three major commercial television networks might disagree. Yet most of Winner's evidence for the centralizing effects of advances in telecommunications is based on his observation of second-generation computer technology. We as yet have no systematic sense of the effect of third-generation, "chip-driven" technology. His conclusion that information technology can separate people from people is also true. We don't, as Winner says, get to visit with the bank teller when we use automatic-teller devices. Yet the time saved by computers can also be used for human interaction. When one of the authors checked two of Winner's books (and a stack of others) out of the library, he got to chat with a student while a holographic sensing device automatically filled out the check-out slips he used to copy by hand – tediously writing author, title, social security number, etc., on a dozen little slips of paper. Certainly the time gained as we are freed by the computer from repetitive tasks need not dehumanize us. We do not gather together in packs to hunt the day's food as we once did, either. To suggest that freedom from hunger incarcerates us in a web of self-centeredness is to demonstrate little confidence in our capacity to use the computer's greatest gift – the gift of time – for human options. This is a pessimism we simply cannot share.

Winner's objection that knowledge is not necessarily power and that, anyway, information is surely not knowledge, is also correct. But information *can* lead to knowledge, and knowledge *often does* lead to power. Worse, information is often used as blackmail. The democratization of information will at least put ordinary people on a firmer footing with their banker, their grocer, and their government. Finally, Winner's most important objection, that somewhere along the line information must be centralized, is more true than false *at this point in our development*. But the trend is in the opposite direction. Besides, those who read, for instance, *Consumer Reports* are in a more powerful position vis-à-vis the car salesman than those who do not, even though that information comes from a centralized source.

Fundamentally Langdon Winner and other critics of tele-democracy have been attacking the kind of teledemocracy that richly deserves it and ignoring the kind that does not. They have been attacking the use of electronic-communications techniques to *shore up* centralized, mass "democracies" based on individualist rather than communalist theory.* For instance Winner takes as his point of departure Etzioni's position quoted above. Etzioni is interested in a process through which "millions of people can enter into dialogue with each other and their representatives and can form the authentic consensus essential for democracy."

No wonder Winner is taken aback. A dialogue of millions? It would produce a din, not a democracy. We nowhere advocate teledemocracy on such a scale. Again, Winner zeros in on J. C. R. Licklider's almost adolescent fascination with computers. "The information revolution," says Licklider, will bring on a "new era of involvement and participation. The key is the self-motivating exhilaration that accompanies truly effective interaction with information through a good console through a good network to a good computer." Yuk! No wonder Winner has entitled the chapter of his attack "Mythinformation."

What is needed are new information technologies for democratic structures that feature face-to-face politics. We must bring the information technology to town meeting rather than try to approximate the characteristics of a town meeting at the mass level via telecommunications. Even Benjamin Barber, whose book *Strong Democracy* has played an important reinforcing role in our own thinking, falls prey to the urge to use technology to democratize the whole rather than its parts. The whole can never be democratized. But it can be governed justly and with competence through representational structures *if* the parts are democratic. The parts are where the focus should be — at the human scale. Using telecommunications, for instance for popular-opinion polling fine-tuned to everyday issues, will only duplicate the evil that has accompanied the massification of the presidential-election process via television.

The utilization of information technology for human-scale pol-

---

*It is noteworthy that Winner uses the nuclear-freeze vote in New England town meetings rather than the macro-approach of the organization Ground Zero as an example of how human-scale decision making is preferable (and more powerful) than organizations based on high-tech, centralized information systems.

itics involves three things. The first, largely ignored in the literature, is the capacity to allow people to do the work of government in the local community itself. This may be more important than all the rest. Computers in the hands of local people will blunt the coercion that centralists have always used to take away local control. "You don't know enough." "It's too complicated." "It would take too much time." Computer technology is at its best when it allows small governments to *do* things.

Secondly, communications technology will bring information to the level of public talk that Barber so rightly extols – but not the public talk of estranged citizens staring into CRTs. As one of us has envisioned (Bryan, in *North By Northeast*), the Vermont town meeting of the future might have a large television screen – much like the ones in ballparks today. There is a debate going on concerning the public funding of kindergarten transportation. A young woman in the middle of the crowd has been punching in a series of instructions on a miniterminal in her hand. These instructions have been queued up on the state's computer system, located in Northfield.

"Mr. Moderator," she calls and stands while her husband holds the baby.

She is recognized to speak.

"You're wrong," she says in the direction of an earlier speaker. "The average cost for transportation to kindergarten in Starksboro is *not* above the statewide average. May I?" She looks at the moderator.

"You have the floor and the computer."

She presses a final button on her terminal, and on the huge screen perched on the basketball backboard there appears a simple chart showing transportation expenses for kindergarten by town size and highlighting Starksboro's position on the chart.

"There!" she says and sits down.

This is no futuristic fantasy. We have the computer technology to do this very thing right now.

Finally, telecommunications can be used to bring people together. This is its least important function. It is one thing to use it so shut-ins can "attend" their town meeting in an interactive way. It is another to use it to count weekly city- or countywide votes on such critical issues as which contestant should win a beauty contest.

The key is to insist that computers and democracy interact on a human scale. In this Langdon Winner may have given us the answer in his earlier book *Autonomous Technology*. Technology, he says, is "a license to forget." He goes on to convince us emphatically that technology needs our constant attention, personal involvement, and moral concern. We must stay close to what we build. Our position is, accordingly, that hands-on, face-to-face forums for real decision making will help us break the habit of ignoring our democracy. Perhaps from time to time we will decide to take it apart and tune it. If information technology helps us do this, perhaps on balance it would be wise to use it even in the face of our incapacity to understand its inner workings – much as we don't really understand what makes this word processor do what it does. At any rate that is what we propose for Vermont.

Part II

A Federation of Shires

Chapter 6

THE SHIRES: GOVERNMENT WITH A HUMAN FACE

The Hobbits named it the Shire as the region of authority of their Thain, and a district of well-ordered business; and there in that pleasant corner of the world they plied their well-ordered business of living. . . .
—J. R. R. Tolkien

WE make three claims. The first is that real democracy is too precious to give up. The second is that communications technology increases the potential for a revitalized democracy. The third is that representational democracy, as *democracy*, depends on the existence of a vital direct democracy.

More than anything else a human-scale politics in America based on these principles needs a place to be—a location of its own. We propose to create one in Vermont by building the housing for a continuing democracy. Fundamental to the design of this new government is the need to address the tragedy of the mass so vividly told by Leopold Kohr:

> When a crowd of New Yorkers not so long ago invited a suicide candidate clinging for hours to a windowsill high on a skyscraper to "make it snappy," one might have been inclined to attribute this monstrous sentiment to the brutalized outlook of insensitive city

dwellers. Yet, the first ones to arrive on the scene displayed quite a different attitude. They were terror-struck and they prayed. But as their number changed, so changed their outlook. The pangs of individual conscience were insensibly drowned in the throb of social excitement. Tragedy turned into spectacle, terror into thrill, and the prayer to desist into the clamor to perform. Only when the spectators dispersed did they return to prayer, not as a result of their better selves but as a result of the transformation of a critical into a sub-critical mass whose tenuous nature makes it impossible for an individual to hide from himself. This indicated that, contrary to current theory, atrocity-loving ideologies in general, such as fascism or nazism, seem again not so much to result from bad leadership, evil education, or metropolitan callousness as from *critical social size.*

A similar giantism is corrupting our political institutions. Overcoming it requires the creation of governments of human scale in which democracy is maintained in the context of communal liberty. To do this, to effect these human values, to preserve our liberties, re-invigorate our democracy, and reunite our communities – and to confound and rebuke the forces of centralism tirelessly at work to undermine that cherished tradition – we propose the creation of a Vermont of *shires*, new units of general-purpose local government to which most of the powers of the state will be devolved and through which our people can express their most heartfelt political ideals.

To achieve these goals the new shires must meet the problems of critical size by integrating seven principles of democratic governance. The first of these principles is that government efficiency must never be defined in terms that sacrifice local citizen judgment. All too often when democratic control conflicts with plans for administrative efficiency, democracy is *automatically* precluded. For us, in contrast, the bottom line is the democratic process. Without that nothing, indeed, can ever be efficient.

Secondly, given this prerequisite, governmental size must be permitted to float free and seek its own level. At present it is encouraged (and often forced) upward but never allowed downward. The question, is a locality *big* enough to provide a welfare *system*, must read, is the unit *small* enough to provide the human *context* without which attempts to care for the needy shrivel and die on the bureaucratic vine of depersonalization?

Thirdly, there is a fundamental difference between direct and representative democracy. Representative systems depend on electorates well versed in the principles of citizenship. These can only be learned in the context of human-scale institutions. Since we can't get along without representational systems, small direct democracies are a requirement, not a luxury.

Fourthly, there is no other way to train democrats other than to give people *total* power to control *some* of the things that affect their lives–from beginning to end–in a government of human scale. Accepting credit for success and blame for failure is the essence of citizenship. Bits and pieces of democracy won't do.

Fifth, the more a particular policy relies on human factors for the proper understanding of its formulation and implementation, the more it ought to be conceived and carried out in governments of human scale. The more planet-based a policy is (that is, the more its proper understanding entails environmental thinking), the more its conception and implementation must come at a centralized level.

By way of example welfare is the most human of all government operations, relying on the most humane instinct, helping others. Centralization has taken welfare away from our people, insisting that this most human behavior can be translated into the most inhuman policy. By taking the giver out of the process of giving, we have lost our sense that as humans we have a *public* obligation to care for others.

Sixth, subdividing policy-making institutions into a multiplicity of one-purpose bodies (school boards, solid-waste authorities, planning commissions), governing over jurisdictions that are seldom coterminous, forces people to seek out influence in a puzzling web. Citizen fatigue and then despair set in. Democracy is lost to the tyranny of complexity and obfuscation. At a time when a complex society demands integration, policy is atomized into camouflaged enclaves dominated by interest groups. The size of jurisdictions must be reduced to the point where the linkages between, say, highways and schools become understandable and manageable. Policy will be better for it. Democracy cannot survive without it.

Finally, administrative decentralization on a function-by-function basis is worse than none at all. Unless democratic processes accompany decentralization, we are left with the worst possible situation, no democracy and lots of complexity. To compound the sin (as Vermont's leaders often do), such a decentralism is often packaged to appear democratic when all it does is divide and conquer local communities.

The Shires

Tucked away in the hills of Vermont are 246 towns and cities. The biggest, Burlington, had a population of 37,712 in 1980, and the smallest, Victory, had a population of 56. Fifty-four towns have a population of under 500. One hundred twenty have populations under 1,000. One hundred and ninety-six (80 percent) have populations of under 2,500. There are also over 50 incorporated villages in Vermont (which are subdivisions of the towns) equipped with taxation and service-delivery powers. Thus the total number of small democracies reaches 348, one for every 1,500 people. No other state comes close to this arrangement.

Why not strengthen democracy by reinforcing the present system? Because with so many units of government a vacuum has been created whereby the state has been free to centralize power. G. Ross Stephens, in an important article in the *Journal of Politics* in 1974, shows that between 1957 and 1969 no other state centralized its government more swiftly than Vermont. When the very smallest towns are incapable of providing services, *all* the towns are apt to lose out, because without home-rule protection in the constitution, they are governed by general law created by the legislature and prescribed for towns as such.

We also need to synchronize political and social structure. Town boundaries were drawn over two hundred years ago. Social and economic influences sometimes crisscross Vermont with little respect for political boundaries. All too often work, play, and home have become estranged from government.

We need new governments bigger than towns yet smaller than Vermont's vestigial counties. They must draw their power down from the state rather than up from the towns. To achieve this, Vermont must change more radically than any other American state has ever changed. The central government must shrink to one quarter its current size – become unrecognizable by current standards. While the authority for laws which must be uniform (and on inspection one finds these are precious few) will continue to reside at the center, the great bulk of state spending programs (education, welfare, mental health, even roads) will devolve to the new shire governments. By giving the shires complete residual power an age-old custom in America will be reversed. In Vermont the localities will no longer be creatures of the state. The state will be the creature of its localities.

These new governments might be given any name, but we prefer "shire." The old English shire provides a rich inspiration for a new, decentralized political structure. Historically that structure was established on a hierarchy of human scale, from warrior to clan to tribe. If we think of Vermont's citizens as warriors and the towns as clans, what is needed is a structure akin to tribes. While the terms "shire" and "county" are used interchangeably by British historians, we prefer the term shire because it is more clearly tied to human (clan/tribe) symbolism, because it will tend to confuse less with the existing county system, and because the term is familiar to Vermont. Counties were first called shires, and "shire towns" still exist in each county.*

Most important though, in history and in literature, the shire's image is of unions of small villages cast in the context of the earth itself—land, water, and the local peculiarities of place which bespeak character and culture, distinctiveness and delineation. When one thinks of "shires," one thinks of them in multiplicity, in constant interaction and creative turmoil. One thinks of the variety on which all art, letters, and science ultimately depend. The shire evokes the sense of communal liberty and environmental consciousness that is essential to the preservation of democracy. It will create the context in which people of all income ranges and social classes will be able to reacquaint themselves with their democracy.

One point must be emphasized most strongly: the shires are not designed as *more government* between the towns and the all-powerful state. Indeed the authors have been in the forefront of the struggle—vocally so—against those who would take away the functions of our towns and vest them in "regional" bodies which would inevitably become the creatures of the state.

On the contrary the proposed shires will be independent polities, accountable directly to their own people, governed by a body elected by the people, having their own independent revenue base adequate to their needs. Shires will represent not more government, but the same amount of government we have now, redistributed from Montpelier to St. Johnsbury, Wilmington, Manchester, Canaan, and Bristol, where

---

*On March 24, 1778, the General Assembly of the Republic of Vermont passed the following resolution: "Voted that the line between Bennington and Rutland *Shires* be the north line of Dorset and Tinmouth." In his path-breaking work on the evolution of Vermont's counties, Virgil McCarty comments, "It is difficult to distinguish between the meaning of the word 'Shire' as it is used here—meaning the extent of territory over which the Shire town of a county exercised jurisdiction—and the word 'county.'" It is interesting that all the records of the colonies of New York use the term "county" while Vermont's very first references used the word "shire." Evidently the word "shire" was considered by these early Vermonters to more appropriately denote the lands of their new-found freedom.

governments can be run the way the people, and not the technocrats, want them run. We want more democracy in the government, not more government in the democracy.

Creating the shire as the primary unit of government raises an essential question about the future of Vermont's towns. We propose that the division of responsibilities between shire governments and sub-shire governments, whether they be towns, incorporated villages, neighborhood districts, or whatever else the local citizenry may conceive—be worked out variously, by the people of the shire. In some smaller shires a unitary shire government may emerge, exercising authority over all former functions of the state as well as all functions currently exercised by the towns. In other shires the town governments may be left intact to do what they now do, while the shire takes on the responsibilities that have come down from the state. It is not inconceivable that some shires will pass powers acquired from the state on to their constituent towns. In yet other, larger shires, new sub-shire districts governed by neighborhood assemblies may be created. The state will have nothing to say about the form of these local arrangements, other than to assure that due process is followed in making decisions.

Put another way our plan calls for a massive enabling of local government. We expect that after fifty years a wide spectrum of variation in shire structure will emerge. The shires will be laboratories for experimentation, where substance (policy) and process (democracy) will work out a natural balance. Vermont's inherent inclination for a public life of human scale should place the towns at the heart of a lively politics of localism. If it does not, and politics rises uniformly to the shire level, we have no complaint, for the evolution will be democratic. And in the worst possible case (the towns disappear altogether and are replaced by forty shires), we still win. For forty shires with real power are better than 246 cities and towns with counterfeit power.

The model best approximating our plan is the Swiss. The Vermont state government would be analogous to the Swiss national government, the Swiss cantons would be our shires, and their communes our towns and cities. As the Swiss communes have their rights and duties defined by the cantons, the Vermont towns and cities will be creatures of the shires. In some Swiss cantons the communes have autonomy in a wide array of policy; in others they do not. This too will happen in Vermont. In Switzerland there are communal assemblies, in Vermont there are town meetings. All of this is wrapped in a strong tradition of communal liberty in Switzerland – as it is in Vermont.

Bounding the Shires

In dealing with the question of space and size in a way consistent with our seven democratic principles above, two problems of language emerge. First, there is no word to modify "community" that means "small" anymore. The great majority of small-city or small-town studies considers a community of 25,000 to be small. But if we are concerned with the size of communities in which democracy is possible, 25,000 is very, very big. It is bigger, for instance, than 245 of the 246 towns and cities in Vermont. It is substantially larger than Vermont's second-biggest city, Rutland, which had a 1980 population of 18,436.

Another problem is that "representative" democracy has come to mean democracy itself. The most thorough look at the subject of size and democracy, by Robert Dahl and Edward Tufte, laments this very point: "Clarity would have been better served if the term 'democracy' had never been transferred from ideals and institutions associated with direct popular rule in the city/state to the ideals and institutions associated with representative government in the nation-state." Madison himself (in Federalist No. 14) warned against the misuse of the word "democracy": "In a democracy the people meet and exercise the government in person: in a republic they assemble and administer it by their representatives."

Keeping these problems in mind and remembering that there is a connection between practicing citizenship yourself and knowing how to elect others to practice it for you, we have established a two-tier framework for democracy in Vermont: (1) the towns, where direct (town meeting) forms of decision making will be used, and (2) the shires, which feature a representational system. Building the shires from the bottom up by combining towns will provide them with a foundation of strong communities. But the shires are also kept small enough to create a clear bond between citizen and legislator and relieve the tension of representation stretched beyond reason. What we need then are criteria for establishing the optimal size for direct democracy and for representational systems.

Beginning with the Greeks there is a long history of optimal-size analysis. Kirkpatrick Sale's recent work concludes that the optimum population size is 500. Robert Dahl, of Yale, one of America's leading political scientists, observes in *Dilemmas of Pluralist Democracy*: "A unit with a citizen body larger than a thousand, let us say, will drastically reduce opportunities for effective participation and individual influence."

In his book *Strong Democracy* Benjamin Barber calls for a national system of neighborhood assemblies which "can probably include no fewer than five thousand citizens and certainly no more than twenty-five thousand." Douglas Yates reviews a long list of examples in *Neighborhood Democracy* and concludes that only where community size was limited to several hundred "did widespread citizen participation occur." Joseph Zimmerman, who writes on town-meeting democracy from the State University of New York at Albany, puts the upper limit at a population of from 8,000 to 10,000.

Two criteria seem to generate these estimates. They are canopied by one overarching control variable. The criteria are: (1) social structure – the Rousseauian premise that "each citizen can with ease know all the rest," and (2) political process – how many people can come face to face and decide issues. The control variable is population density, what Sale refers to as the "walking distance" criterion.

Our judgment from Vermont is that the optimal population size for direct democracy is in the 500-to-2,500 range. Towns of over 2,500 people quickly come to fail the social-structure requirement – that is, one cannot know everyone else "with ease" in them. The record of what happened in hundreds of town meetings we studied between 1969 and 1989 shows a strong and consistent relationship between size and participation. There is a remarkable dropoff in attendance at about the 1,000-population level. There is also a dramatic decrease in the percentage of citizens that speak out in larger town meetings. Nevertheless there are enough cases of towns in the 1,000-to-2,500 range that attain, say 20-percent attendance to warrant a faith in population sizes of up to 2,500.

Thus the assessments of both Barber and Zimmerman need some adjustment. Neighborhood assemblies in towns of over 5,000 will soon become debating forums for a tiny few. Stretching the town meeting form over communities of from 2,500 to 5,000 reduces attendance well below the 10-percent range. At the same time we don't accept the notion that 500 is the optimal population for the democratic unit, although it is absolutely clear that the tiny communities of 500 are more purely democratic than those of 2,500. With the shires made up of towns or neighborhood assemblies of 500-to-2,500 population,

20 percent of the towns in Vermont will be too *small*. Our limit also means that some of Vermont's larger towns, which are too big to meet the requirements of direct democracy and too small to become shires, will need to subdivide. Yet over 50 percent of Vermont's towns are in the 500-to-2,500 population range and thus already fit our prescriptions for optimal democratic governance.

Surely the communities in this array seem tiny. It is legitimate to ask how much togetherness is too much togetherness? This question, however, has less relevance in small, town-meeting democracies than in utopian communal arrangements. Town-meeting societies have always been based on a balance of personal and impersonal behavior. Small-towners know it is essential to preserve the capacity to act together even in the face of sharp disagreement. That is why strictly applied "rules of order" in town meeting often astound the newcomer expecting a "touchy-feely" 1960s atmosphere. Small-town life has always maintained rituals and institutions that let diversity exist in the context of community – to allow the private and public person to coexist in each citizen. Vermonters understand that it is frightfully difficult to offer your neighbor a smile and a "good day" when her hogs have recently rooted out a perfectly good row of your beets. "Good fences make good neighbors" in politics too.

While the towns will remain the fundamental unit of Vermont's democracy – the place where politics will be learned through practice in centers of deep-rooted history and tradition – the primary unit of Vermont's government will be the shires. While the distinction is somewhat artificial, one might think of the towns as the heart of Vermont democracy, while the shires are the heart of Vermont's governance.

The size of the shires (75 percent will fall in the 5,000-to-15,000 population range) and the small number of towns in them (from five to ten) will give every town considerable weight in the shire. This will create a condition whereby the arguments made by representatives of even the shire's smallest towns (which will receive face-to-face consideration in the shire-moot) will be hard to dismiss. Opponents will not be able to hide behind the anonymity of social distance. Consensual decision making will replace the kind of adversarialism which is apt to rely on the brute force of numbers.

The populations of the shires are smaller than that recommended by Sale – 50,000 people for the intermediary level of governance between the community and the state. One reason for the smaller population size is topography. In Vermont geographical blankets governing populations of 25,000 would, in most cases, stretch the density too thin even if the "walking-distance" criterion is changed to a driving-distance criterion (and then amended by a mud-season variable). Large land masses would also violate the natural configurations of watershed, ridge line, and valley. We are not, for the most part, discussing optimal cities. We mean to create optimal *countryside* governments.

The small size of the shires also provides a needed human base for representation. By applying what some have called an optimal number of citizens per neighborhood (200) to a reasonably sized shire legislature of, say 50, we arrive at shires with populations of about 10,000. The intention is to maintain a neighborhood base for representation in the shires by creating a kind of representative town meeting at the shire level. The average shire in our prototype map (see Chapter 7) has a population of 10,229. The median has a population of 8,533. This is an appropriate compromise dictated by topographical constraints and democratic principles. Our rural plan may be contrasted to Sale's more urban model as follows:

Sale's URBAN MODEL

Unit	Optimal Population
Neighborhood	500
Community	5,000
City	50,000

Bryan and McClaughry's RURAL MODEL

Unit	Optimal Population
Town	1,500
Shire	10,000
Federation	550,000

No sane social scientist would claim too much for optimal-size analysis. Nevertheless, there is an amazing consensus of scholarship in different fields over, indeed, the last four thousand years on the size question. Our thinking, for instance, comes very close to that of Christopher Alexander and his colleagues, who published from the Center for Environmental Structure, at Berkeley, a trilogy designed to "lay the basis for an entirely new approach to architecture." The third book in the series was entitled *A Pattern Language* and concludes "every city needs to be made of *self-governing groups* [italics ours] which exist at two different levels, the communities with populations of 5,000–10,000 and the neighborhoods with populations of 200–1,000." Given Vermont's very special circumstances our figures on optimal size seem to square with the Berkeley studies. It is important that this agreement, coming through two different disciplines (architecture and political science) resulted from the same desire to expand human options.

•

Witness: Bill and Sally Jones were cramped into the cab of their 1967 Ford two-ton. Even in Vermont it gets hot in August, and Bill couldn't turn the heater off. He'd meant to cut and splice the heater hose, but he hadn't gotten to it. The truck's body had been home-built many years earlier. A peavey and two chain binders lay with the logging chains on the back between the bunkers. Vent windows directed some cooling to Bill and Sally's faces, but at thirty-five miles per hour it didn't help much. The right front wheel wobbled slightly on a bald tire as the dust from the road filtered up through the floor.

About a month earlier they'd purchased a 1976 Ford with 120,000 miles on it from a neighbor for $150 and a load of hay (seventy-five bales). To register it they had mailed the sales tax to the state capital along with the registration fee. Sally did that. Forty-five dollars to register the car and $6 tax (4 percent of the sale price of $150). With the car registered they wouldn't have to eat up gas with the truck whenever they had an errand. They'd already picked up a junk Ford for $50 and parked it across the road from their place. That would serve for parts.

But now the Vermont State Department of Motor Vehicles (fifty-six miles to the south in Montpelier) had sent the Joneses a form letter with the list price of a 1976 Ford at $1,200. They said the Joneses still owed $42 in tax on their new vehicle. Their neighbor drafted a letter to the DMV saying he'd sold Bill and Sally the car for $150 because it was falling apart. "It probably wasn't worth the $150," he wrote. (The seventy-five bales of hay he chalked up to the hidden economy.) Sally mailed the letter. Time passed. Then came a second form letter: Please pay the $42, or you don't get your registration. The Joneses said, to hell with it, we'll pay the $42. They needed the car. The neighbor said, "Stand up for your rights. Drive down there and get it settled once and for all."

The trip to Montpelier is the Joneses' longest by far this year. The Motor Vehicle Department is across the street from the capitol. There is traffic, and there are parking meters (for cars – not logging trucks). The Joneses parked some distance off. Sally is fifty-eight years old and walks with a cane. Her legs don't support her weight any more. Bill, partially bald, long unkempt beard of gray and huge hands – so callused the joints seem to have disappeared – walks straight but slow. He is relieved their truck held together on the trip to Montpelier; his mind is on the trip back. The sidewalk shimmers in the heat. They sweat. Inside the building there is a long line before the registration window. Bill and Sally know they look different. Time passes, and the urge to go home becomes overpowering. When the clerk behind the glass says $42, Sally lays down several sweaty bills and pays on the spot. It's time to leave.

That evening at a supper table crammed with bread, rolls, fried hotdogs, fried potatoes, and little brown cupcakes – seconds from a local bakery – the Joneses were happy. They'd made it down and back. Nothing bad had happened. They explained the day's events to their neighbor over coffee. He was struck by the fact that Sally had been, more than anything else, impressed with the number of police cars she'd seen in Montpelier. Bill said, with a smile and perhaps just a trace of apology, "Didn't save any money, but what t'hell." The neighbor said, "Yeah, what the hell." He'd caused the Joneses enough trouble already.

Once again people who most needed and deserved their government's help got, instead, the shaft. For those for whom reading and writing are a chore, for whom the sound of their car *starting up* is a joy (one that is most often problematical), for whom hope has withered away in the gloom of chances lost, the "interface" with government cannot be routinized and bureaucratized. It is a truth of the twentieth century that policies which transformed the great low-income working majority of 1900 into the income-secure middle class of 1990 will not work for the substantial residue of truly poor people that were left behind.

Bureaucracies are not evil, but they are inhuman. They are *fashioned* that way: they work *because* they are capable of inhumanity on a massive scale. This is not to criticize bureaucrats. In fact the greatest complaints bureaucrats have about being bureaucrats is that they are forced by routine to treat people as numbers. When Bill and Sally Jones reached that window in Montpelier, they had a tale to tell – a very human tale. It involved a neighbor and a special circumstance.

93

It involved a dying little hill farm. It involved two people who are uncomfortable dealing with strangers.

It is our task to reintroduce everyone – but especially people like Bill and Sally Jones – to their democracy. The middle class is taught to deal with lines and schedules, routines, forms, and faceless functionaries. That is why program after program intended to help the poor ends up helping, instead, the secure. Middle-class citizens fudge forms to secure low-income housing. Well-to-do parents of college students borrow low-interest money from the government for college bills instead of cashing in their stocks. Conservatives often latch onto the extremes (the tiny percentage of the poor who cheat the system) and tout them as typical. Liberals, because they have no capacity to separate an admission that the old technologies have failed from the implication that the conservatives are right, overlook the fact that the secure are benefiting at the expense of the poor. Spend more, they say, and a good portion of the benefits will fall into the lap of the poor. Liberals have their own "trickle-down theory."

Rather than in Montpelier, picture Sally Jones down at the town clerk's office in the town where she lives. The town administers car registration and collects the tax that goes with it. Sally knows the town clerk. True, there is a class difference between them. Sally is poor, and the town clerk has "done better." But there is no way the town clerk can ignore Sally. There is no need for a form letter. There is plenty of time and space for tales to be told. Besides, Bill sells wood to the town clerk's sister-in-law. Bill's grandchildren are in school with hers. And there is something else. Bill and Sally Jones *won't take it* if they are treated badly by "the town." They'll raise hell. Finally there is town meeting. Bill seldom goes, but Sally and her daughter-in-law were there last year. When the Joneses get riled up, they can account for at least a dozen votes at town meeting. They did that eight years ago when they opposed the plan to move a one-room school house in their part of town down to the village. Town clerks pay attention to a dozen votes in a town with less than a thousand registered voters.

•

Distributing Power

Designing a code for the redistribution of power between state and shire in Vermont involves a complete turnabout in the way Americans approach government. To wit: policies that most directly affect people are most appropriately decentralized; policies that most directly affect the planet are most appropriately centralized. Our reform abandons the way of government currently in favor: education by megastandards, welfare by mailbox, police protection by radio, and health care by stranger.

If we can build the "complicated and dutiful" relationships of true human interaction back into governance, most of our problems in these areas will shrink to manageable size. Thus the power of the state government as the protector of the environment and guarantor of basic civil rights and liberties should be preserved. But the shires should be the repository of authority in matters in which success or failure depend on face-to-face interaction of human beings.

There is a need for state presence in other concerns that transcend local boundaries, such as transportation, disease control, information gathering and dissemination, technical assistance, and shire-federal relationships. But even in areas such as transportation there should be a substantial shift of power to the shires. The bottom line: If when traveling through Vermont one encounters variations in the quality of the roads, that is the price one pays for democracy. If local speed limits are different, that is a quirk produced when self-government is given more than lip service. While many may see these as problems, we see them as an affirmation of the human condition, a condition that thrives on variety, innovation, spontaneity, and the deep-seated and long-lasting cultures generated by people in charge of their own destinies.

In all areas where law making is shared between state and shire the *administration* of policy should be at the shire level. Here is where information technology offers its greatest hope for democracy. During the 1970s the decentralization of administration to the face-to-face level was called "street-level bureaucracy." There have been problems with building human transactions back into administration. But the process should not be abandoned, for the course of events is moving in its favor. If advances in information technology – especially in the field of "real-time" decision making – continue to develop as they have over the last two decades, we will soon be able to administer nearly all governmental functions at the shire and sub-shire level.

In this way citizens will be required to do the *work* of government as well as making the decisions. An officer like the environmental constable, a local citizen with the power to poke around the shire and make sure laws designed to keep the countryside clean are being obeyed, is an example.* In fact Vermont not only has a deep historical tradition of local office holding – hog reeves, fence viewers, scalers – it has also developed more and more roles for citizens in recent years. One such is town energy officer. Quasi-public functions are remarkably strong, too. Volunteer fire departments and rescue squads in Vermont provide an infrastructure of local organizational vitality. With the shires in place a whole range of administrative services now run by the state will become the work of local people.

The case for a complete redirecting of human-scale policy to the localities and a parallel redirection of environmental policy to the bioregional level seems obvious. People *need* the human touch. Welfare without love is impossible. With environmental concerns, however, the case is otherwise. Nature does not know love. While it must be treated *with* love, it will not react *to* it – as anyone will tell you who has asked a team of oxen to perform out of love. The nationally-based welfare bureaucracy doesn't take this critical distinction into account. It, therefore, quite literally, treats the poor like something inhuman – like dirt.

Individuals get lost in the aggregates created by centralized institutions. Statistical absurdities lead to equally absurd public policy – both in design and implementation. On the other hand the planet is an aggregate. If we learned anything from the environmental revolution of the 1970s, it is that the environment *is* an interrelated, interdependent whole. It cannot be protected in bits and pieces – by letting each community deal with it on its own. Human beings, on the other hand, cannot be protected and served outside the context of a community where each individual can be treated as a unique case having unique needs to be met and unique contributions to be made.

There is a second, reinforcing, proposition: People are more resilient to the damage caused by the "mistakes" democracies will inevitably produce than is nature. The human race is more capable of withstanding tragedies caused by governments. Case in point: Several years ago one of the authors was asked to be on a panel that would discuss the question of democratizing the "nuclear-dump" question in Vermont's Northeast Kingdom. The idea was to establish committees to put resolutions on the agendas (called "warnings") of the forty-

---

*"Bounty hunting for trash" is not such a wild idea. After all, Vermont's returnable-bottle law kept one of the authors in spending money as he was growing up in the late 1940s and 1950s (and is keeping the other in spending money now).

nine town meetings held in the area. These resolutions would outlaw the disposal of nuclear waste in each town. Yet when it was speculated that one or two towns, seduced by the benefits that would inevitably be offered to any municipality welcoming the placement of a nuclear dump within its borders, might vote for a nuclear dump, the organizers began to reconsider the entire strategy, and the movement fizzled.

Democracy is risky business. We would not dream of letting the towns along the Connecticut River decide whether or not to allow chemical wastes to be dumped into the water. This is not because the quality of the decisions made by these towns would not be higher, on average and over time, than the quality of, for instance, decisions made by the state legislature or, certainly, by the United States Congress. It is the *range* of impact of a decision that is of concern. We cannot *risk* a mistake *by even one unit* when an entire river is at stake. Better (in cases involving the potential for massive damage to the environment) to live with the mediocrity of centralized decisions – where one cannot hope for the best decision but neither fears the worst.

In these cases the progress that comes through the trial and error and experimentation of a multiplicity of units making decisions over time, the consciousness raising that would occur, an invigorated global awareness, and a heightened sense of citizenhood in each town must be sacrificed because the impact of a mistake by one unit would come crashing down on the entire region.

In contrast consider the issue of risk in education: Who wants to put rosy-cheeked school children in jeopardy? Education is also a good case because it is a profoundly human undertaking. Suppose the question of a totally creationist curriculum were placed on the warnings of our town meetings, and two of the forty-nine towns in the Northeast Kingdom voted "Yes"? We are biased, but there is little doubt in our minds that the children served by such a curriculum would be poorly served. Yet on all counts, quality, quantity, and range, the harm done would not amount to much. The effects of a creationist curriculum in one town are not automatically transferred to another. The risk of *societal* harm would be massively outbalanced by all the benefits that would occur from local control of education in all forty-nine towns – the innovations in curriculum design, parental involvement, political efficacy, community building, and – most important – in the children's own *awareness* of public debate over the issues, and in their perception that their parents were involved in the very

97

heart of their education.

In education as in art, variety is in and of itself a positive good. Warren Johnson is eloquent on this point in *The Future Is Not What It Used to Be*. He argues that variety and diversity in public affairs are not simply *useful* to society, they are *necessary* to it: "It is rare that a single quality is valuable in all circumstances; even the best of things usually have some disadvantages. But with diversity, the disadvantages are hard to find, while the benefits seem to be universal." Added to the many values of diversity, especially in the area of policy making, says Johnson, there is "a much more fundamental advantage for survival: *It contributes to stability, to the ongoing continuity of life and the avoidance of devastating breakdowns* [italics in original]." Johnson understands that "diversity means that no part of a system is so dominant that its collapse would be a catastrophe for all. . . . Diversity also allows change to occur smoothly since individuals can shift to modestly different ways without making big, risky changes, to experiment with greater safety, and thus encourage it." In environmental affairs, of course, nature *makes its own variety*, and when governments try to interfere they generally screw it up. The role of planetary policy *must* be uniform in order to match the conceptual simplicity of the earth's charge to us as stewards: let the planet be.

While it is unfortunate that diversity may mean some inequality in human transactions, education is not possible without it. If we really believe that a totally creationist curriculum in a school system here and there will become a serious impediment to the march of scientific progress—if we fear a wrong doctrine might infect the entire nation and that society might "melt down"—then we might as well jettison all notions of democracy and burn this book on the grounds that the people are too incompetent to govern themselves.

It is also true that under conditions of human-scale decision making, where a community's own children are at stake, great care is usually exercised. We are less apt to do harm to each other under conditions of localism than we are to the planet, because we *care* more about ourselves. It confounds reason and usurps all sense of instinct to argue that there is any mechanism which is apt to treat children more humanely than a close-knit community of parents and neighbors. Education without humanity is a farce. Humanity without community is impossible. One has only to watch the eyes of a six-year-old standing in a holiday chorus, searching the audience for her parents, to know this. To be that parent is to know too the incredible power of the primeval urge to protect and to care. If we treated the planet with equal concern, there would be far less need to centralize environmental decisions.

Finally, we tend to forget that massive harm can be done by centralized instruments. In fact decisions made by the institutions of adversarial, representative liberalism are almost always wrong, by definition. Compromise, which is essential to centralized decision making in a complex society, may work, but policies produced by compromise in mass societies are seldom correct. Moreover when adversarial, compromising liberalism breaks down, centralized decisions can end up deep on the down side of their intended goal of an acceptable mediocrity. When this happens everyone (not just a local district or two) is harmed. Centrists often wrongly assume that the choice is between a system that always works perfectly (and consistently produces mediocrity) and a system that can work very well and can work very badly. We concede that local decisions can be very bad. But so too can centrist decisions. When centrist decisions are good, they are average; and when they are bad, they are horrid.

To summarize: What will the shires do? The answer? Nearly everything. We have outlined the general characteristics of a radical redistribution of power in this chapter and will have more to say on the matter in Chapter 9 when we deal with the remaining role of state government. Also we will treat specific types of policies in individual chapters further on. Until then the pivotal *structural* concept to bear in mind is that whereas before the localities were creatures of the state, in the new system the state will be a creature of the shires. In other words Vermont will shift from the unitary model to the federal model. The pivotal *functional* concept to bear in mind is that human-services policy will be localized, while environmental policy will be centralized. In all our plan we were guided by Benjamin Barber's description of a strong democracy: one that requires common deliberation, common legislation, and common work.

It is now time to discuss in some detail what the shires will actually look like.

Chapter 7

THE SHIRES: ARCHITECTURE FOR A NEW DEMOCRACY

When in some obscure country town, the farmers come together to a special town meeting, to express their opinion on some subject which is vexing the land, that I think, is the true Congress, and the most respectable one that is ever assembled in the United States.

—Henry David Thoreau

THE shires will bring the work of government back home and thereby counter a major problem of advanced technology – the separation of neighbor from neighbor, a lessening of the need for mutual aid. Barns don't burn down as often. New barns are therefore raised less frequently, and when they are raised it is done by machines not neighbors. Better tires and improved roads mean we don't have to help as many of our friends out of ditches.

Earlier we argued that mutual need and the attitudes it generates are major components of community cohesion and human-scale behavior. Creating shires with heavy governmental responsibility will replace physical interdependence with political interdependence. Until now both kinds of shared work have been taken from the community – the physical by technology and the political by the state. The shires will give one back. While before we joined around the village green to graze our cattle, now we will gather around the green to solve our political problems. We'll need each other again.

100

Specifically, what kind of governmental apparatus will allow this to happen? Two fundamental notions ground our answer. The first is that Madison's fears of tyrannical majority factions occupying the halls of government are no longer as relevant as they once were. It follows (secondly) that a complex system of "checks and balances" which has sentenced our democracy to a future of endless conflict is no longer a structural imperative. Accordingly the shire governments we have proposed do not feature the separation of powers between legislature and executive. The judicial system will not be set apart from the people and "protected" from them by executive appointment. The concept of representation as a means of isolation from "popular passion" will be severely curtailed. In the electoral system "approval voting" will work to select consensus candidates rather than ensure that this or that group is represented.

We do not claim the shires will be populated by angels. Therefore elements of the old politics such as the secret ballot have been preserved. We have also protected the little towns in the shires from takeover by majorities in the bigger towns through votes requiring large and geographically diffused majorities. We agree with Jane Mansbridge who concludes in her book *Beyond Adversary Democracy* that democracy needs a combination of adversarial and nonadversarial forms. But as she also points out, these nonadversarial, more communalistic forms are far more appropriate in small jurisdictions. Like shires.

Face-to-face communal decision making, by its very process, mitigates the "evils of faction" Madison so rightly abhorred. The adoption of Madisonian principles (which were designed for a large national federation) for use in communities has intensified the problems of democratic government at the local level throughout American history. In Burlington, Vermont, for instance, power is divided among the mayor, the board of aldermen, and various municipal commissions. The mayor in Burlington does not hire the fire chief; a commission appointed by the board of aldermen does that. This tripartite arrangement creates a quagmire of confusion, rendering citizenship impossible for all but those who spend most of their waking hours involved in public matters. In addition it is time we paid more attention to an important empirical reality: the probability that this or that jurisdiction will house a "class" majority that might usurp a consensual process has diminished with time. Vermont's towns today, each and every one, are far more likely to contain the multiplicity of interests that *by nature* reduces the likelihood of mischief by factions.

It is now appropriate to step beyond the pessimism of the founders, who increased the size of government to make sure the people could not act in concert at the base and then set in place an intricate system of checks and counterchecks to make it difficult for them to govern effectively at the center. In short let's proceed with the business of trusting ourselves.

Fundamental constitutional changes are needed to set the shires in operation under a model structure of governance. This done, a home-rule clause will allow the people of the shires to alter the model by creating their own charters. The towns will be preserved precisely as they currently exist and with the powers they now have; becoming creatures of the shires even as now they are creatures of the state.

Once established in their shires, the people may subdivide, combine, or eliminate the towns altogether, but only if they meet the requirements of the *state* constitution. (Three-fourths vote of the shire-moot and three-fourths vote of the shire's population must approve.)* This places the future of each town in the hands of the people of the shire in which it is situated. At the same time it gives the town more protection against the larger authority. The state legislature may currently abolish, combine, or subdivide towns by a simple majority vote. Yet in the common sense of shire jurisdiction, there will be more incentive to treat town status innovatively than there was under the overlord mentality of the state.

The second kind of change needed to start our system involves all other matters of governance. If the people of the shire want to abandon the town meeting, change the ratio of citizens to reeves in the shire-moot, replace the shire council with a single executive, adopt a different ballot system, or in any other way alter its basic frame of government to make it more appropriate to its own circumstances, it may do so through a constitutionally prescribed method of charter change, a process requiring approval of a two-thirds vote of the shire-moot and a two-thirds vote of the shire's citizens in a referendum.

Governmental functions will also be distributed between state and shires by the state constitution. The general features of this division of powers include: (1) shire and town: all town powers will remain

---

*To ensure that referenda are not dominated by the voters from the larger towns, any charter change will bear the additional requirement that the three-fourths vote occur in half the towns of the shire. The shire-moot is the shire's legislative body.

intact at the outset, but they will be subject to shire takeover through charter change; (2) shire and state: the shires will become the depositories of all reserved powers. They, like the states under the original federal constitution, may do *anything* they please as long as they do not invade guaranteed human rights or wander into areas denied them by the state constitution. Vermont will thus become a true federal system. The state and the towns will both be creatures of the shires.

The shires may *empower* the towns to do things currently done by the state and for which they, themselves, will, under the new constitution, be given ultimate responsibility. For instance operation of the welfare system will revert to the shires. They may keep it themselves or subdelegate it in part or in whole to the towns.

The state-shire distribution of power will be maintained by a new constitutional-amendment process that includes proposal by a two-thirds vote of the state legislature and ratification by three quarters of the shires. The constitution will also contain a "necessary-and-proper" clause and language that instructs the supreme court to interpret it in favor of the shires. We said at the outset of this book that the early crises of American government called for centralization of political power but that the contemporary crisis demands the opposite. The tradition of interpreting "necessary-and-proper" extensions of delegated powers in favor of the center, set by Chief Justice John Marshall in 1823, must be reversed if we are to make progress in our quest for decentralized communal liberty.

The General Structure of the Shire

Each shire will be governed by a shire-moot. The term originates from the early English governing bodies, composed of representatives from the first towns. The Vermont shire-moot will resemble the representative town meeting, which features face-to-face decision making by a relatively large number of citizens, each one "standing in" for a relatively small number of their fellow citizens. All legislative authority will lie in the shire-moot. It will meet on a given day of each quarter and stay in session until the shire's business is settled.

Members of the moot are called reeves. Under the old English system the reeve was a representative elected by the people to the shire-moot. The shire will pay a per-diem salary which will equal the average individual income for citizens of the shire. Thus there will be a disincentive for the better-off to participate and an incentive for the poor to do so. It will be unlawful for any employer to discriminate against a worker elected to participate in moot meetings. Moot meetings will be held in a different town each quarter and, although it is expected that business will be transacted in a single day, meetings may extend over several days if needed. Mileage expenses will be reimbursed by the shire.

Reeves will be chosen at the town meetings of the shire's several towns or by ballot in cities with a council system. Reeves will serve yearly terms and be elected at large—one for every two hundred people of the town, with each town entitled to one reeve and the remainder based on the one-person-one-vote principle. Thus a shire of ten thousand people will have a moot of fifty.* No reeve shall be allowed to serve more than five consecutive terms; the shire system is designed to spread out the *work* of democracy.

Between moot meetings the shire's business will be conducted by the shire council, a body of from three to fifteen members (depending on the size of the shire) elected from the shire-moot for a term of three years with staggered terms. The shire manager, hired by the council, will carry out shire policy. Abandoning the separation-of-powers principle for a system more parliamentary in nature will blunt the kind of adversarial decision making that limits the capacities of small governments to build consensus. Council members will be paid a per-diem salary equal to the average salary of the citizens of the shire. Meeting times may be set by the council, but it, like the shire-moot, should rotate its meeting around the shire. Council members will elect a chairman who will be the presiding officer.

This moot/council arrangement approximates the town meeting/selectman process that exists in Vermont's towns today. It is a more efficient process than it might at first seem. With the people gathering yearly in their town meetings, a considerable amount of authority is typically given to the selectmen. This is power that has been *legitimized* by the town meeting. While town officers have to face the voters "out in the open," this very process siphons off a lot of hostility and frees them from much of the guerrilla tactics used when local citizens organize single-issue committees to bring pressure on a city council or aldermanic board. At the same time the town meeting is

---

*In the largest shires, like Burlingshire, where city government predominates, the shire may decide to have the elections in their larger jurisdictions by districts.

MODEL SHIRE STRUCTURE

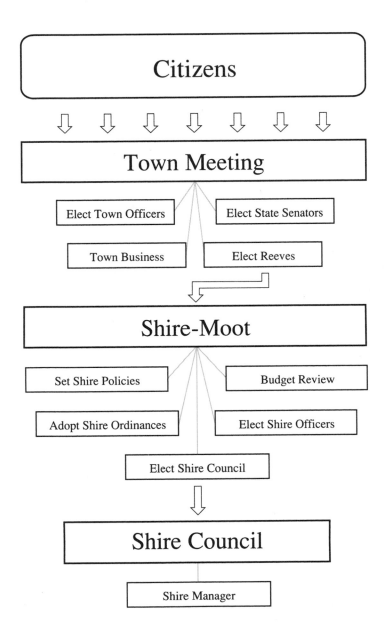

capable of powerful, honorable, and effective action on important issues. We expect the same set of circumstances to develop in the moot/council system with a manager.

The largest of Vermont's shires, Burlingshire, will have 54,709 people, a shire-moot of 273 reeves, and a council of 15. At least one day a quarter, as many as 273 citizens will enter a hall somewhere in the shire to make shire policy. The moot meeting itself will display the ambiance of a traditional Vermont town meeting. If one imagines a mood of spontaneity, even rowdiness, no alarm should be taken. For Vermont's strong tradition of public order – a refined chaos secured at the edges by a fundamental sense of fairness – will never be far off. Let the shire-moot resound to the passion of free debate that prevails when real choices are being made. Why should the citizens of the larger shires be denied the nourishment of communal democracy? Are 273 reeves too many? Indeed the number is nearly consistent with many present town-meeting assemblies.

The general form of the town meeting government is well known in Vermont, although several "improvements" have been made over the years – most of which have been dysfunctional. The new constitution will preserve the character of the traditional model which features daytime meetings, no Australian ballot, and the election (not appointment) of all town officers, including road commissioner. If a town wants to change this, it may do so in the constitutionally prescribed manner.

Although the constitutional convention called to put the shire system in place under a model charter will have to work this out (just as it will deal with all matters we are "prescribing" in this book), we recommend consideration of approval voting for elections in the shire, in the town meeting as it elects town officers, reeves, and state representatives, and in the shire-moot as it elects council members and judges. The model for approval voting has been developed by Steven Brams, of New York University. It is a very simple system that allows each voter to "vote for, or 'approve of' as many candidates as he or she wishes."

For instance, if three candidates were running for the post of reeve, each voter could vote for one, two, or all three candidates – in short all those candidates she or he approved of. The candidate with the most "approvals" would be declared the winner. Brams has worked the plan out carefully, and it seems to suit democratic choice at the level of human scale. Especially geared for a nonpartisan environment, approval voting is nonadversarial in tone and in practice leads "to the election of candidates with the most widespread support among voters."

Town meeting and with it the election of town and shire officials will take place on a state holiday ordained by the constitution called Democracy Day, a paid holiday in Vermont with the force of the present Labor Day. It should be set at the third Tuesday in April instead of the first Tuesday in March, Vermont's traditional Town Meeting Day. The later date would come during a time of better weather for travel on the roads. Vermont's fifth season, mud season, would be over. Sugaring time would have passed, but "spring work" for the farmers would be only just beginning. And it would be too late for winter sports (ice fishing, skiing, snowmobiling). The only outdoor sport available would be crow- and woodchuck hunting and some limited fishing. Baseball and golf would still be waiting for the sod to dry.

We see Democracy Day as a part of a great state celebration of public life. This could be accomplished by holding Shire Day (discussed in Chapter 7) on the weekend before Democracy Day. Thus Democracy Day would be accompanied by public festivities sponsored by schools, churches, and civic groups and, as the decades pass, it would evolve into a spring festival that would coincide with May Day, Vermont's present "Green Up" Day, and Shire Day. Parades, concerts, and plays would be held along with other outdoor activities that bespeak a rural mountain kingdom. Sporting events, such as ox draws, horse pulling, and plowing contests, might well become a part of the celebration lasting over the weekend and through Monday. During the evening, panel discussions, political debates, public lectures, and educational forums would be held on subjects that were current on the political agenda. Democracy Day would be looked forward to as a good time of the year, a springtime release of civic pride, education, and activism – a Beltane of citizenship and a popular affirmation of the importance of democratic governance.

Elections will be held at town meeting, in neighborhood assemblies in the cities, or by ballot in the cities that maintain their council systems. While there will be no Australian ballot, absentee balloting will be allowed. Therefore, except for those who secure an absentee ballot and those in hospitals or similarly unable to attend – to whom ballots would be carried by ballot beadles – one must attend a Democracy Day assembly to vote. The beadle was an elected town officer in the old English system who served the function of messenger. There is no reason why school children could not serve in this capacity, thus learning to participate in politics at an early age.

We do not hold the view that nonattendance and nonvoting are evils to be avoided at all costs. Absence from town meeting can be consistent with a well-developed sense of citizenship. It is more apt to reflect the view that all is well in town and shire than the view that "it doesn't matter anyway, and besides I don't count" – an attitude which is behind the current American movement away from citizenship. Strong democracies do not fear for participation. It will occur naturally in the ebb and flow of public passion.

Current arguments in Vermont for a state holiday for town meeting, which are made on behalf of working people who will lose a day's pay if they attend, are often met with the claim that working people will go ice fishing or snowmobiling on their holiday instead of to town meeting. Our response is that if this were to happen it should surprise no one, given the depths to which political efficacy has fallen. Dynamic and creative localism in shire and town, however, and the rearing of citizens in the atmosphere of civic education that the shires will inspire, will ensure full meeting halls. The cry, "if you don't participate, you have no right to complain," will once again be a reasonable proposition rather than what it has become today – a cheap, guilt-inspiring accusation by elites desirous of shoring up enough legitimacy to keep themselves afloat in a leaking system.

When their names are placed in nomination and seconded, town officers will stand before their neighbors for election as they have done throughout Vermont's history. After nominations are over, the secret ballot will be used, and a majority will be needed to win. Reeves sent to the shire-moot from the town must also be *nominated from the floor*. After nominations are completed the vote for reeves will take place exactly as will the vote for town officers. Anyone not present at the time of the voting will simply be out of luck. Following this any special balloting called for (such as town, shire, or state-wide referenda) will take place.

Representatives to the state legislature will be nominated and elected at a special evening town meeting scheduled for the last week of October. This means that anyone seeking to represent the shire in Montpelier will have to *plan* to be nominated and seconded in every town in order to get votes from that town. Ideally, as years pass, this meeting will expand and become a fixture in the shires. Other matters besides the election of state representatives will be taken up, and a tradition of holding a town meeting in both the spring and fall will develop.*

By electing all officers at a face-to-face grassroots assembly, a sense of community and shared responsibility will be returned to the electoral process. A home ground will be established that will entail a sense of unity and communal decision. People who go on to represent the town at the shire level, and those who go on to represent the shire at the state level, will have in memory an organic portrait of union rather than one of individuals traveling alone to polling places to cast their vote (as in a cameo appearance) as quickly and painlessly as possible in a world that begrudges still another interruption on still another busy day. In this way, too, a coherent design will be maintained among levels of government, and the presence of civic roots will be reaffirmed.

The Shire Judicial System

The reorganization of Vermont into self-governing shires will necessarily involve sweeping changes in the means for providing justice. Like the rest of government, a judicial system ought to be close to the people, in harmony with their values and beliefs, and under their own control. Accordingly the shires will have their own judicial system, operating within the broad framework of state law and under the guidance of a state supreme court.

The present Vermont judiciary is a not altogether happy product of long evolution. At the top sits the supreme court, which has centralized administrative power over the whole system. Below the supreme court is a dual system of superior and district courts (the former dealing mainly with civil cases, the latter criminal cases plus minor civil disputes), as well as probate courts, which have jurisdiction over such matters as administration of estates, trusts and guardianships, and name changes. Vermont's justices of the peace, an ancient town office dating back to the twelfth century, have had their judicial functions stripped away over the years and now are limited to counting ballots, marrying people, and swearing in town officers.

Those peculiar creatures of the superior courts, the assistant- or

---

*Voting for governor, congressional seats, and other state-wide offices will take place as usual in November.

"side" judges, require explanation. In the state's earliest days much ire was directed toward the lawyers employed by New York land barons to separate free Vermont settlers from lawful title to their land. Indeed all lawyers were suspected of being at best innocent of any modicum of common sense or justice. Ethan Allen, faced with a state's attorney on the verge of dropping charges against some pro-Yorker sedition-ists, marched into the courtroom and declared to the astonished judge and prosecutor, "I can upset his Blackstones, his whitestones, his gravestones, and his brimstones." Here perhaps was Vermont's earli-est proclamation by a side judge.

It was conceded – grudgingly – that courts ought to be presided over by persons trained in the law, but it was never conceded that lawyer judges should have the sole power to judge. So from the beginning of the Vermont court system it was required that the freemen elect assistant judges, two lay citizens who would flank the lawyer judge and correct any rulings which would offend the simple sense of jus-tice known to every honest Vermonter. In addition to their judicial duties, assistant judges also have executive powers (they maintain the court house and hire the assistant court clerks) and legislative powers (they levy a countywide property tax to finance the county's share of superior court expenses). This tripartite public responsibility is unique among elected officials in the United States. It is the *spirit* of the side judges that we wish to reincarnate in the shire judicial system.

For starters the current superior and district court systems must be replaced by shire courts, presided over by the shire judge and administered by the shire judicial clerk. Criminal prosecutions will be brought by the shire attorney. The shire court will sit in a court house, or equivalent quarters, within each shire, unless adjacent shires decided to establish a joint shire court by inter-shire agreement. Beneath the shire court would be lay magistrates, resurrecting some of the former powers of the justices of the peace. Finally there would be a shire family court, built upon the present probate court.

Shire judges will not be transient strangers picked by the gov-ernor, but shire citizens chosen by election in the shire-moot. The people of the shire would thus have the opportunity to choose judges whose general outlook approximated their own and whose standing in the community inspired public confidence. The shire court will combine most of the criminal and civil jurisdictions of both the present district and superior courts. At the state level the supreme court will retain the power to convene special ad hoc superior courts to handle cases of great import or complexity, naming judges from a panel of the most distinguished private lawyers and retired judges in the state. The shire family court will include all of the present functions of the probate courts, plus matters of divorce, child support, and guardianships now handled in district and superior courts.

Beneath the shire court, in addition to the family court, will be a magistrate's court to resolve the countless relatively minor matters which once fell under the jurisdiction of justices of the peace. The magistrate, who will usually be a layman, will become the heir of the present side judges. Unlike them, however, the magistrates will have no executive or legislative duties; those will be handled along with all other shire matters by the shire-moot and the shire council. The magistrate's court will dispose of small claims, fish-and-game violations, uncontested divorces, boating and snowmobile infractions, minor traffic tickets, and low-level misdemeanors. As in New Hampshire, arresting officers will be allowed to prosecute their own cases in magistrate's court, thereby easing the burdens of shire attorneys. If a case came before the magistrate which seemed to involve larger or more complicated issues, the magistrate would normally transfer the case to the shire court. Such a system has long been used in Great Britain.

The shire judicial system will feature an institution not currently known in Vermont, the judicial review board. This board, composed of local citizens elected by the shire-moot (or by towns), will have several important duties. It will examine and rate candidates for appointment to all judicial positions and maintain a close watch on the operations of the shire courts, reviewing the appropriateness of sentences and punishments, the efficiency of the courts in settling cases, and the propriety of judges and court officials, issuing such review to the people of the shire. The judicial review board will also have the power to recommend impeachment to the shire-moot in serious cases.

The judicial review board will help redress the virtual inability of citizens or legislators to obtain sufficient information to justify the retention or rejection of a sitting judge. Only in cases of gross abuse – conviction of crimes, wildly erratic behavior, senility, or frequent reversals on appeal – are sitting judges now likely to be denied re-election. Procedures for judicial review have been highly developed in Minnesota and are now making an appearance in some Vermont superior courts.

A special task of both magistrates and shire judges will be the encouragement of informal mediation and arbitration of disputes. Not surprisingly, staggering backlogs and long delays, which make civil justice costly and time-consuming, have resulted in disputants' seeking alternative ways of settling their problems. The result has been a sharp increase in programs for what is called "alternative dispute resolution." Some, such as the community mediation centers, have been initiated by traditional "peace" churches such as the Church of the Brethren. Others, so-called neighborhood justice centers, are sponsored by local bar associations in two hundred locations around the country. Better business bureaus have long offered mediation services between merchants and customers. A mediation service went into operation in 1985 in the district court in Barre, Vermont, and has produced uniformly positive results.

We do not intend to dictate an immutable model for the shire judicial system. Two or three sparsely populated shires might agree to share a shire court, keeping magistrate's courts under their separate control. Or a shire might choose not to have a magistrate's court, expanding the shire court to perform all functions. Shires might agree to exchange judges, much as district judges are now rotated for six-month tours of duty. A shire might have a unitary law-enforcement system under the sheriff's authority, or it might have a sheriff, a town police force in a larger town, and constables in the smaller towns.

Nor do we propose that each shire develop its own criminal code; that will remain a function of the state legislature. We do propose, however, that the usual level of municipal ordinance powers be conferred upon the shires. Finally, we recognize the need for the Vermont Supreme Court to remain as the supreme judicial authority and the court of final appeal under state law. However, in the spirit of Vermont's new liberty, supreme court judges should be elected by the legislature, not appointed by the governor with the advice and consent of the senate. The supreme court will have no administrative control over the shire courts.

The Shires: Some Examples

In order to provide a fuller understanding of what a shire will look like in the new Vermont federation, we offer the following hypothetical descriptions.

112

Lincolnshire (A Rural Agrarian Shire)

Lincolnshire begins at the top of the Green Mountains and slopes westward to the shores of Lake Champlain, following the watershed of the New Haven River, a mountain stream of great beauty, and the historic Otter Creek into which the New Haven empties in the southern part of the shire. From there Otter Creek flows northwest until, along with Little Otter Creek and Lewis Creek (which drain the northern part of the shire), it enters Lake Champlain in the town of Ferrisburg. The shire thus enjoys the diversity of mountains and lake-basin. Its highest peak in the east is Mt. Abraham at 4,052 feet. To the west are foothills such as Mt. Pleasant (2,040 feet), Hillsboro Mountain (2,560 feet) and Shaker Mountain (1,920 feet). These drop off quickly, and broad, fertile fields lead to the shores of the lake, which is about 175 feet above sea level. As the crow flies, it is twenty-five miiles from the peak of Mt. Abraham to Lake Champlain. Lincolnshire will encompass an area of roughly 355 square miles and will be home to 14,127 people (1980 census). With about sixteen acres of land available for every man, woman, and child, Lincolnshire will have a population density which for the people of New York City to achieve would require an area the size of all of New England, New York, New Jersey, Pennsylvania, Maryland, and Delaware, plus another parcel the size of Vermont and New Hampshire.

The shire contains ten towns. This number includes the combination of the present adjacent towns of Panton (population 537) and Waltham (population 394). They are the two smallest towns in the shire both in terms of area and population. One is below minimum town size and one barely above the lower limit of 500. Otter Creek forms the border between Waltham and Panton. Combining the two towns will turn this river basin into a joiner rather than a separator of jurisdictions and preserve the environmental integrity of the area. The largest town in the shire is Bristol, with a population of 3,993. The smallest is Weybridge, with a population of 667.

Lincolnshire's government will consist of nine town governments and one small city government (Vergennes).* The town governments use the town meeting as legislature and board of selectmen as executive. The Lincolnshire-Moot will contain seventy-one reeves from the

---

*Vergennes is an anomaly in Vermont. It is a town with a "city" government. It has 2,273 people and a land mass of less than two square miles.

ten localities. Bristol will send fifteen; Weybridge will send five. The shire council will consist of seven reeves who will hire a shire manager. The shire will have its own shire court, family court, and magistrate's court.

Kingdomshire (A Rural-Wilderness Shire)

Kingdomshire is named after Vermont's fabled Northeast Kingdom. The shire lies on the border of Canada to the north and New Hampshire to the east. Hunters travel to Kingdomshire for the big bucks and the black bears that are plentiful. Forestry and some agriculture along the Connecticut River are the chief economic sectors, and the summer tourist business is good. Kingdomshire will have 327 square miles of territory and only 1,858 people. The population density is six per square mile, one-seventh that of Lincolnshire. The shire's eastern border is the Connecticut River. Its highest point is Mt. Monadnock, at 3,140 feet. The rest of the shire is heavily forested rolling hills stretching off to the west, broken by swamps, sliced by streams, and dotted with ponds, bogs, and several large lakes. There is only one word for it: rugged.

Kingdomshire presents a perfect example of the social cost of space. Only one of the shire's six towns has over 1,000 people, and each of the other five has less than 200. Yet combining towns to meet minimum levels of population mass (500 people) automatically triggers density problems. It may be that the 1,858 citizens of Kingdomshire will scrap the towns in the region altogether and govern themselves simply as a shire. Another alternative is to diminish the role of the shire and consolidate into two geographically huge towns, one centered in the south, combining the towns of Maidstone, Brunswick, and Bloomfield, the other in the north, combining Canaan, Lemington, and Norton. As the decades pass the people of this wide land will have time to work out the best situation for themselves.

Kingdomshire clearly tests the limits of the model for communal democracy we have outlined. For instance the shire-moot of Kingdomshire would consist of only nine reeves. Perhaps the shire might adopt a direct town meeting format instead of the representational structure. If this meeting were held in Lemington, for instance, citizens from the farthest towns could still reach the meeting in about a half-hour.

Despite its population-density problems, there is great potential for Kingdomshire. Pride and tradition are deeply ingrained throughout the region – as can be seen in the pages of Robert Pike's classic of the north country, *Tall Trees, Tough Men.*

Kingdomshire contains some of the few truly wild places left in Vermont, unmarked by camp sites, trail markers, or other guide-like obstructions. Some would like to see it remain that way – a reminder of what the land was like when the settlers first heard the wind in the hemlocks. It is one thing to hunt whitetails over hill and dale in rural farmland. It is quite another to be alone in the huge tracts of unmarked timber, ridge, and swamp of the Kingdom. Whether or not the Kingdom remains as it is, however, must be decided by the people of the Kingdom. That is what shires are for.

Burlingshire (A Neighborhood-Based Metro Shire)

Chittenden County, one of Vermont's fourteen counties, is profoundly dissimilar from the Northeast Kingdom. It is the communication, educational, and industrial center of the state. In 1980, 115,534 (almost one quarter) of Vermont's 511,131 people lived there. Its population density (180 per square mile) is about four and a half times that of the rest of the state. It contains the state's largest city, Burlington (population 37,712) as well as several more of the state's largest communities: Colchester, Essex, and South Burlington. But Chittenden County also includes smaller towns, such as Charlotte, Hinesburg, and Huntington (formerly farming towns), bedroom communities such as Jericho, and a ski town, Bolton.

Given such a population mass, the solution for governance in Burlingshire is the same as that advocated for Vermont as a whole: build a political structure that allows for the consolidation of those governmental functions that *naturally* need centralized administration and the decentralization of those that are best met in neighborhoods. The formation of one large metro-shire will, over time, allow a sensible reordering of government functions. Highways, waste disposal, and energy are examples of policy that could use shire-wide attention. Now, with so many jurisdictions compacted into such a small area, it takes herculean efforts even to plan for a bike path.

On the other hand, especially in the city of Burlington, there is a real need for a creative neighborhood system of decentralized governance that is involved with such things as setting school policy, caring for the poor, policing the streets, and creating recreational and cultural opportunities. This kind of natural inclination to reorder the levels of government at which policies are made is everywhere evident. We need shires big enough to rationalize traffic systems while *at the same time* allowing for neighborhood control in matters of human interaction.

Burlingshire will be such a shire. Containing the cities of Burlington, South Burlington, and Winooski, it is the largest shire in the state, with 54,709 people. The geographic features that dominate Burlingshire are the beautiful harbor on Lake Champlain and the Winooski River. The Winooski, Vermont's most important east–west waterway, runs through the shire between the cities of Winooski and Burlington and empties into the lake at the northern end of Burlington Harbor. Protection of river and harbor is the shire's greatest ecological concern, and one which has historically caused difficulties between Winooski and Burlington.

Since the shires are all-powerful, it would be possible for Burlingshire to keep the present city of Burlington as it is. It might also replace the city with a number of neighborhood governments or "towns," equipped with town-meeting-like neighborhood assemblies, and empowered to deal with neighborhood concerns. Indeed we would expect this to happen as Burlington's mayor and board of aldermen are caught in the middle, with area-wide policy developed by the shire and pressure from the grass roots to establish their own human-scale policies in the neighborhoods.

This arrangement would provide the best of both worlds for the citizen – a shire to deal with more area-wide concerns, and small community councils to take care of those matters that depend on human-scale interaction. In high-density living places like Burlington the key is to give neighborhoods *some* things in which they have *absolute* control and the civic responsibility that flows from it. The approach in favor today is to give neighborhoods an advisory role on *everything* (from leash laws to thermonuclear war) but to entrust them with *nothing* completely. People in cities understand that a neighborhood should not have final say on where a landfill should be located. What they don't understand (quite correctly) is why they should not have control over the education of their children or the care of their elderly. We have been telling our citizens for fifty years that no one is responsible for anything, that there are always "higher levels" that will take care of society's problems – and we wonder why people go hungry on the streets?

By the year 2025 we see Burlingshire as a vibrant metropolitan center for Vermont. It will have responsibility for physical infrastructure – major roads, waste disposal, energy plants, bike paths, and the like. It will have an important partnership role in neighborhood-based services like fire- and police protection. It will have a simple, low-visibility, coordinating role to play in the delivery of human services. In this way the shire will provide its citizens with both a livable physical environment in which to work and play and the variety, excitement, and creatively competitive spirit that exist in cities where neighborhoods are allowed to grow, flower, and become self-assertive.

Brattleshire (A Big-Town-Small-Town Shire)

We have discussed a typical rural-agrarian shire (Lincolnshire) and the two shires that will be the most atypical of the lot, Kingdomshire and Burlingshire. In southern Vermont near Massachusetts and bordering the Connecticut River is the town of Brattleboro, with a population of 11,880 people. It will form the hub of another kind of shire – a large town center surrounded by several smaller communities. Even though it's a large town, Brattleboro is typically Vermont in its topography. The western part of town is dotted with hills, over ten of them above 1,500 feet, while the downtown on the Connecticut River is about 300 feet above sea level. The hills are full of game and crisscrossed with streams and valleys. The other towns of the shire are quintessential hill towns. Brattleshire is also the place where the sparkling West River empties into the Connecticut. Town and village, farm and forest. Brattleboro is Vermont.

Brattleboro is the only town in Vermont with a representative town meeting. Its chief administrative duties are performed by a town manager. It has a feisty daily newspaper, a strong tradition of progressiveness, and a cosmopolitan atmosphere. The four small towns surrounding it are Dummerston, Marlboro, Guilford, and Vernon. Brattleshire might wish to form several smaller neighborhood structures within the town of Brattleboro. These subunits would then make decisions involving certain human-scale policies in their areas, while the outlying towns would continue to function as they do now.

Yet concessions to high density and small mass may need to be made. Although we have suggested that there are optimal numbers for community size and that *some* form of face-to-face decision making for *everyone* is best, Brattleboro is currently doing very well indeed with its representative town meeting. Perhaps it is the case for high-density towns and cities of, say, between 5,000 and 15,000 population, that the combination of small-town life, a healthy community communications system (Brattleboro also has two radio stations and a myriad of civic networks and organizations), and a street-corner ambiance creates an environment of open, human-scale decision making without formalized town-meeting-like neighborhood councils.

Brattleshire also demonstrates the classic problem of political power when small communities surround a larger town. Brattleshire will have a total population of 16,862. This means that the shire-moot will contain eighty-four reeves, and fifty-six of them will come from the town of Brattleboro. This is another argument to dissolve Brattleboro into several neighborhood structures with the approximate power of towns. On the other hand there is no certitude that reeves elected from Brattleboro will be any more disposed "against" the smaller towns surrounding it than would be reeves elected from several neighborhood governments that have taken the place of Brattleboro. These are the kinds of considerations that the people of the shire will have the opportunity to debate in their own time. The key is to establish shire home rule. What happens then is the people's business.

Creating the Shires

The ultimate boundaries and configuration of each shire will be decided by the people of the shire as it comes into being. The transition process, however, needs careful attention.

Obviously it won't do to have a central convention or legislature dictate the boundaries of the shires. Most of the members of any such body would not have workable information about most of the state; and in addition the people of the shires would resent being collected into new political bodies by a central mandate. Our commitment to local democracy requires that the shire should be defined by those who will inhabit and govern it.

But some kind of starting point must set the process in motion. That starting point will be the election of representatives to the constitutional convention called in 1993 to work out the new Vermont government in its entirety. Among its actions the convention will sort the existing towns and cities of the state into "proto-shires," first-order approximations of what are likely to be shires in the new Vermont. The criteria to be used would include first a population base appropriate for shire democracy. Other criteria are bioregional identity, with heavy emphasis on what geographers call "population nodes," and particularly watershed boundaries, which have silently controlled human behavior since the dawn of time. Patterns of human activity – where people work, shop, worship, send their children to school, and attend band concerts – will also be important in defining proto-shires, as will communications patterns – newspaper readership, radio listening areas, and telephone exchanges. Proto-shires may also correspond, perhaps only roughly, to historical and cultural perceptions of political community, such as the Upper Valley of river towns around Norwich or the Islands of Grand Isle County. Environmental variety, where possible, would also be a factor; a town on Lake Champlain might, therefore, be placed in a shire without access to the lake, rather than in one with it.

These proto-shire patterns, arrived at in 1993, will of course be very different from what Benning Wentworth might have imagined when he handed out the New Hampshire grants in the 1750s. Patterns of human activity have changed radically since then. Nor did Wentworth consider geography. His sharp quill simply subdivided Vermont into more-or-less rectangular plots all with more-or-less the same area. Perhaps in another two hundred years the shires of the 1990s will seem hopelessly out of touch – in which case the political machinery will exist for once again bringing them back into line with the reality of human life and its interaction with the environment.

Over the two-year sorting-out period following the constitutional convention, the people of the towns in each proto-shire will participate in a process of boundary adjustment. The citizens at the center of a proto-shire will probably be satisfied with the designation, but in some cases there will be dissatisfaction at the edges. The people of some towns may wish to associate with an adjacent proto-shire instead of the one in which they were put by the convention's first approximation. Even more likely, the people in some remote part of an "edge" town – the people on "the other side of the mountain" or "across the river" – may prefer to join an adjacent shire, while the majority of people in their town will be content to remain in the shire to which they were assigned. In some cases there might be a strong desire to construct a new shire from parts of one or more proto-shires.

There is a large and well-established body of law in most states which governs the process of municipal annexation. Usually that law applies to a central city seeking annexation of suburban or rural land. This is not the case in Vermont. Unlike most states outside of New

England, Vermont does not have incorporated cities separated by unincorporated areas subject to annexation. We have wall-to-wall towns and a few cities, and no supervening county government. Thus our problem is to create a new means for the people of a town or part of a town to secede from one proto-shire to join an adjacent shire.

A suitable procedure can be adapted from the experience of other states (in this case, the Minnesota Municipal Commission Act). A Vermont Shire Boundary Board will be created by the constitutional convention. The people of an entire town or of a part of a town would apply to this board for permission to redraw the final shire boundaries to put their town or area into a different shire. In the case of an entire town the petition would be presented by the selectmen, following approval of the idea at a town-meeting vote. If the area concerned is only part of the town, 20 percent of the residents of the described area would be required to sign the petition, or, as an alternative, the owners of 20 percent of the grand list included within the proposed area would be required to sign.

The shire boundary board would review the proposal in light of the criteria outlined for creating the original shires. These would be fine-tuned on such items found, for example, in a Washington State statute of 1967: natural neighborhoods and communities; physical boundaries such as bodies of water, highways, ridges, and land contours; and logical municipal-service areas.

If after the required public hearings the boundary board finds that it is reasonable – not necessarily compelling, but merely reasonable – for the change to be made, it will organize and supervise a vote within the affected town or area. If a majority of the voters voting in a duly warned election approve the proposal, the board will certify it, and the ultimate shire boundaries will be adjusted accordingly. Neither the rest of the proto-shire containing the area, nor the rest of the proto-shire receiving it, plays a part in this process except to present testimony to the shire boundary board.

Once this sorting-out period is complete, the new permanent shire boundaries will be confirmed. In a few cases some present-day towns may lose a section of territory to a town in another shire because the townspeople of different parts of the town saw advantages to joining different shires. So be it. With the shire called into life as a general unit of local government where democracy can live again, there is no compelling reason to forbid the division of towns if that is what their people prefer.

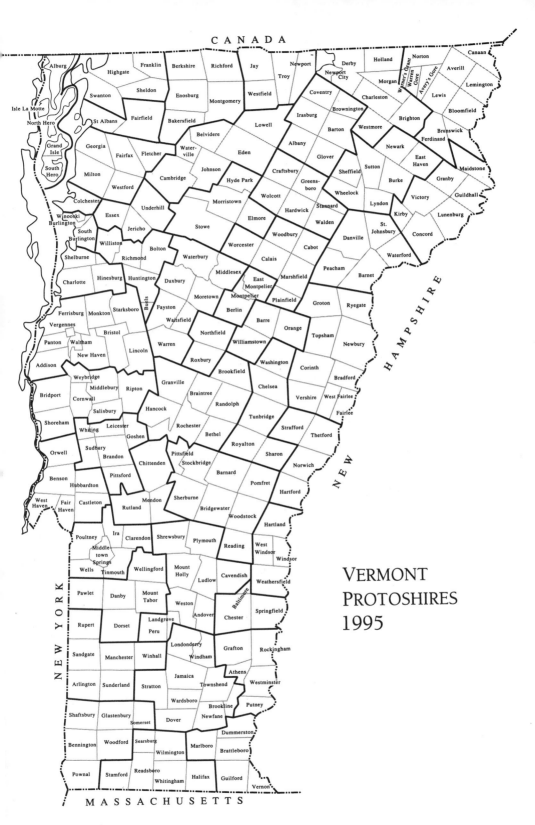

VERMONT
PROTOSHIRES
1995

Finally a permanent secession policy will be written into the state constitution, along the lines of the California Local Agency Formation Councils, which supervise the incorporation of unincorporated areas. Under those procedures (about which there is an enormous body of literature), parts of shires could hive off to join new shires without having to secure a formal act of the state legislature. Since such boundary changes would be more complicated once the shires are in full constitutional operation, we think relocation under the modern shire system would be minimal, especially since the two-step process of original shire creation would be far more rational and far, far more democratic than the process that created Vermont's original town boundaries in the first place.

Our first map shows proto-shires as they might emerge from a constitutional convention in the 1990s. This map will help define the debate about the final form of the shires and provide a starting point for people to use in making decisions. The result of those early decisions and the continuing capacity for shires to readjust over time may well result in a map like the one on the next page. Note that there are lots of deliberately imprecise curved lines in this second map. It is drawn to emphasize that the people of the proto-shires have the power to round off the edges to accommodate their needs and desires.

The town of Newbury provides an example. On the northeastern corner of Newbury, on the banks of the Wells River, stands the village of Wells River. As late as the 1960s, both Newbury and Wells River had their own high schools. Now Wells River Independent School District children attend Blue Mountain Union, up the Wells River on Route 302, while most of Newbury's high schoolers attend Oxbow Union, in Bradford to the south.

A case could be made for creating a very small, rural "Wellshire" along Route 302 and the Wells River watershed, including the towns of Groton and Ryegate and Wells River village, all linked economically to the larger town of Woodsville in New Hampshire. The remainder of Newbury would remain in Oxbowshire along with Bradford, Corinth, Fairlee, West Fairlee, and Vershire. The McIndoes Falls area of Barnet to the north, and the Mosquitoville area at the town's southwest corner, might prefer to join Wellshire instead of remaining in Caledoniashire to its north.

A careful inspection of a physical map of Vermont will reveal many other instances of parts of towns where the residents relate more to other towns than to their own – towns which might turn out to be in

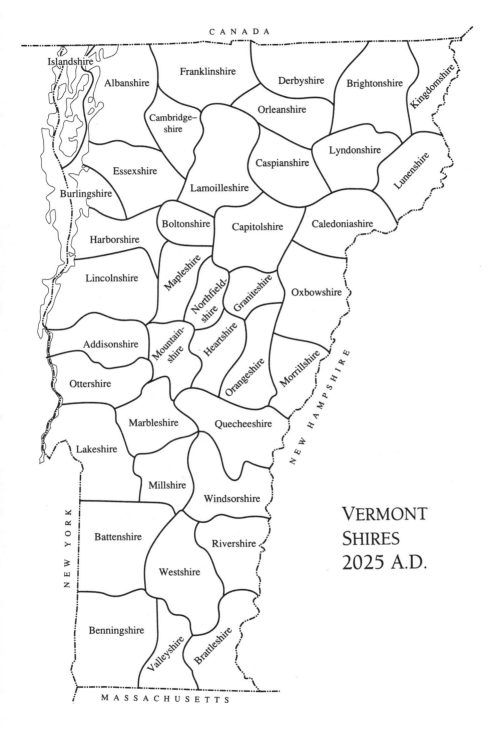

CANADA

Islandshire

Franklinshire

Albanshire

Derbyshire

Brightonshire

Kingdomshire

Cambridge-
shire

Orleanshire

Essexshire

Caspianshire

Lyndonshire

Lunenshire

Burlingshire

Lamoilleshire

Boltonshire

Capitolshire

Caledoniashire

Harborshire

Mapleshire

Northfield-
shire

Graniteshire

Oxbowshire

Lincolnshire

Addisonshire

Mountain-
shire

Heartshire

Orangeshire

Morrillshire

Ottershire

Marbleshire

Quecheeshire

Lakeshire

NEW HAMPSHIRE

Millshire

Windsorshire

NEW YORK

Battenshire

Rivershire

Westshire

VERMONT
SHIRES
2025 A.D.

Benningshire

Valleyshire

Brattleshire

MASSACHUSETTS

other shires. For instance there are three houses in the town of Wheelock on Route 16 between Greensboro Bend and Glover. These three houses clearly belong in a shire with Greensboro and Hardwick and not with Wheelock, whose town office is a nineteen-mile drive from Route 16. More than likely the three families in this tiny corner of Wheelock would prefer to be part of the shire with Greensboro rather than with Wheelock, which would logically attach to Lyndonshire to the east. Similarly the village of East Granville might prefer to join with Roxbury and Northfield, while the rest of Granville might prefer to go with Rochester and Hancock.

The town of Kirby presents another example. The North Kirby and Burke Tongue parts of town relate to Lyndonville and East Burke, both parts of a proposed Lyndonshire. Mud Hollow, Severance Hill, and South Kirby relate more to East St. Johnsbury, which we conceive as being part of Caledoniashire. How the people of Kirby sort this out will remain to be seen, but it is possible that some would prefer to go one way and some another. A similar analysis could be made for towns like Weathersfield, Mt. Holly, Fairfax, Morgan, Jamaica, and Bolton.

After the smoke clears, the map of Vermont would show maybe forty shires instead of the original forty-six proto-shires, with boundaries determined by the people themselves, not by the Supreme Mapmaker in Montpelier. Within those shires the people will again choose whether to retain the original towns, to create a unitary shire government, to establish new subdivisions such as wards or neighborhoods with their own democratic assemblies, or to set up almost any conceivable variation. The guiding principle is to allow the people to design their own governments. The time of the creation of the shires will be an enormously exciting and fulfilling period, for citizens will be able to take part personally in the heady business of choosing the boundaries of their own government instead of being forced to accept what has been parceled out to them. The process of making those decisions will once again allow them to be citizens in the fullest sense of the word.

Chapter 8

CELEBRATING SHIRE IDENTITY

In the summertime on Brendon
The bells they sound so clear
Round both the Shires they ring them
In steeples far and near
A happy noise to hear.

— Alfred Edward Housman

LET us reiterate: our central purpose is to fortify traditions of liberty and democracy in the face of relentless pressure for the centralization of power in the state capitol. To effect that purpose we have proposed the creation of a new political structure — a federation of shires.

But to create such a new structure does not mean that the shires will correspond to a perceived human community. And if they do not they will be little more than functional special districts in the minds of their people. In old England people created the *wapentake* to defend their homes and farms against the Danes, sort of a special-purpose military district. But it never claimed the loyalty of the people, who saw themselves as citizens only of their *tun* (town) and parish. More recently in Vermont the legislature, by edict of the U.S. Supreme Court, grouped towns into legislative districts to meet the one-man-one-vote criterion. After two decades most Vermonters today probably could not even tell you which towns are in their district.

By what means, then, will the people become patriots of their shires? Happily there has long been in Vermont an awareness of community larger than the individual town. Many rural townspeople necessarily relate to another larger town where they shop and sometimes work. Town governments have often cooperated with their neighbors on matters of snow-plowing routes and planning decisions. The existence of the shire will accentuate this outward-looking habit, and in time citizens will come to confer increased allegiance to this new body.

While creating shires will not, at one stroke, dispose of the systems mentality and suffuse the souls of rural people with a new communal identity, the existence of the shires will influence the values and perceptions of their citizens. By providing the political tools to construct countryside communities, they will place the solutions to a far larger number of civic problems within hand's reach. People are apt to take pride in their own handiwork.

Beyond the activity of self-government itself several steps can be taken to establish community identity in the shires.

Shire Symbolism

Foremost among these steps is the creation of a shire symbolism. Charles Merriam tells how identity is preserved in the cantons of Switzerland:

> The role of symbolism in Switzerland is an important one notwithstanding the democratic simplicity of the government. In a long series of impressive ways, the local and national political events are brilliantly pictured and brought home to the citizen from day to day .... The localities are full of celebrations of various kinds. ... The open air mass meetings of the Landesgemeinde [cantonal assembly] are among the most impressive and colorful spectacles of the political world. Gymnastic societies, shooting societies, costume demonstrations, flags and songs enliven the scene, and tend to impress upon each generation the cultural and political values of the Swiss group.

It takes but a little imagination to conceive of an emerging shire symbolism. To begin with, the shire will have well-defined boundaries. Where the highways – and even the byways – enter the shire, travelers will see the shire's distinctive welcome sign, featuring the shire heraldry and colors. Once a decade, on Shire Day, a relay of young citizens who have come of age since the last occasion will carry out the ancient Anglo-Saxon custom of perambulating the shire perimeter – perhaps on snowmobiles, if there is still snow, or on bikes, or by runners – an act reaffirming the shire's traditional territorial bounds.

126

In front of the shire's public buildings, its assembly halls, town halls, schools, and community centers, will fly the unique and colorful shire flag. In Orleanshire with its many French descendants the flag might resemble the scarlet oriflamme of Charlemagne. In the shire including the now unorganized towns of Glastenbury and Somerset, the flag might look like the dragon pennon of King Arthur. Over Lakeshire one might spy the red gryphon of Wales. Other shires would have flags as distinctive as the climbing bear of Berne, the bull's head of Uri, the great key of Obwalden, the gold lion of Brabant, or the leaping dolphin of Anguilla. In a conservative shire in the Northeast Kingdom – who knows? – the flag might resemble the nine-tasseled gyrfalcon flag of Genghis Khan.

The shire colors will appear in many places as well as on its flag. They will be emblazoned on its road signs and annual shire reports. They will be found on the decal which appears on all car, truck, and snowmobile license plates, a more eye-catching version of the county name which appears on the license plates of Kentucky and Florida. The colors will be found on the shire band uniforms and on the shirts of the shire athletic teams. The flowers carefully planted around the shire building may seem to have been chosen for the same colors.

Symbols of proud local history will abound. On a shady street in Old Bennington stands a statue of Vermont hero Colonel Seth Warner, whose Green Mountain Boys helped defeat the Hessians at the Battle of Bennington. On Route 302 at the foot of Orange Heights in the town of Groton is a modest monument to William Scott, the "sleeping sentinel," whom President Lincoln pardoned during the Civil War. At a dusty crossroads near Shadow Lake in Concord, a marker reminds passersby that there in 1823 Samuel Read Hall founded America's first normal school. Off Route 9 in Searsburg a simple, faded stone records that on that spot Solomon Rich, "a kind husband, affectionate father, and enterprising citizen," was thrown from his wagon and killed on an April day in 1848. Similarly each shire will have its monuments to commemorate shire residents or even sad events in the shire's history. As in modern Boston, small corner parks or crossroads commons will bear the names of servicemen and -women who gave their lives in war, or citizens distinguished for their learning, achievements, or long service to the shire community.

In each shire there will be one or more places of assembly, a common or muster field where public events can be held. There, beneath the waving flags, the shire elder, elected by the shire-moot to be the ceremonial greeter and presiding officer for shire events, will conduct the shire's ceremonies and welcome its distinguished guests. There, as in the town square in Vergennes, the people will pay their respects annually, on Memorial Day, to the townspeople who went off to war. It is there that the shire's lacrosse and soccer teams will do battle and the all-shire softball team will prepare for the state tournament. It is there that the strains of the shire anthem will often be heard.

Shire Citizenship

Shire citizenship is not just an empty phrase, denoting the arrival at age eighteen of its young people or the registration of newcomers as voters. Shire citizenship is intended to have a far more profound meaning. It will be a stepping forward to full membership in a community and a conscious accepting of responsibility for the civic affairs of one's own self-governing republic.

Accordingly shire citizenship will differ somewhat from state and national citizenship. Shire citizens will be initiated in a public ceremony, held once a year on Shire Day. On that day all those choosing to accept shire citizenship publicly will take the Shire Oath, which binds them to the shire just as the freeman's oath was written to bind new citizens to the young State of Vermont. Of course federal and state governments would continue to determine who may vote in their elections, but only those who have accepted shire citizenship shall have the right to vote in shire elections and on shire public questions.

Each shire will set its own requirements for citizenship, subject only to the overriding conditions that citizenship could not be denied for reasons of race, creed, color, sex, or national origin. A shire might choose to reinstate the former Vermont residency requirement. It might require citizen candidates to demonstrate an understanding of the shire's history and traditions and form of government, a sort of secular equivalent to confirmation or bar mitzvah. Such a demonstration ought to be easy to make, since the shire's high schools will provide a course in shire history, citizenship, and service opportunities, open to adults as well as high schoolers.

With shire citizenship the new citizens will customarily volunteer themselves to a position of civic responsibility or community self-help. It might be to serve as an apprentice to the pound keeper, or as a perambulator, or as a trumpeter in the shire band, or manager of the

shire computer bulletin board, or as an aide in the senior meals program, or as a deputy sheriff or volunteer fire department member, or
as an organizer of the Shire Day activities, or as a recruit in the shire
militia. It would not be imperative for a new citizen to choose a mode
for making a contribution to the shire, but it would be expected that
he or she do so. Indeed, in a fully functioning shire, young people
would most likely have been involved even before reaching the age
of majority, e.g., as ballot beadles (Chapter 7).

In addition to its ceremonial and service aspects, accepting shire
citizenship will be an important signal to the leaders of society that
a young person or newcomer had exhibited seriousness of purpose
and commitment to the well-being of his or her local community. Such
persons would quickly find themselves accepted into shire society and
will find the doors open to economic and social advancement. Those
who declined shire citizenship, or who merely chose to vote without
contributing, would find that they had made a mistake – happily, not
an irremediable one.

In these ways, then, shire citizenship, the modern embodiment
of the ancient civic-humanist ideal, would be defined as the opportunity, and responsibility, to participate fully in the affairs of one's shire.
As such it would have far greater importance than the relatively meaningless and empty coming-of-age ceremony of today – a trip to the post
office to register for the draft, and a visit to the town clerk to get on
the check list.

Cultural Life in the Shire

Vital to knitting together a strong community within the shire will
be a wide array of cultural events. Those events are already familiar –
they have been held in one or another Vermont town for many years.

In December 1910 a group of Thetford townspeople came together to begin to plan a suitable observance for the town's sesqui-
centennial the following year. It was proposed that the town create
a pageant of its history, to be performed on a hillside overlooking the
Connecticut River. In due course scores of townspeople joined in con-
structing the amphitheater and performing the pageant, which drew
large and enthusiastic crowds from miles around. The pageant had
three themes: the New Agriculture, the New Education, and the New
Life, the last of which sought to describe life in Thetford's future.
The pageant interwove the spirits of nature with the determination

of the settlers to portray a tableau of Thetford life over 150 years.

But more important than the pageant itself, which was performed only in the summer of 1911, was the recrudescence of town life. As a direct result of the pageant there sprang up within the town all sorts of improvement activities: a cow-test association, a forestry association, Boy Scouts, Campfire Girls, union church services, a town orchestra and chorus, a women's home-crafts league called the Thetford Kitchen. Renewed civic commitment to the venerable Thetford Academy was also evident. As its historian reports, the pageant was "not a celebration, but a civic movement for the reinvigoration of local life."

Of course a pageant of this sort cannot be offered in every shire every year, but such an event can do much to generate a sense of shire community even if performed once a decade or quarter-century.

Other public events and activities would also contribute to the shire's sense of identity. A shire band, with uniforms in shire colors, preceded by a shire color guard with state, national, and shire flags, are obvious examples. Shire athletic teams, composed of men and women out of the high schools, could carry on the spirit of pride and competition associated with high-school athletics. Already there are town basketball teams, and a Connecticut Valley Hockey League, which boasts youth teams from Kearsarge, New Hampshire, and from Brattleboro, Hartford, and other Vermont communities. In 1986 the league crown was won by the Rutland Area Hockey Association, a proto-shire team composed of youths from six Rutland County high schools.

Preserving historical buildings and townscapes will be an important function for a shire committee. The Old Stone House in Brownington, the Old Tavern in Grafton, the beautiful old churches in Rockingham, Barnet Center, Richmond, and West Newbury, and the rehabilitated Main Street in Danby are examples of inspiring historic preservation, as is the restoration of The Square in Bellows Falls.

The shire's intellectual life could be stimulated by bringing back the institution of the lyceum. The lyceum movement began in 1828 as a way of diffusing useful and practical knowledge, cultivating the moral and intellectual faculties of the citizenry, providing in-service education for teachers, and supporting town histories, maps, and surveys. At the lyceum citizens could listen to lectures on a wide range of topics, including, in the lyceum of Concord, Massachusetts, attended by Emerson and Thoreau, presentations on "such uncompromisingly intellectual topics as 'Miasma.' " Two years after its founding in Boston,

Thomas Palmer founded a lyceum in Pittsford, Vermont, the first of some twenty-five to appear around the state. The closest modern Vermont counterpart is the historical discussion series organized and supported through the Vermont Council on the Humanities.

A first cousin to the lyceum is the academic inn, now regaining popularity in England and Europe. The inn is a dinner gathering at which a speaker introduces a topic of common interest to be debated by all members present around the table. And of course shire debate teams could challenge teams from other shires on topics of civic interest.

Shire Day

In August of 1901, by declaration of the Vermont legislature and proclamation of Governor Stickney, Vermonters in forty-five towns celebrated the first Old Home Week, in later years shortened to Old Home Day. As in New Hampshire, where the idea originated, Old Home Week or Day was an occasion for the return of natives from distant parts and for a celebration of the town's history, identity, and virtues. A typical Old Home Day offered concerts, parades, picnics, bonfires, dances, dramas, boat-, foot-, and horse races, literary events and historical commemorations, family reunions, and even an occasional balloon ascension. It was also an occasion for emigrants who made good to return and bestow some benefaction upon the town, such as the new town hall dedicated in Pittsfield on Old Home Day in 1934.

The very process of preparing for Old Home Day had a salutary effect. Former residents were tracked down and invited by letter. The sprucing-up of the village in preparation for the great event often led to lasting improvements, and interest in town history and historic preservation bounded upward. "Perhaps the greatest contribution of these occasions," wrote Harold F. Wilson, "even though it was indirect in its effect, was the influence that the celebrations had in bringing people into the hill regions of New England in the most delightful part of the year, and thus spurring the growth of the summer recreation business."

Shire Day will be a modern combination of Old Home Day and town field day, participated in by all the people of the shire. In addition to the traditional Old Home Day activities, Shire Day will feature a special ceremony, conducted by the respected shire elder, to welcome and formally initiate new shire citizens. It will be an occasion to recognize worthy achievements of shire citizens during the preceding year, such as the fireman who rescued a child from a burning building, a student who won a state oratorical contest, or a retiring public servant. It would be an occasion for the proud display of the shire band and militia, and the honoring of some returning shire native who had succeeded in the world beyond the shire's boundaries.

The Shire Center

Every community needs a focal point, a place which serves as its nerve center and, in modern parlance, its networking node. Such a place should be different from the shire manager's office, which is concerned with the operation of the shire government.

A model for the shire center can be constructed out of numerous examples from around the country. The Community Self-Reliance Center, in Ithaca, New York, can serve as one such example. The center is a joint office for eleven grassroots organizations, including groups dedicated to ecology action, the farmer's market, energy conservation, the community gardens, and self-help for poor people. The center offers normal office services, telephone answering, duplication equipment, a meeting room, and a lending library of useful materials on community improvement and self-help.

To this sort of operation can be added a community memory project, pioneered in Berkeley, California, in the early 1970s. Originally only a computer installed in a laundromat where people could come in off the street and leave messages as on a bulletin board, the idea later emerged as the computerized Denver Open Network. Members enter their particular interests on the network's computer and invite others to share them. The network operator then tries to put people in touch for joint efforts. Successes include matching a rancher who needed to learn about windmills for water pumping with an inventor of a new, more efficient windmill system who needed a place for testing. In another instance a request came in for a person with firsthand knowledge of child-rearing practices in Borneo. Within twenty-four hours the network had located three such people in the greater Denver area.

Computer bulletin boards already exist in a number of places in Vermont, although not in any kind of a community center. The Memphremagog BBS in Newport and the Hilltopper BBS in St. Johnsbury

132

are examples. Anyone who has used a computer bulletin board is well aware of the willingness of participants to share expertise with novices. Certainly this talent and spirit of service could be well employed in designing a computerized community data base to help shire residents learn of and use important resources and information within the shire.

Another useful model is the Baltimore Neighborhood Resource Bank, launched early in 1982. The bank locates noncash resources for community self-improvement projects carried out by seventy-five neighborhood self-help organizations throughout the city. Supported by a long list of Baltimore businesses, the bank systematically collects surplus furniture, supplies, pro bono professional services, and useful information for its groups, matching needs with available resources. When the steps of the East Baltimore Public Library deteriorated to the point where senior citizens and children scarcely dared go in, and city budget cutbacks precluded municipal repairs, the local neighborhood group used the resource bank to solicit design and construction expertise and materials for making repairs. Through the bank they got what they needed from construction companies, and the steps were fully repaired.

Miller's River Trade Service in South Royalston, Massachusetts, was patterned after the barter networks that sprang up in many parts of the country during the Depression. Its motto is "Discover Who Has What You Need and Needs What You Have." The trade service organizes barter exchanges for goods, services, skills, knowledge, labor, interests, and friendships. In addition it runs a car-pooling and ride-matching service, an apprenticeship program, a garden-produce exchange, a tutoring exchange, and a roommate or house-sitting service. The trade service requests donations from successful users of 5 percent of the estimated value of each transaction. It also publishes a sixty-four-page catalogue of services offered and needed.

The Shire Militia

When in 1782 John Adams was asked the secret of the success of New England's communities, he was ready with a four-point answer: "towns [local self-government], congregations, schools, and militia." Three of these still exist, but the local militia is long gone. Perhaps it is time to bring it back. Since it is no longer necessary to repel Indian raids or ship out for foreign climes to fight for the nation, the shire militia would concentrate on local emergency and disaster relief services.

There are already numerous organizations which fill part of this role. Typical of these is the Danville Emergency Ambulance Service, perhaps the finest in the state, which offers immediate response to accidents and emergencies with trained volunteer paramedical personnel and fully modern equipment. Thousands of Vermonters serve in volunteer ambulance services and fire departments, much of whose equipment can be seen proudly passing in review in annual Fourth of July parades. There is the REACT organization, which patrols highways on heavy traffic weekends and maintains an effective amateur radio network. There is the network of several hundred sheriffs' deputies. There are the search-and-rescue units of local snowmobile clubs and flying clubs. There are Explorer Scouts, first-aid teams, and sportsmen's clubs throughout the state. And of course there are the members of the American Legion and VFW, all of whom have had military training.

Conceive, then, of a shire militia whose membership includes all of these participants, integrated into a coordinated organization along with National Guard and other more formal emergency units. Like the militia of old, the shire militia will serve the shire's young women and men by offering a route into the responsibilities of shire citizenship. Membership will give shire citizens the opportunity to make a useful contribution to their shire, receiving from it the identity, status, and opportunity necessary for their integration into a strong shire community. Needless to say, there is little point in attempting to recreate some semblance of a fighting force in an age when it is no longer needed, but the idea underlying the shire militia remains valid, and it could become an important factor in the civic life of a shire.

It is often said that "Vermont is just one big community." The implication, always felt, never expressed, is that we therefore don't need local identities. But we do. It is true that a Vermonter feels a warm glow when crossing the border by the WELCOME TO VERMONT sign on the interstate, a sentiment common to state residents across America. But the notion that this is enough to satisfy the citizen's longing for a place to be is promoted mostly by people with immense *political* power.

As a percentage of the population this cadre of influentials – in the legislature, the governor's office, the state bureaucracy, the media, and Vermont's higher business circles – is much larger in Vermont than it is in most states. Its members travel extensively, make decisions affecting lots of people, and have friends all over the state. To these elites the notion of Vermont as just one big community is understandable. But for the other 95 percent of Vermonters, especially the poor, the real Vermont is a bend in the river, a long dirt road in the bottom of a hollow, a shadowed pasture on the sunset side of a ridge. It is neighborhood and town, both of which have suffered grievously over the years. For them the cultural identity and political cohesion offered by the new shires will fill a void caused by modernism and the systems view of life.

What the shires will do is provide, in Richard Goodwin's phrase, "a mooring for the human spirit." They will create an opportunity for developing one's personality and abilities in service to the common good. The shires will be a crucible of true human freedom in that they will nurture that sense of self-restraint which flowers into ordered liberty. The shires will build the kind of community that integrates the individual into a matrix of land, society, custom, belief, and hope without which he or she is prey to alienation and despair. These manifestations of shire identity will, in time, strengthen this vital spirit of community and make the shire into a spiritual home for its people.

Chapter 9

THE STATE GOVERNMENT: DOING MUCH LESS, MUCH BETTER

We cannot put everything up to the
government without over-burdening it.
— Calvin Coolidge

W ITH domestic affairs returned to the hearths of the people in their shires, Vermont's state government will be free to address the other issues that must have its attention in the coming century. America will see how a lean, effective state government can be both democratic and competent in meeting the new challenges of the post-modern world.

Our design for state government welcomes the hopefulness of consensual politics. It attacks policy fiefdoms in the bureaucracy and features a unicameral legislature, an executive capable of measurable accomplishment, and an end to the proliferation of bureaucratic structures that over the past century have been set one against the other in the name of protecting democracy from itself.

The legislature will be enlarged and its policy-making capacity strengthened in those areas that remain under state control. Thus state policy, although limited in scope, will once again be fashioned by citizens, not public-sector technocrats. Administrators armed with better law will be able to concentrate on management (as, indeed, the best ones like to do) rather than remain preoccupied with second guessing the legislature.

The key to this model is contained in one fundamental observation: The *range* of state government activities will be drastically curtailed but not necessarily the *amount* of activities. Those things the state does it will do better. The new central government – crisp, efficient, and innovative – will maintain the purity of the environment, establish Vermont as a new actor in global affairs, and help coordinate relations among the shires, and between the shires and itself.

Distributing the Work of Democracy

Remember that we are following the federal model. Delegated powers go to the state, reserved powers to the shires. The new Vermont Constitution will instruct the courts to interpret a new necessary and proper clause as narrowly as possible, always with the presumption that power resides in the shires. The supreme court itself will be made up of judges elected by a legislature which is in turn elected by the shires. The amendment process, discussed earlier, likewise will be structured to favor the shires. The combination of these factors will mean that power placed in the hands of the shire in the first place will remain there. Thus protected from overload, the state can go about its own very important business.

Let us discuss, therefore, what the state *can* do and the apparatus needed to do it. To some this may seem to be a lot of new activities and attendant bureaucracy for a plan based on a radical reduction of state responsibility. This is because we are in the habit of thinking of state power in terms of residual power, not delegated power. We are about to list what the state government may do and *only* what it may do. This list will include some new functions, but these will hardly replace the tremendous amounts of public responsibility the state has assumed over the last century that are to be reassigned to the shires.

Delegated Powers

To begin, the state will remain responsible for overhead functions traditionally conducted by officers like the secretary of state and the attorney general. It will, of course, house the supreme court and establish a criminal code. It will also supervise such things as workmen's-compensation policy. A Department of Administration, much reduced in size from the current agency, will handle purchasing, taxation, personnel, and budgeting. Most important, the state will be given primary responsibility to protect the civil rights and civil liberties of its people.

Beyond that it will be delegated powers from the constitution in four major areas. First, it will have the power to operate an Agency of State Life through which it will publish the state magazine, *Vermont Life*, and it will operate the Office of Historic Preservation to ensure that Vermont does not lose the precious remnants of its historical heritage. In addition it will maintain the state library, and the state college system.

Secondly, the new Vermont Constitution will delegate primary responsibility for environmental protection to the state. There is room for local activity but there is no room for local *control* of environmental affairs. We do not, however, envision statewide zoning. If a shire wants to look like hell, let it. For too long the environmental movement has been weakened by the insistence by some that "visual pollution" be given equal status with things like water- and air pollution. But the state must have power over the shires to keep the air and water clean and the land free of contaminants that may work their way into either. While shires may be creative in their approach to environmental policy, the state must have ultimate power to step in and demand compliance with its own rules and regulations. Environmental policy will be administered through what will probably become the largest state agency, the Agency of Natural Resources – to include the departments of Forests; Fish and Wildlife; and Environmental Protection.

A new Agency of Vermont Affairs will administer a third delegated authority – to take bold steps to increase Vermont's influence beyond its own borders. Within this agency, the Office of Global Involvement will administer policy set by the state legislature in world trade, international cultural exchanges, technology sharing, and initiatives to promote world understanding and development. This agency will also have offices of National Affairs and Subnational Affairs; the latter to develop bioregional cooperation and interstate compacts and agreements, and the former to promote our concerns in the U.S. Congress and the executive branch. We foresee a robust state presence in Washington but not a presence as it is now – individual agencies operating as entrepreneurs for their own interests in a hit-or-miss search for money and power. The Office of National Affairs will thus be an important counterbalance to the special-interest politics the present situation encourages.

Finally the state government will be delegated dramatically improved capacities to provide technical assistance, establish information banks, engage in collection and disbursement services, and operate a central communications clearinghouse. These will be located in a new Agency of Shire Support Services. Thus a shire might hire the state to evaluate an educational program or seek technical advice on facilities for the care of the mentally ill.

Government agencies have built-in, institutional biases that affect the outcome of any technical services they provide, such as measurement. By removing the provision of technical services from special-interest agencies (e.g., departments of education, fish and wildlife, etc.) and placing them in the hands of an agency whose *only* mandate is the provision of technical services, the shires and their citizens will be far better served.

The Office of Federal Contracts within the Agency of Shire Support Services will receive and distribute federal funds to the shires when such funds are prohibited from going directly to them. In cases where federal funds are earmarked for state programs only, this office will contract with the shires to spend what will only nominally be state money.

Shared Powers

In addition to these delegated powers, the state will be involved with policy that it shares with the shires, and that complements rather than controls shire functions. The Agency of State–Shire Partnership will conduct two kinds of activities. It will design and administer programs concurrently with the shires, and it will regulate the private sector.

The Department of Implemented Policy in the Agency of State–Shire Partnership will deal with powers given to both state and shire. Small offices in this department will carry out the state's responsibilities in such fields as transportation, public health, agriculture, police, and corrections. To keep these offices small the constitution will instruct the Vermont Supreme Court to rule in favor of the shires in all matters where clear definition of jurisdiction between state and shire is lacking.

For instance the Office of Transportation will be responsible for maintaining federal highways in Vermont. But it will also administer policy from a specific grant of power in the constitution to maintain state highways in cooperation with shire highway departments.* All "state-aid" local roads will revert back to total shire control. If the state government decides to change a two-lane state highway into a four-lane highway, the constitutional clause directing the court to interpret "maintenance" in favor of the shire will preclude the state from doing so. Likewise the constitution may delegate the state power to maintain a state prison in cooperation with the shire in which the prison is located, or cooperate with the shires to maintain the integrity of Vermont's public-health system. The Office of Agriculture might be given the power to assist in maintaining the health of Vermont's dairy herd. Thus the state could test for brucellosis but would have no power to promote Vermont farm products as it does now, unless it were specifically so empowered by the constitution.

The other department in the Agency of State–Shire Partnership is Licensing and Regulation. It will include offices, now attached to the secretary of state's office, which license architects, doctors, pharmacists, public accountants, and so forth. The role of this department will be to provide administrative support to all such regulatory bodies. The constitutional convention called to create the new Vermont federation of shires will have to decide which of these will remain under state control.

In sum the state government will be radically smaller, retaining only five responsibilities: (1) technical services to the shires; (2) environmental protection that transcends locality in a *fundamental* way; (3) foreign policy on a far-ranging array of issues from the Connecticut River Valley to Washington, D.C., and beyond; (4) the maintenance of small departments and licensing and regulatory offices in areas of state–shire cooperation; and (5) the protection of basic civil rights and liberties.

Needless to say a wide range of decisions regarding the organizational structure of the state government will have to be made as Vermont puts the shire system in place. What to do with the Vermont Student Assistance Corporation (VSAC) is a case in point. At present it helps deserving Vermont students go to college. Money for scholar-

---

*If this language seems too specific, remember the number of such statements in the constitution will be very few, since the list of shared powers will be limited.

VERMONT STATE GOVERNMENT UNDER THE SHIRE FEDERATION, 2025 A.D.

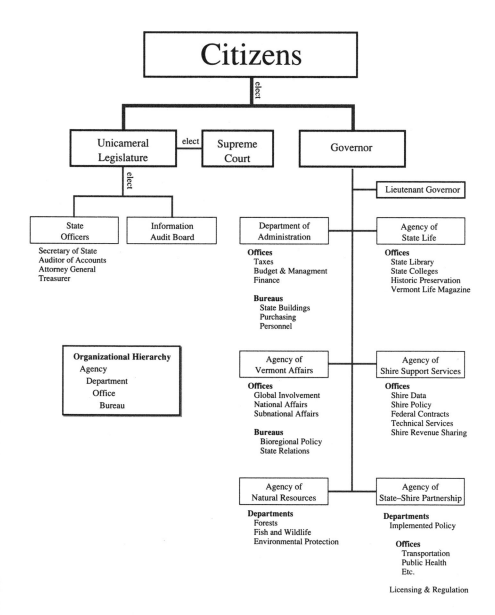

Citizens

elect

Unicameral Legislature — elect — **Supreme Court**   **Governor**

elect

Lieutenant Governor

State Officers
Secretary of State
Auditor of Accounts
Attorney General
Treasurer

Information Audit Board

Department of Administration
Offices
Taxes
Budget & Managment
Finance

Bureaus
State Buildings
Purchasing
Personnel

Agency of State Life
Offices
State Library
State Colleges
Historic Preservation
Vermont Life Magazine

Organizational Hierarchy
Agency
  Department
    Office
      Bureau

Agency of Vermont Affairs
Offices
Global Involvement
National Affairs
Subnational Affairs

Bureaus
Bioregional Policy
State Relations

Agency of Shire Support Services
Offices
Shire Data
Shire Policy
Federal Contracts
Technical Services
Shire Revenue Sharing

Agency of Natural Resources
Departments
Forests
Fish and Wildlife
Environmental Protection

Agency of State–Shire Partnership
Departments
Implemented Policy

Offices
Transportation
Public Health
Etc.

Licensing & Regulation

ships goes to VSAC, not the University of Vermont or the other state colleges. Qualifying students can then apply the VSAC money to their tuition at whatever college they attend. VSAC is very well run but very, very isolated from the democratic process. Our recommendation would be to eliminate it and let the shires decide how to help their children go to college. On the other hand a case could be made that this is an issue that could remain a function of a quasi-public corporation at the state level.

Or what about the Vermont Public Service Board and the Public Service Department? We do not feel Vermont will be able to work toward the strong network of small-scale local energy sources it needs until the political control over energy is decentralized. On the other hand a case can be made that the shire system will be too diffuse to manage energy policy. While we might bet that continuing break-throughs in technology are trending toward decentralism, this is another debate that will undoubtedly go on in the constitutional convention called to hammer out the constitution for the shire federation.

We have no wish to *weaken* state government, but to narrow its scope severely. While the state has been strong enough to bully power away from the towns, in so doing it has not strengthened itself – it has overburdened itself. Reordering traditional functions downward will do more than deal with the incapacity of the central government to treat human problems in an effective, humane way. Devolution of authority to the shires frees the state to tackle the complex and enormously important duties the future is already demanding. If Vermont's state government can meet its new responsibilities in national and world affairs, environmental protection, information gathering and dissemination, the protection of civil rights and liberties, and technical assistance to its localities, it will be doing plenty, indeed. Conversely, as long as the state continues to expend its greatest energies on those matters that can be performed better and more effectively at the local level, it will remain unable to meet the challenges of the coming century. The same is being said more and more about the national government. It is time to *share* the work of democracy. There is enough to do for everyone.

•

Witness: In 1984 the Vermont Board of Education decreed that there should be a system of basic statewide standards for local schools. These standards were to be designed and implemented by the board and the Department of Education. In Vermont educational policy is made by a seven-member Board of Education appointed by the governor. Board members serve staggered six-year terms. Its policies are implemented by a Department of Education headed by a commissioner who is appointed by the Board of Education, not the governor. The state educational establishment is for all intents and purposes beyond democratic control.

In every way the design and implementation of the state's Public School Approval (PSA) process demonstrates a central axiom of this book: when human-scale policy is crammed into a system-scale paradigm, the process is unavoidably dullwitted, inefficient, and undemocratic. First of all it is dullwitted because large-scale approaches to policy making cannot escape the law of size and mediocrity. In this case the state acted in precise accord with the fundamental model of policy making in America today: it covered all its bases and sought the lowest common denominator. The result was a formula whereby every interest made sure no school would be approved in Vermont if it did not do at least some of what that particular interest thought it ought to do. From the beginning the PSA process had no chance to be progressive.

Secondly, the process was grossly inefficient. The state arrived at the schoolhouse carrying thick packets of regulations. As local schools and school boards were forced through hoops they neither needed nor appreciated, more and more slack appeared in the rules. Exceptions and postponements and qualifications flowed like sap on a warm March afternoon. The result was a well-known pattern: teachers and administrators waited patiently for the state to leave and then set about cleaning up the mess. The energy of reform was lost in the dance of deceit. The original intention of the PSA was to train paid evaluators to visit local schools to assess whether or not state standards were being met. This approach proved to be too expensive, and volunteers were recruited. The state had bitten off more than it could chew, and the original goals of the program were further diminished. The entire process is a textbook example of how size is, at its very core, inefficient.

Finally the PSA case demonstrates that system-level policy fashioned on a web of special interests can never be *democratic*. At the state level the legislature was left out of the PSA process. The policy was designed by the educational establishment. While this establishment is by no means harmonious, it exists, nevertheless, like all policy subsets in America (including the military, highway, and agricultural policy establishments) in its own little eddy while the great river of citizenship flows onward essentially unaware and uninformed. Public hearings were attended only by the self-interested. Testimony was taken, but nearly always it was from representatives of special-interest groups: the Vermont School Boards Association, the Vermont Superintendents Association, the Vermont chapter of the National Education Association. This kind of process may be a necessary condition for democracy, but it is far from being a sufficient one.

In the vacuum caused by an overworked state bureaucracy attempting to put in place a complicated set of policies, democracy at the community level is tarnished as well. In the PSA debacle local educators were tempted to turn the process to their own advantage, using the old "the-state-made-me-do-it" ploy to develop programs that the voters (rightly or wrongly) had previously turned down again and again. While one might say it is better to get the shaft from locally elected officials than from state bureaucrats, that is saying very little indeed for democracy.

•

We turn now to a description of the state's legislative and executive structures in the shire federation. These are designed to weaken adversarialism, strengthen more unitary forms of decision making, and neutralize the capacity of special interests to operate freely within the government.

The State Legislature

It has been some time since Alexander Hamilton said of state legislatures in general: "Will [the people] suffer their legislatures to be reduced to a shadow and a name? The idea is shocking to common sense." But the growth of bureaucracy and the diminishing of the legislative process by special-interest politics has produced just such a shock. Indeed historian John Lukacs argues that "while the main phase of the transition from the American legislative to the American administrative state may have occurred in the 1930s, the main phase of the transition from an American democratic state to an American bureaucratic state took place in the 1950s."

Thus the most important thing to be done to preserve *representative* democracy (beyond the building of a base of real democracy in the shires) is to revitalize the legislative process. This must be done in accord with the fundamental principle that grounds this book: citizens can govern. As Vermont entered the post-modern period with

its communities intact, its legislature entered it with citizens still holding most of the seats. As Vermont's local democracies can use technology to take back the power they lost to the State, so the Vermont
legislature can use technology to reestablish the influence it sacrificed to the bureaucracy.

For the idea that citizens are unfit to govern is not limited to local
government. It is more and more the case that when legislative bodies
snatch power from the localities, they quickly give it up to the bureaucracy, and they do so under a gun of argumentation that looks exactly
like the one they themselves trained on the communities: legislators
are not experts; they lack the capacity to make policy judgments in
a complex world; it is better to turn over the "details" to professionals who will act in the name of the public good.

When a recent speaker of the Vermont House of Representatives
referred to floor discussion on a fish-and-game bill as "raccoon debates"
and wished aloud that they would go away, he provided a clear snap-
shot of what happens when the systems axiom gains control of politics: wild-game management is a scientific process that is best left
to fish-and-game experts who know what they're doing. Besides, it
is implied, what do "raccoon debates" have to do with the politics of
a modern state, anyway? There is, too, in this mindset a not very well
camouflaged disparagement of country ways.

The sharpest manifestation of the bureaucratic, antirural, systems-
axiom attitude in Vermont has been the debate over the deer herd.
Should the herd be controlled by the Fish and Wildlife Department
or by the legislature? Behind this question the real issue was always
whether or not to shoot female deer. The "doe-season" debate was invariably hot and always involved the question of bureaucratic (spell that
"professional") control as opposed to legislative control. Sophisticates
derided the whole process as the most embarrassing of the many issues
that brought out the "woodchucks" (spell that "native Vermonters").

The game managers' argument reeked of techno-imperialism, the
expansion of specialization over decision making. Every American who
has ever left his car at a garage and been given the "pay-me-now-or-
pay-me-later" routine knows all about it. Techno-imperialists use their
understanding of complex phenomena to force their way into the free
territory of the mind. In the case of the Vermont deer herd, the question was simple enough. The professional game managers said there
were too many deer. Doe would have to be "harvested" to bring the
herd down to a size that would fit the range available. Deer hunters

said there were not enough deer and that the doe should be spared.* Now the only data on numbers of deer were gathered, analyzed, and reported by the same people whose livelihoods, indeed whose very professional existence, depended on there being too many deer. Asking the fish and wildlife officers to census the deer herd was thus like asking a homeward-bound fox how many chickens there were in the chicken house. We bear wildlife managers no malice. Highway engineers like to build roads. Educators like to educate. Neither should control the information on which society's decision whether or not to do these things is based.

Faced with no capacity to generate data of their own (such as on the number of deer found in the spring that had died from starvation), the legislature turned the deer herd over to the bureaucracy, which immediately established a series of doe seasons.

The wildlife biologists may be right about the deer herd. All their studies say they are. Yet it is hard to forget the words of Robert McNamara, secretary of defense in the 1960s, when he commented on Vietnam: "Every quantitative measure we have shows we are winning the war." Or listen to General William C. Westmoreland in 1968: "The enemy has been defeated at every turn." Like our Vermont deer experts, McNamara and Westmoreland were the only ones counting the bodies.

Why shouldn't the Vermont legislature debate the fate of the deer? What is wrong with "raccoon debates"? Wildlife is as important to Vermont as oil is to Texas. Why are so many of our leaders ashamed to be seen discussing fish-and-wildlife policy? Why is it that the Fish and Wildlife Committee of the legislature is considered by many to be one of the least attractive committee assignments? Why do we deny what we are? Hooray for raccoon debates!

Abdicating the people's rightful authority to experts doesn't stop there. About a decade ago a group of legislators thought that what then Governor Richard Snelling called "the most important energy decision Vermont would make in the remainder of this century" should

---

*They also had their safety in mind. In the buck-only seasons, hunters could shoot no deer unless it had antlers at least three inches long. Without this restriction there was no need to take a close look at a deer. Great Danes, heifers, other hunters, fawns, and good-sized house cats were thereby jeopardized. In fact the most dangerous hour in Vermont for any given year since the beginning of doe hunting is between 4:00 and 5:00 P.M. of the last day of the deer season, when frustrated hunters are apt to empty their magazines at damn near anything. Our advice to anyone in Vermont during that hour is: Don't leave your houses. If you must, be careful that as you go about you make no sudden movements whatsoever.

not be left up to the Vermont Public Service Board. The speaker of the house responded: "What do 180 legislators know about power lines, anyway?" When the Board of Education decreed the Public School Approval standards, the act was called by one official "the most important development in Vermont education in twenty years." When asked what the legislative input was, he said, "Next to nothing."

Education. Wildlife. Energy. Colonization of the legislature by the bureaucracy must end. Those things left to the state under the shire federation will be fashioned by the citizens in their parliament assembled.

The heart of Vermont's new State government will be a unicameral legislature of about two hundred members. A "unicam" has many appeals. Vermont is one of the few states in the Union to ever operate one. We did so until 1836. Additionally Vermont's upper house represents counties, and counties have become virtual nonentities. Finally the limbs of true bicameralism – one house based on place, the other on population – were axed by the U.S. Supreme Court in 1964, when it held (with remarkable dimwittedness) that both houses must be based on population.

In the age of special-interest politics, bicameralism exacerbates the problem of complexity and makes the governing process still more invisible to the public. Worst of all, bicameralism, which was designed to contain an adversarialism that was considered inevitable, now ensures the inevitability of adversarialism where none need exist.

To give everyone in our shire federation a fair shot at election to the "unicam," salaries will be set (as they are for the shire-moots) at the statewide average, and constitutional guarantees will ensure that employers give time off. Terms will be for two years with a limit of five. We are told that continuity of office holding is a good thing. Continuity of democracy is better. The intent here is to promote the notion that service in the state legislature is a public duty. Vermont's tradition of citizen lawmakers will be preserved.

Once in place, the legislature must address the most fundamental weakness of law-making bodies in the post-modern period – a lack of access to information. As a Vermont state senator said recently at a public hearing, "We are in the dark most of the time over there [in Montpelier], and we are kept in the dark." In the new Vermont the organization with the most sophisticated data-processing system and data-access capacity in the entire state must be the legislature. This will mean the creation of new and robust staff.

147

Conservatives oppose improvement in legislative-staff services, arguing that it means "more" government. Whether or not that is true is arguable. What is not arguable is that lack of staff means more power for bureaucracies and interest groups. Opponents of staff services also claim that big legislative staffs mean the end of the "citizen legislature." Poppycock. Citizens are fully capable of using information-based staff services. You don't have to be a professional legislator to legislate professionally. Some say staff services can be used by legislators to advance their political careers. Perhaps. But there are things one can do about that – tying staff securely to committees or establishing an ombudsman's office are examples.

Vermont has a population about the size of greater Tulsa, Oklahoma. The new unicameral legislature will have as many as two hundred members. Is this too many?* No. It is time to do something about a modern irony of American government: the more power we give to government to establish rules that control our lives, the fewer people we elect to work out what these rules will be. Keeping legislators overworked does not mean there will be less law in our lives, it only means there will be worse law. We reiterate: it is time to spread out the *work* of democracy. Narrowing the scope of legislative concern, increasing the number of legislators to two hundred, and creating a modern staff structure will bring more talent and wisdom to bear on specific issues. This will increase the potential to build more effective policy, which will have a greater impact on public life and in turn enhance legislative efficacy. All of this will lead to a more positive public view of legislative service, more competition for seats, and ultimately a healthier democracy.

One problem in creating a legislature that is both democratic and effective is the district problem. Vermont, like other states, has been told to mold its legislative districts to fit the imperatives of "one person, one vote." The result has been the disappearance of the concept of place as an element in representative democracy. Every ten years the legislative districts dance to the tune of the mathematician's flute. It is little wonder that the people lose sight of their representatives and that the lawmakers themselves begin to conceive of legislative districts as arbitrary clusters of numbers and interests, rather than long-living communities with an identity defined by the contours of history, tra-

---

*The current legislature has 30 senators and 150 representatives.

148

dition, and the land itself. In order to rebuild our democracy we must bring new meaning to the concept of representation.

The idea that all one has to do to prevent "invidious discrimination" favoring some districts over others is to carve, graft, and append communities into quantitatively pure "totals" of people will go down as one of this century's great absurdities. What a shallow concept "democracy by ratio" is! What a fundamental depreciation it is to recede from any notion of content to a blind attachment to percentages when we set about putting into practice this definition of representation. First the slide rule and now the computer modeling software package have supplanted the communal identity that is absolutely germane to the notion of representation. Madness.

And for what? Political scientists are in near-unanimous agreement that rural people got a bum rap in the first half of this century, when state legislatures contained many more farmers and rural people than their actual numbers in society dictated. They were accused of pushing American cities into crisis in the 1950s. But it wasn't so. When the analysis was finally over in the 1970s ("reapportionment" took place in the 1960s), and the empirical dust had settled, it was found that rural legislators had seldom "ganged up" on city interests prior to the "reapportionment revolution," nor did they often channel funds in disproportionate amounts to rural areas. The dramatic rearrangement of seats that took place through reapportionment set urban and suburban interests to battling with one another as votes flowed out of the countryside into the urban *fringes*, not the inner cities.

Instead of demanding that our districts chase after quantitative purity every ten years, our intent is to keep the legislative districts solid and let the ratios do the running around. Each shire will always have at least one representative – by itself. If this means that another larger shire gains one, that is better than combining shires or, worse, carving off a chunk of one shire and appending it to another. It is also better to let the size of the legislature float than to chop up the districts. This will most likely mean that Vermont will have to petition the Supreme Court to uphold substantial deviations from the one-person-one-vote rule.

Vermont has several advantages in restoring permanent legislative districts. More than any other state, Vermont began as a federation of localities. Thus the federal analogy with the U.S. Senate makes more sense here. Also, the effect of deviations from one-man-one-vote will mean less in a state government that does very little. Since the approval process for the new system will begin in a legislature based strictly on one-man-one-vote, Justice Frankfurter's dissent in *Reynolds v. Sims** will be persuasive; that is, states may vote themselves geographical representation as long as the vote to do so is based on population.

The U.S. Supreme Court is no longer under the pressure of the "urban crisis" that led it to endorse reapportionment in the 1960s. Its latest decision on the matter (*Brown v. Thomson*) allowed a deviation of 89 percent from perfect ratios of population to numbers of representatives. More significantly the Court's criteria for fair apportionment were more lenient. It allowed states to consider such things as the integrity of political subdivisions and the compactness of districts. If deviations from one-person-one-vote are more than 10 percent, the burden is on the state to show that such deviations are the result of a rational, consistent, nondiscriminatory policy free of any taint of arbitrariness. It must also show that there is no way its objectives could be furthered by an alternative plan.

The new Vermont legislature will have as many as two hundred members, and each shire is guaranteed at least one representative. The smallest shire has 1,856 people and the largest 54,709. This discrepancy creates serious problems. Significantly, however, the challenge in the *Brown* case came because Wyoming gave every county *at least one* representative. Yet the Court was sympathetic, because the intent was only to enfranchise even the smallest county. Our plan in Vermont will result from this same concern – giving the larger shires all they deserve but giving each shire at least one representative. Thus we have reason to be hopeful.

The plan could be made more acceptable to the courts by using a floterial district system, as in New Hampshire and Idaho. In a floterial system some representatives would be elected from more than one shire, in addition to those elected from a single shire. For instance in the 1982 New Hampshire house reapportionment, 90 of the 145 house districts were placed in 17 floterial districts. Voters in many towns thus voted for one town representative, and for one additional representative who represented two or three towns together.

The size of the Vermont legislature could also be made to vary with each apportionment to bring the deviations within bounds. As a last

---

*This was the case that stipulated *both* houses of a state legislature must be based on population.

resort, weighted voting in the legislature might be considered. It is a logical alternative for meeting an equal population standard, but one which raises peculiar psychological objections. If all this fails, Vermont will have to ask the American people to amend the Constitution to allow Vermont to do its thing. If universal change is not deemed advisable, let the country pass an amendment for Vermont only.

What Vermont should absolutely *refuse to do* is to carve legislative district lines across shire boundaries in the pursuit of some mathematical Holy Grail which ignores human experience and the integrity of the shires as social, economic, cultural, and political units.

Once the legislative-district problem is resolved and guarantees that people from all walks of life have access to the legislature are carved in stone, the new Vermont Constitution should stay out of the legislature's way. Let the legislature establish its own schedule. Let there be no limitations on how much it taxes or spends. Give it free reign to experiment where it has the authority to make policy. Let it especially be the conscience of Vermont as a state, protecting its heritage, exalting its history, and carrying its message around the nation and the globe. Most of all let the legislature think outward and leave most of the day-to-day problems of governance to the shires.

With such a legislature in place, there will be no need for a statewide referendum procedure. On the desirability and usefulness of referenda we part company with many with whom we usually sympathize. Referenda are used by *frustrated* democrats. They are subject to mass-media manipulation and interest-group pressure. They gut the politics of human-scale deliberation and perpetuate the delusion of popular governance while the real decisions continue to be made as usual. Referenda are opium.

In the October 1986 issue of *New Options*, David Schmidt, executive director of the Initiative Resource Center in Washington, D.C., claimed that "the initiative and referendum is the perfect vehicle for Green activists." Martin Peretz, editor-in-chief of *The New Republic*, challenged Schmidt: "The genius of American politics, such as it is, is the genius of representative government. The single-issue passion provoked by referendum undermines representative government and civility as a whole." Schmidt replied: "I think representative democracy is not all that it's cracked up to be. We have a system that despite all its democratic trappings, is not all that different from the monarchial and centralist government system that the American Revolution was against." We hold that Peretz is right if the representative system were all it is "cracked up to be." But Schmidt is more right, because it's not. Given the state of decay in representative institutions he describes (we think with understatement), the reformers' support of referenda is not only understandable, but justified. Our approach, however, is to fix representation and thereby make direct voting in referenda unnecessary.

Surely a two-hundred-member legislature, representing just over a half-million people with a fully democratized election procedure that operates from a platform of real direct democracy, can create better public policy than a mass of 200,000 voters making one decision at a time in a polling booth. All things democratic are related to scale. The concept of democracy is not demeaned one whit if it doesn't work at the mass level. On the contrary, it is elevated. To insist that direct democracy must be kept small is to insist that it be kept human. Let the legislature be radically democratic. Then let it be.

The Governor and the Bureaucracy

Vermont's executive branch features one of the last two-year terms for governor in America. This will be preserved. The case for executive efficiency does not conflict with the two-year term. The reasoning for longer terms is based on a classic misperception about modern governance – that public scrutiny *causes* inefficiency. Inefficiency is caused now, as it always has been, by a host of factors which fill the textbooks of political science. Using democracy as a scapegoat for bad government has got to cease. When in 1962, for instance, Vermont elected by a narrow margin its first Democratic governor since the Civil War, Republican leaders, considering the election to be a fluke, planned to throw the new governor out of office in two years. But Philip Hoff won a resounding victory in 1964 and used that mandate to good advantage, overcoming his weak mandate as a first-term governor and building a solid record of achievement from the strongest of all foundations for effectiveness in governance – democratic legitimacy. Without the two-year term Vermont would have gotten four years of weakened executive power instead of two.

One of the principles that anchors this book is that real democracy cannot, by definition, be writ large. Democracy's value is in its capacity to provide the home ground for a governance that can produce citizens capable of operating a representative republic. With the creation of larger governments, this principle was continually violated.

We began, for instance, to hold elections at the mass level (such as referenda on policy questions) in the forlorn hope of preserving something precious we sensed was being lost.

Every two years Vermont voters face a very long state election ballot. Once they get beyond governor, most have little idea of the qualifications or even the identities of the candidates for many of the remaining five state offices on the ballot. Aspiring candidates spend large amounts of money and criss cross the state looking for support, and when elected frequently use these offices to milk publicity useful for a run at higher office. Furthermore many capable people will simply not consider taking any of the lower five jobs, because they are unwilling to submit to a costly, tiring, and often maddening political campaign. Worst of all, in the long run the long state ballot demeans the electoral process by creating a habit of voting in the dark.

We propose a single-office state ballot, where the voter casts one vote for his or her preferred candidate for governor. The gubernatorial candidates would designate their prospective lieutenant governors after the primary election – perhaps subject to ratification by their party's convention – and the two would run and be elected thereafter as a team (as in Maryland). The lieutenant governor would step in for an absent or deceased governor. Since there would be no senate over which to preside, it will be necessary to give the lieutenant governor something to do. Vermont doesn't need a vice president. Fortunately the present Vermont Constitution provides for a position that would serve perfectly – the Secretary of Civil and Military Affairs. This office has evolved into a very active one that might more accurately be called chief of staff.

The other four offices, secretary of state, auditor of accounts, attorney general, and treasurer, would be elected by the legislature, much in the way the legislature now elects trustees of the University of Vermont. This would ensure these officers an indirect base of authority from the people. It would also bring them more in line with legislative politics and move the whole system toward the parliamentary-like consensual framework at the state level that is becoming both more desirable and more possible as time passes.

The most important way to reform the governorship itself is to beef up its administrative role. A major theme of this analysis is that democracy gets lost in the mist of the complexity which often settles over the framework of government. Citizens must be able to assign blame when things go wrong and credit when things go right. The traditional word for this is "accountability." The popular metaphor is the buck that reportedly ended up on Harry Truman's desk. In America today the buck usually slips from sight. It doesn't stop at the desk of the chief executive. It never gets there.

Worse, Americans have been led to believe that inefficiency is democracy, or at least it is the best that democracy can offer—a hedge on tyranny. We deserve more. True, an inefficient despot is better than an efficient one. But the argument that the best we can do is to slow down the authoritarian urge by a complex system of checks and balances leads to the birth of an all-too-familiar figure in American public life: the executive who cannot (truthfully) claim real credit for much of *anything*, takes credit for *everything* good, and ducks (usually justifiably—because he or she really can't be blamed) everything bad. The opposition, which can't in truth blame the executive for anything, blames it for everything. The public watches this asinine crossfire and waits for someone like Dan Rather to tell them who's really at fault. Enough. In Vermont we intend to strengthen representational democracy by strengthening the executive.

Vermont's present system, like most others around the country, exhibits all the signs of executive degeneration. The administrative branch of government is a horror of confusion, obfuscation, and misdirection. It looks like eight teams of soccer players competing in four matches at the same time on separately marked fields that intersect at the center.

Several things can be done about this. The first is to reduce what the governor does. Overload has been discussed for a half-century by scholars of the American presidency. Even governors of little states like Vermont are not immune. It takes as much time to give an order to one thousand people as it does to ten thousand. True, the range of decisions is smaller at the state level but not that much smaller. Taking, for instance, Clinton Rossiter's list of presidential functions and applying them to the office of governor of Vermont reveals that Vermont's governor is involved on nearly as many fronts as the president.

Even those areas generally believed to be unimportant to the governor are becoming more and more relevant. The governor of Vermont, for instance, is fully involved in the "presidential" role of "chief diplomat." Vermont's previous governor, Richard Snelling, chaired the National Governors Conference and conducted important energy negotiations with Canada. The present governor, Madeleine Kunin, spent three weeks in Japan negotiating trade deals soon after taking office and traveled to Europe in her second term to promote Vermont as a business site.

Faced with a massive array of responsibilities and having severely limited means to deal with them, the governor is apt to spend too much time in roles such as the ones Rossiter calls "voice of the people," "chief of state," and "leader of the party." To a governor these are immensely more satisfying roles than trying to manage a bureaucracy, and they seem more democratic. Unfortunately popularity is not democracy.

Vermont's new federation of shires will cut the governor's role down to size. By so doing that office will be made more (not less) important in the scheme of public order. In governance, as with nearly everything else in this century, scale has been the forgotten ingredient. As the governor's role becomes more focused, it will become more involved with the workings of specific policies. As this happens it will become more possible for the governor to do real things, make *measurable* contributions, and leave visible marks on the body politic. Most importantly these marks will be apparent to the public and open to its judgment.

A second solution to the chaos and invisibility of state government is to dissolve the great policy fiefdoms, which have become estranged from the governor. Agencies having their own sources of funding is one way this occurs. In the world of adversarial liberalism, this makes sense. The argument is, as ever, plausible. Highways should be supported by those that use them. Thus there is a "highway fund" based on taxes and fees related to motor-vehicle usage. Hunting and fishing should be supported by those that hunt and fish. Thus the money from the sale of hunting and fishing licenses is set aside for the Fish and Wildlife Department.* In each case agencies are funded directly and so are more independent of both the governor and legislature.

All this may sound good until one considers what it does to the polity as a whole. When policy is cut loose from democratic structures through its independent sources of revenue, it quickly enters the magnetic force fields of group interests and fades from public sight in a dark political universe of specialization. Vermont's new executive branch under the shire federation must avoid this pitfall.

---

*Now Vermont allows the Fish and Wildlife Department to ask for "contributions" directly from the voters through a check-off system on their income-tax forms.

Another factor promoting executive fiefdoms is the structure of the state government itself. It would be hard to name, for instance, a policy area that has more concerned Vermont governors in recent years than education. Yet, as explained earlier, the institution responsible for education policy is largely divorced from the governor. When Madeleine Kunin took office the commissioner of education was a political appointee of a previous board. Policy decisions were made by this same board which was entirely appointed by the previous governor. In time Governor Kunin was able to make her own appointments, but even with her own appointees in the majority, it was very difficult for the governor to manage education policy in a way that allowed a reasonable person to attach credit or blame to her. The only thing she could affect was spending. This is the kind of executive arrangement that must be eliminated in the shire federation.*

But even many of the departments the governor can manage directly are equipped with policy-making, "citizen" boards. The Department of Fish and Wildlife is an important example. Although the governor appoints the commissioner of fish and wildlife, the commissioner's attention must be also directed to the Fish and Wildlife Board, which sets policy for the department. We could continue this analysis for much of Vermont's bureaucracy, and it would grow even more complex. Footnotes of every conceivable variety would be required. Asterisk would follow asterisk. And that's the point. Confusion is not democracy, although elites would have us believe it is since confusion comes in handy when they need to cover their trails. Bureaucrats seek structural complexity the way a white-tailed deer seeks the cover of the deep slash on a frosty November morning.

How does one defend the call for an end to citizens' boards in a book committed to the radical democratization of the political process? First of all these boards were created long before the arrival of specialization, the atomization of the political process, and the resultant ascendancy of single-interest politics. These factors have increased the probability that appointed boards will become caught up in the influence of special interests. Secondly, it is wrongly believed that the "citizen" role dominates when one becomes a nonelected "volunteer" policy maker recruited from the public. Often citizen board members are selected as repayment for electoral support. Often they bring

---

*We emphasize the word "kind" since under the shire federation Vermont's state educational system (including both board and department) will disappear.

with them narrow, policy-specific interests and expertise. Thirdly, these boards are not *structured* to be true citizens' boards, if only because it is very difficult for working people to meet their schedules. In short there must be a place for experts to give testimony on a continuing and more-or-less institutional basis in democratic systems. But they must be satisfied with giving advice only. They must not be allowed to make decisions or render managerial directives.

More important, if governors know that the people they appoint will never actually be making decisions, they will be more apt to appoint people they don't *have to trust to agree with them*. They may, in effect, appoint persons whose advice they need, rather than people they are sure will "do the right thing." Finally, eliminating citizens' boards at the state level will free up people to do the work of the shires. Local policy making will require deep pools of talent. Much of it will come from those people whose services are no longer needed at the state level. They will quickly come to realize that it is far more satisfying to be part of coherent shire governments than it was to sit on specialized boards lost in the chaos of state politics.

We have made one exception to our abolition of state policy boards, an Information Audit Board patterned after the General Accounting Office in the United States Congress. Information is, indeed, power. In a society driven by information we feel as justified in fearing its unfettered monopoly in the hands of government as our ancestors feared any government that held all the guns. Thus a citizens' board at the highest level, armed with the tools and the authority to expose bad information, is a necessity. In fact it should be created and charged in the state constitution, and its members should be elected by the state legislature with the requirement that they hold no public office and be on no other public payroll when they serve. We expect the Information Audit Board to be staffed with a large, well-paid group of highly trained research specialists, charged with delving into every aspect of state operation. Working for such a board should be one of the state's most prestigious jobs. Board investigators will arrive at public offices unannounced and ask questions like: "How do you know that? Where did you get that information? How come you used the median instead of the average in this case? What was the N in this survey?" This board would have no authority to do anything with their findings except publish them.

For instance the Information Audit Board might take it upon itself to independently investigate statistics on the deer herd provided by the Fish and Wildlife Department. If the Office of Public Health provided figures on the number of AIDS cases reported in Vermont, the IAB might do a thorough check of these data. If the Office of Transportation claimed that a certain state highway was so heavily traveled it needed widening, the IAB might monitor the highway itself. Let the bureaucracy live in fear of the IAB.

A final problem of executive inefficiency is the insistence that bureaucracies hold hearings before decisions are made. The great bulk of this problem will be solved when policy making is sent back to the shires or returned to the legislature. A major reason for the grafting of direct democracy to the administrative process in the first place was the natural tendency for legislatures to want to include some method of "representation" as they handed their constitutional duty to make law over to the bureaucracy.

The erroneous belief that democracy is happening when, say, the Department of Education holds a public hearing on mandating state-wide student performance tests is another result of our blindness to the implications of scale. As long as legislatures are required to make all the decisions for everyone, they will subdelegate most of them to bureaucracies. In so doing they subdelegate *representation*, and representation is the best substitute we have for democracy in large governments. Grafting direct democracy in the form of public hearings onto the tail end of the political process is no more than a sham and a delusion. The trick is to give the legislature much less to do, increase their capacity to do it, and then insist that they *themselves* fashion public policy through the making of good law.

•

Witness: As we pointed out earlier, energy decisions in Vermont are made by three political appointees on the Public Service Board. In deciding whether or not to build the Hydro Quebec power line through Vermont's Northeast Kingdom, several public hearings were conducted. But the Public Service Board wanted expert testimony. It asked for technical reasons, related to specific dimensions of public policy (health, wildlife, esthetics, etc.), why the line should not be built. Suppose one were to reason that even if the power line wasn't going to hurt the deer, even if it wasn't going to curdle the milk in the udders of dairy cows, it still should be opposed on the grounds that Vermont must risk energy "brown outs" in order to *force* itself to develop scaled-down sources of energy? This kind of view would be deemed inappropriate to the public-hearing process because (aside from the fact that a huge majority of the actors in the game would consider it extremely weird) it didn't fit any of the hearing's prearranged categories. The argument is "designed" incorrectly. It is too general. It is too "citizenlike."

Secondly the hearing process (which is defined in part by law) was stacked against the notions of polity and citizenship since hearings were held principally in that part of the state through which the power line was to pass. Even though the electricity would be used by everyone, those not *immediately* affected by the power line were *assumed* to be uninterested. The issue was not seen in societal terms but in technical terms. Citizen perspectives were not needed or desired.

The public hearings on the Northeast Kingdom's power line exemplified elite control of policy making in another manner. To watch the lawyers (plural, many times over) for the power companies cross swords with the lawyer (singular) for the opposition – this time the Coalition for Wise Power Planning – was like watching a dog fight between a squadron of F16s and the World War I Red Baron all alone in his wire-and-paper biplane. But even if the sides were evenly matched, democracy is not served when hearings, ostensibly held to elicit facts, take on the character of a trial. The characteristics of adversarial politics assume dominance. A format that features lawyers talking to one another does little for citizenship.

Worse still, at the time of the hearings the Public Service *Department* (the state agency created to voice the interests of "the people") was administered by a lawyer and political appointee who was totally in support of Canadian power. In fact he was appointed *because* he was in support of Canadian power. Irrespective of its position, though, could we ever say that the Public Service Department "represented" the polity? That department is essentially a cluster of energy specialists. It is not geared to make *societal* decisions about energy; it is geared to make decisions about *energy* for society. In sum there was no way the public could be represented in this critical decision if the public hearings didn't provide it. And they didn't even come close.

In the new Vermont, therefore, the bureaucracy will no longer need to use public hearings, because what limited policy making remains at the state level will revert back to the legislature, where it belongs. This does not mean public hearings should be eliminated, but it does mean they should be returned to legislative sponsorship where they will become once again a *part* of the democratic process, not an addendum to managerial life.

159

If the constitutional convention which decides the final distribution of power decrees, for instance, that energy policy should be made at the state level, then let it be made by the legislature instead of the Public Service Board. Let the Public Service Department report to the Governor, let the legislature hold hearings, let the Public Service Department be brought into the hearing process – and then let the legislature decide. With far less to do in the overall policy picture, legislators will have the time and capacity to become expert enough to make sound judgments. There is no reason why legislators cannot "regulate" as well as "legislate." The distinction between the two terms has become hopelessly confused. Since the regulation of the power companies will never exist in a vacuum, let it be captured by the people's representatives rather than by an interlocking directorate of energy specialists. Americans have got in the habit of hedging their bets on democracy. We don't trust ourselves to provide services through the legislature, but we don't trust the private sector either. So we regulate, through quasi-judicial boards, and often end up with the worst of both worlds.

•

To summarize, the problems of the executive – work overload, the lack of clear lines of administrative control, and a preoccupation with special-interest "publics" through the hearings process – will all be solved at least in part by the federation of shires. Workload will be reduced both by limiting the activities of the entire state government and by re-establishing the legislature in its proper position of chief policymaker. The elimination of autonomous departments, policy-making boards, and perhaps even regulatory commissions will nail down accountability and provide order and therefore visibility to the public's business. The transfer of the public-hearing process back to the legislature where it belongs will allow managers to go about the business of management.

Our plan is for a state government that is less adversarial, less complex, more accessible, more open, more competent, and more accountable. In this way it will become more effective doing the things that will be needed to be done in the coming century: protecting civil rights and liberties, promoting Vermont's interests and vision throughout the world, keeping our environment clean, and helping out the shires when they need it. That's all. Indeed, that's a load in itself.

PART III
HUMAN-SCALE
DEMOCRACY
IN ACTION

Chapter 10

FINANCING SHIRE DEMOCRACY

> *Taxation, for the maintenance of civil*
> *government or the national defence, will*
> *also take away property; but then it may*
> *bestow liberty.*
>
> —John Taylor of Caroline

OVER the years no question of public policy has been more controversial and vexing in Vermont—or for that matter in any state—than how to raise the funds to pay for what the public wants. At its center is the core issue: what *level* of government should raise the funds for what public programs? The reconstruction of Vermont into a federation of shires thus involves some of the most fundamental questions of political life.

Who among those that pay attention to such matters has not been caught on the horns of the following dilemma: Small governments want services, but they haven't got the resource base to pay for them. Accepting funds from higher levels of government with strings attached has the effect of destroying the fiscal independence of the smaller government. But funds given to small jurisdictions with no strings attached compromise the principle of accountability which is so essential to democracy.

In our case this dilemma has a new twist, since under the massive devolution of governmental functions we have proposed, the shires will have, in the aggregate, a budget dwarfing today's state budget. It is now time to turn to the thorny question of reordering the public revenue base so that state and shires may raise the funds to pay for their respective programs while satisfying the demands of liberty and democracy.

The largest revenue base is that occupied by the state, which in recent years has imposed virtually every tax the mind of man has been able to conceive (including even a tax on taxes – the income surtaxes of 1969 and 1984). Today (Fiscal Year 1989) the state's general-fund revenues are made up of the following major items: personal-income tax, 37 percent; retail-sales tax, 25 percent; corporation tax, 7 percent; meals-and-rooms tax, 9 percent; other taxes, 16 percent; other revenues, 6 percent. In addition the state has a substantial Transportation Fund, based mainly on motor-fuel taxes, motor-vehicle fees, and federal grant receipts, and a Fish and Wildlife Fund made up of license fees and federal receipts.

By contrast the only tax base of any consequence enjoyed by Vermont's town governments is the property tax, levied on real property (land and buildings) and, by local option, on personal property like machinery and inventories. A significant portion of town revenues, however, comes from transfers from state government. Chief among these are town road and bridge funds and state aid for elementary and secondary education. Additional state funds are paid to the towns for school construction and for special education for the handicapped. While the state also pays over to the towns some fines collected, part of the property tax due from landowners in the current-use and working-farm tax-abatement programs, and a small amount of civil-defense funds, town-highway aid and aid for education are the big-ticket items.

In a small state with 246 towns and cities having no effective tax base other than real property, there are certain to be wide disparities in available tax base and thus in the capacity to finance public services. Stratton, a southern Vermont town with a huge ski development and few children, has an aggregate real-property fair market value of $1,435,754 per inhabitant, while low-income Hardwick has only $18,381. Despite large amounts of state aid for education, which in Hardwick makes up over 70 percent of the education budget, property owners there pay a property tax rate of 3.72 percent of fair market value per year, compared to Stratton's 0.40 percent. This disparity has regularly excited the envy of reformers, who have urged the state to tax property in towns like Stratton and bestow the proceeds on towns like Hardwick.

Transferring functions from state to shire obviously means that the property tax will be insufficient to meet shire expenditures, especially if the people decide to transfer current town functions to the shires. What source of revenue, then, would the shires have to carry out these substantial new responsibilities?

Quite obviously, as the principal unit of general local government, the shire would have the power to levy a property tax on all property within the shire, although when the shires come into being their constituent towns and cities will still retain the property tax exclusively. Grouping towns into shires tends to level out the present disparity of taxable property among towns. Unfortunately, though, the state's rich towns are not scattered evenly among the state's poor towns. Collecting half a dozen adjacent towns into forty or more shires throughout the state will not produce relatively equal property wealth per inhabitant. There will be rich shires and poor shires.

One possible remedy would be to give the shires the option to claim a portion of various taxes collected by the state, at uniform rates, within each shire. For instance suppose each shire was entitled to have the state pay over to it half the income tax paid by the shire's residents, half the sales tax collected by shire merchants, and so on. This would certainly expand the revenues of the shire. It would not, however, assure resource equality among shires, and the shire which chose to exercise such an option would run the risk of seeing its better personal-income earners relocate to a lower-tax (richer) shire, with very unfortunate social and economic results.

A better alternative—because it allows the people of the shires to decide what mix of taxation they prefer—would be to give each shire the power to levy taxes on five of the six tax bases now the sole province of the state: income, sales, meals and rooms, property transfer, and motor fuel. The shire rate would be in addition to the state rate (which might be zero). The state could conceivably set the ceiling on the total rate, i.e., the total sales tax could not exceed, say, 5 percent.

This would offer the advantage that the shire could determine for itself the tax rates prevailing within its jurisdiction, but it would also mean that all the taxes involved would have local rates that varied from shire to shire. This would not pose any administrative problems in the computer age, but as with the previous "uniform state rate with shire rebate" alternative, the amounts per capita that could be raised by shires would still vary. This is so because the distribution of taxable resources will not be equal no matter how the shire boundaries are drawn and no matter what rates the shires choose to impose. In short even though the combination of grouping towns and allowing a wide array of local-option taxes would alleviate inequalities substantially, shires rich in things to tax would continue to have lower rates, and poor shires would have higher rates.

Both of these schemes founder on the disparity of resources available to the various shires. That leads to the idea of state revenue sharing according to some formula. The state would raise the funds and hand them out again as it does state aid to education, with the neediest shires getting disproportionately more and the richest shires getting little or no payment. Redistribution of this sort, however, brings with it several serious problems. The most obvious is that any distribution formula favors some and injures others. The perennial quarreling over the "fairness" of the state aid to education formula in Vermont is convincing testimony on this point.

A further drawback to making the state tax collector for the shires is that when the state redistributes money, it gains control. The shire would gradually become a state dependency, subject to whatever mandates and demands might be attached to state-aid payments and to the amount the state legislature votes to appropriate for the revenue-sharing program. This danger was incisively noted by President Andrew Jackson who, in vetoing a proposed federal revenue-sharing measure in 1833, declared that such handouts would make the state and local governments "the mere instruments and stipendiaries of the Central Power." Since we intend the shires to be, within broad limits, independent of the state government, conventional state revenue-sharing devices must be looked at with considerable skepticism. Are we, then, stuck with a choice between substantial inequality of resources and shire dependency on the state for much of its revenues?

The choice is not quite that grim. There is a way of equalizing resources which, although it still has the form of revenue sharing, minimizes these problems. It is the Canadian system of financial-equalization entitlements. This interesting and indeed clever system has been in effect since 1957, and since 1983 has been incorporated into the Canadian Constitution. Although it is relatively complex and unfamiliar to North Americans south of the border, we believe that it offers the most suitable solution to the problem of the disparity of shire resources.

The constitutional provision in Canada (Section 36.2) reads: "Parliament and the Government of Canada are committed to the principle of making equalization payments to ensure that provincial governments have sufficient revenues to provide reasonably comparable levels of public services at reasonably comparable levels of taxation." The best way to encapsulate the Canadian equalization system is to put it into the vernacular. In effect, the federal government says to each province, "You obviously have a wide disparity of tax bases. If you had to raise funds to meet ordinary governmental requirements strictly from your own resources, some provinces (like Newfoundland) would be very heavily taxed and some (like Alberta) very lightly taxed.

"Therefore we, the federal government, agree to guarantee that all provinces shall have at least a 'standard' level of resources to draw upon for governmental needs. We have devised a Representative Tax System (RTS), which is based on a weighted average of the provincial tax rates throughout the country. If the RTS were applied to all the tax bases of all ten provinces, it would yield what actually was collected by the ten provinces.

"First, we'll apply the RTS to our five 'standard' (that is, middle) provinces, and see how much revenue that would yield per capita. Then we'll apply the same RTS to *your* province's taxable resources, and calculate how much per-capita revenue you could raise by using the RTS. If your province falls short of the average revenue yield of the standard provinces, we'll make up the difference with a single, no-strings-attached annual grant. That way your province will have enough resources—your own plus the RTS equalization grant—to meet public needs at a level which is an average for Canada as a whole."

Note that there is no requirement that a given province actually make use of the RTS in its own tax system, and none in fact does. Each province can use any combination of tax schedules it chooses. What it receives from Ottawa has nothing to do with what it actually raises through its own tax levies. That payment depends only upon things over which an individual province has very little if any control: the RTS, the "standard" province's actual tax base, and the actual tax base of the province in question. What the federal government does is to ensure that each province has enough resources (its own tax base plus the federal grant) to meet standard needs and service levels. How the province taxes itself, what public needs it chooses to meet, and how well it meets those needs are the concerns only of the citizens of the province, not of the federal government.

The Canadian RTS originally took account of only three taxes: individual income, corporate income, and estates. In 1967 it was expanded to include thirty-nine separate types of taxes, rents, and fees in use in one or more of the provinces. Even though four of Canada's ten provinces get no payments under the system (Ontario, Alberta, Saskatchewan, and British Columbia), it appears to be well accepted and well managed.

Now let us apply the principles of the Canadian system to a Vermont of shires. Under our proposal the statutory definition of each of the five revenue bases involved—personal income, retail sales, meals and rooms, motor fuel, and property transfers—would be identical in every shire. The shires, however, would have the power to set the tax rates within the shire. A possible schedule of allowable rates might be the following:

Tax Base	Sample Shire Rate (Voted by Shire)	Minimum State Rate (Set by Legislature)	Current State Rate (1989)
Personal income (percent of federal liability)	20%	8%	25%
Retail sales	0%	2%	4%
Motor fuel (per gal.)	8¢	6¢	13¢
Property transfer	.5%	1%	1.25%
Meals and rooms	3%	2%	6%

In each case the state would handle the tax collection and administration, and would rebate the appropriate amounts to the shires on a monthly basis.

A sample shire, for example, might decide to impose a personal-income tax rate of 20 percent of the federal tax liability, the maximum allowed. But the shire's shire-moot might decide that a 3-percent meals-and-rooms tax rate was enough, and if the shire bordered New Hampshire, a zero sales tax. It might choose a half-percent property-transfer tax and would probably choose the full 8-cents-per-gallon tax on motor fuel. Whatever was necessary to meet the budget requirements after setting the rates on the five specified taxes could be obtained through a shire property tax. The state would retain exclusive jurisdiction over all other revenue sources, such as motor-vehicle use taxes and license fees, alcohol and tobacco excises, the lottery, the corporate income tax, the estate tax, etc.

The fact that the tax-base definitions would be identical in all shires is a very significant advantage. In Canada, where each province has different statutory tax bases as well as different rates, defining revenue categories has proven to be a difficult technical task. Each time a province makes a significant change in the way it collects a given tax, or adds a new tax, the RTS must be revised. With all tax bases in question being the same throughout Vermont, and only the rates differing, all the complications of adjusting the RTS to reflect provincial differences would be obviated.

What is known – the raw data for the schedule – is the amount of revenue base within each shire. In any given shire the state knows the dollar amount of individual taxable incomes, the value of taxable real property, the dollar volume of covered retail sales, the dollar amount of property transfers reported, and the dollar amount of meals-and-rooms transactions, and it can at least estimate the number of gallons of gasoline sold. (It would not be difficult to obtain precise numbers by asking retailers to report their sales.) Also known is the total state revenue base for all of these taxes.

To apply the Canadian RTS system to Vermont, then, the state would calculate the Representative Tax Schedule by dividing the total tax revenues collected by the shires for each tax by the total tax base of all the shires. This gives the weighted state average tax rate applied to each base by the shires. For example the average state property tax rate is 1.65 percent (in 1987), which is the total property tax receipts divided by the total property tax base of the state.

Our hypothetical RTS might then come out looking like this for all the shires taken together:

Income tax	.1623 of federal tax liability
Sales tax	.032 of covered purchases
Property-transfer tax	.0098 of amount of sale
Meals-and-rooms tax	.051 of covered transactions
Gasoline tax	13 cents per gallon
Property	.0165 of fair market value

Now let's take a present-day county (Lamoille, with 3.3 percent of Vermont's population), and see how the system works. Assume these economic facts are for a given year (they are not strictly accurate, but are close to actual for 1987):

Tax Base	Amount ($ millions)	RTS Rate	Yield ($ millions)
Taxable income	155.6	.1623	25.2
Retail sales (covered)	70.8	.032	2.3
Property transfers	88.6	.0098	0.9
Meals and rooms	49.7	.051	2.5
Motor fuel	9.0	.08 $/gal.	0.7
Property	892.7	.0165	14.8
TOTAL			46.4
Population			16,800
Total per capita			$2,761

Using the RTS, then, a shire like Lamoille County (which would be a near-average shire) ought to be able to raise $2,761 per capita by applying "average" rates to its tax base. Let us suppose the "standard" shire – the hypothetical median shire – had 13,500 people and could raise, using the RTS against its revenue base, $44 million, or $3,259 per capita. The difference between this amount and Lamoilleshire's $2,761 – $498 per capita – times 16,800 people, would yield $8.4 million. This would be the amount of Lamoilleshire's annual equalization-grant payment from the state.

Note that, in our example, it makes no difference how much Lamoilleshire actually chooses to tax its people. The amount of the equalization grant depends only on how much Lamoilleshire *could* raise if it applied the state RTS to its revenue base. If it could not raise as much as the state average, the state would pay the difference.

The foregoing formula is, of course, the same principle used today in calculating the "Foundation Grant" for education in Vermont, as adopted by the 1987 legislature (and also in use from 1963–1970). But instead of keeping the state in charge of setting a uniform rate for each tax throughout the state, our proposal would allow the shires to set their own tax rates. We are not advocating an add-on local-option tax, but a true sharing of the revenue base among the shires, which would then vote their own taxes to support their activities. Remember, too, that state expenditures will drop dramatically when public services are transferred from state to shire. This will free up revenues to fund the formula.

Our proposal provides some basic level of revenue base for each shire. That level is not, however, determined by a political vote in the legislature, or worse yet, by an agency of state government like the Department of Education, which unilaterally controls the key foundation amount figure in the state education-aid formula. Our basic revenue level is established by economic facts which no one shire, and no legislature, can manipulate. And the automatic nature of the equalization means that the legislature cannot tack on mandates and conditions or withhold funds to force compliance.

To sum up: the shires vote their desired rates on five revenue bases now under the sole control of the state, and the state rebates the amounts thus calculated on a monthly basis. The shire may also levy its own property tax if it so desires. The state makes an annual formula-determined payment to ensure each shire a minimum level of resources for its public needs. The formula is determined by actual economic facts from the previous year, not by political or bureaucratic fiat. The payment comes without mandates. How much the shire chooses to raise from its revenue base, to add to the annual state equalization payment, is up to the shire-moot. How much it chooses to spend on, say, education, is up to the shire-moot. How it chooses to organize its governmental services is up to the shire-moot.

The distribution of tax bases among shire, town, village, and special district poses yet another question of public finance, but one which need not detain us long. The shire-moot would simply allocate funds from its tax base (including, of course, the state equalization payment) to its component governments. Or it could choose to leave the property-tax base to component governments and use only the proceeds of the other taxes and the equalization payment to fund programs operated at the shire level. (We consider it highly unlikely that the shires would give the towns a local option on taxes other than the property tax, but that possibility would exist if the shire-moot wanted to take advantage of it.)

We do not expect that such allocations of funds or tax bases within the shire would be noncontroversial. They might be highly controversial, as they have been whenever a town and village merger is debated. But if democracy means anything, it means that the people incorporated into a polity have to come together to make public choices. The shire-moot is their arena. Unlike the state, the shire is very close to home, and it is composed of people many of whom the ordinary citizen will be likely to encounter in the course of a normal month. There will be as many decisions about intra-shire finances as there are shires. There is no "correct" decision, but the system as a whole will reflect the democratic wishes of the people it is designed to serve.

It seems likely that in time the shires would be able to achieve considerable efficiencies in public-service delivery. By reorganizing the road-maintenance districts, for example, it would probably get more out of its road equipment than would its component towns. (Of course, certain remotely located selectmen might not get plowed out quite so quickly after a storm, but that is a price that we – not being selectmen – are willing to pay.) By managing its own welfare system, freed from many of the rigid requirements and bureaucratic overhead of the present state welfare system, and by making flexible use of non-governmental resources, the shire welfare department ought to acquit itself very well in holding down welfare costs without penalizing those who deserve society's aid.

Certain functions, like keeping land records, will probably end up with the shire computer system, where they will be far more accessible than they often are today. Forsyth County, North Carolina, for example, has installed a county land-record system which at the touch of a computer key produces information on chain of title, deeds, mortgages, liens, property taxes, zoning classifications, and even incidence of fire- and police calls. Citizens may have access to this data base in the town clerk's office (as they do now), in bank lobbies, real-estate offices, police stations, and various other government offices, or for that matter, via home computers.

In addition to the efficiencies resulting from the decentralization of large-scale bureaucracies and the passing of their functions to the shire, and from achieving better coordination of functions now performed by town governments, it is likely that shires will become laboratories for finding innovative and economical ways of providing public services. As the Advisory Commission on Intergovernmental Relations (ACIR) pointed out in its report on "The Organization of Local Public Economies" (1987), providing public services is not the same thing as producing public services. The former term refers to raising public funds to pay for certain services. The latter term refers to actually delivering those services, a task that need not be performed by government itself. The most common way of separating provision from production is the increased use of contracting with private vendors to produce and deliver a wide range of public services.

In recent years much research has been carried on to judge the effects of contracting for public services by city governments, notably in California after the adoption of Proposition 13 in 1978 put severe limits on the use of the local property tax. In 1984 a celebrated study of the results of contracting was conducted by a firm called Ecodata,

171

directed by Dr. Barbara Stevens. The study provided for a "matched-pair" comparison of similar small cities in the Los Angeles area with respect to eight specific areas of government services. The effects of area, population, land use, and other variables were controlled.

The result was that in seven of the eight comparisons the city that contracted with the private sector achieved sizable savings to the tax-payers. Street cleaning and tree maintenance performance by city employees cost 43 percent and 37 percent more, respectively, than the same services performed by contractors. Asphalt paving by city crews was 96 percent more costly than when done by private contractors. Traffic-signal maintenance cost 56 percent more when done by the city, janitorial services 73 percent more, and turf maintenance 43 percent more. Only in payroll preparation was the city government competitive with private contractors.

In all cases, the researchers found, the private contractors, which had won a bidding process to get the jobs, showed greater efficiency in the use of labor, gave more authority to foremen, and made better use of their equipment than their counterparts on the public payroll. The contractors, unlike the city departments, lived in fear of not having their contracts renewed and thus were very much attuned to the need for tight cost control and good service delivery.

The ACIR report cited above also emphasizes that different services can be produced at different levels and on different scales. Some governmental units may be too small to deal with air-pollution control or forensic criminal investigation but may be perfectly adequate to operate water systems or control mosquitoes, especially when they are free to contract with private contractors. It might well turn out within a shire that some functions are operated by the shire employees, others by employees of sub-shire towns or districts, and yet others by private contractors hired by various governmental units to produce services paid for by the public.

With this kind of state-shire fiscal system in place, we would expect that public services will be far better tailored to the desires of the people of the shires, as will the mix of taxes chosen to pay for them. The equalization-payment device ensures that every shire will have enough resources available to it to provide services as good as those provided in the "standard" shire. The opportunities for achieving both efficiency and consumer satisfaction in service delivery, compared to the present state-town system, are likely to be very substantial.

But most of all, the proposed fiscal system will restore to the people, in their own shire governments close to home, the true power and the essential resources to act to meet a wide range of public concerns, in ways they themselves have designed and approved. It would be hard to ask much more.

Chapter 11

EDUCATION ON A HUMAN SCALE

*Wherever is found what is called paternal
government, there is found state education.*

−Benjamin Disraeli

I N education lies the hope of a working democracy. If there is
any governmental function which ought to be kept close to the
people and under the control of their communities, it is the education of their children. The new shires of Vermont are designed to
ensure that this will be so. They will provide a nesting place for small,
decentralized schools democratically controlled, schools that are part
of the social ecology of the shire landscape and a true reflection of
local culture and tradition.

As a general rule, small schools are better than big schools. But
small schools are not enough. They must also be neighborhood
schools − community schools. And the heart of the community school
is democratic control. Dartmouth College's Faith Dunn concluded after
an exhaustive study of differences in school financial resources and
community control: "We might well ask why the school in 'Clinch'
should have so little, when the school in 'Rogerville' has so much. But
we run a serious risk when we begin to ask whether the citizens of
Clinch have a right to decide whether their school should continue
to exist."

Dunn's study contrasts urban and rural schools. Noting that "for the bulk of the population, urbanized, centralized, systematic, standardized, and expert-dominated schooling is wholly consistent with the rest of their lives," Dunn concludes: "For most of the country, this is fine." She then observes: "Lay people do not feel that they have the time, the knowledge, or the authority to make decisions about the education of their children. They feel it is appropriate to leave such decisions to experts, just as they leave decisions about fire fighting equipment and public transportation largely to experts in those fields."

Dunn's all-too-correct assessment is nothing less than a funeral oration, not only for education in America, but, more important, for *democracy* in America. Much of the passion that drove us to write this book arose as we watched systems manipulators strip democracy from education in Vermont. In no small measure the shires were designed to do something about this very problem. But empowerment in education must not become a luxury reserved for rural states like ours. It is a necessity, as Vermonter John Dewey used to say, for the survival of American democracy.

Education in Vermont

Even in Vermont the last century has seen education become increasingly a function of the state. The town governments, in theory, retain control over their own public schools. But to the chagrin of more and more local school boards, the framework in which they operate is determined by the state, and they have long been under relentless pressure to consolidate under state control. In the shire system, responsibility for elementary and secondary education will be returned, firmly and decisively, to the people.

Vermonters have long evidenced the traditional New England passion for education. Vermont's 1777 Constitution provided that "a competent number of schools ought to be maintained in each town unless the General Assembly permits other provisions for the convenient instruction of youth." Also created was a system of county grammar (high) schools, and a state university. The University of Vermont was in fact chartered by the legislature in 1791, on the recommendation of a legislative committee which seems to have included seven of the approximately ten college graduates known to be at large in the state at the time. Jedediah Morse, writing in his *American Universal Geography* (1792), observed of Vermont that "in no country is common

175

schooling more attended to. A family of children who could not read, write, and understand common arithmetic would be looked upon as little better than savages."

The early Vermonters saw no particular reason why the state should meddle in the educational process. That was a matter for the freemen and parents of each town, or each school district within a town. After all who knew better what sort of education their children needed? And who knew best the character and efficacy of the school teacher?

What followed from that sound beginning, however, was the slow and painful process now so familiar to citizens across the country. It involved two dynamics: (1) education came to be increasingly centralized; (2) at the center education came to be captured by the professional educationists. This tale, so often told, has a special poignancy in rural areas. For it was to these places that the methods of the cities were applied. Theorists (mostly imported) used the power of the state and the people's desire for progress through education to impose theories which didn't work, and took little account of the importance of human scale.

•

Witness: At 5:30 A.M. on a weekday in December 1986, Martha White got out of bed. She lived in a trailer on a back road in a town in Caledonia county. It was twenty-two degrees below zero. By 6:30 Martha had herself ready for work. Her daughter, Stephanie, five years old, sat in a pool of light at the kitchen table sleepily playing with her Cheerios. Mrs. White hurried her along, directing her plump legs into an oversized snowsuit. Then Stephanie's hair disappeared under the hood, and soon only a nose and two great brown eyes were visible under the folds of clothing. Clutching a colorful little lunch pail, she grabbed her mother's hand as they snapped out the light and stepped into the pitch black of a Vermont winter morning. It was 6:45 A.M.

Mrs. White prayed, and her car started. Five minutes later it began to warm. But five minutes sitting in sub-zero temperatures will make you shiver. At that moment distant headlights appeared in the slowly graying dawn. Letting her car idle, Martha and Stephanie walked to the edge of the road. The school bus stopped, and Stephanie disappeared inside, turning to wave goodbye to her mother. The bus was already crowded with students, little and big, from age five to eighteen. Lots of things happened on that bus that little Stephanie didn't understand. She sat quietly next to a window and wondered where the frost came from. At least it was warm inside the bus.

By 7:15 dawn was underway. The bus stopped at a school, and Stephanie got out, walking across to the other side of the snow-covered school yard. The temperature had risen to eighteen below. She was surrounded by several other tiny human chimneys puffing steam in the gray of first light. Five minutes later a second bus pulled up, the door opened, and a wave of children spilled out. Stephanie waited until the last big kid rushed past so she wouldn't be pushed by mistake. Then she climbed on, found a seat, and sat down. Her cheeks began to get warm again.

Thirty minutes later, at 7:55, Stephanie got off the second bus at a second school, still clutching her lunch pail. She had forgotten it once before. Once, also, some big kids had eaten her apple. She had already been up two hours and traveled twenty-three miles. In the school library she waited for kindergarten to start at 8:30. At noon she had her lunch, then went to a "free room" where several other kindergarten kids played until 3:15 when the bus came. Again Stephanie got on the bus. Again she changed to another bus. Again she got off this second bus. It was 4:15 and getting dark. Stephanie knocked on Mrs. Livingston's door. She was to wait in her kitchen until 5:15 when her mother, who got out of work at 5:00, would pull up outside. During the day it had warmed up to four degrees below zero, but now it was back down to nine below. At 5:55, Mrs. White and her daughter stepped back inside their darkened trailer and turned on the light.

That is how Stephanie, a five-year-old girl, spent her days. Wondering if the bus would come. Wondering if her mother would be on time. Worrying about the big kids, her lunch, her mittens. That is how Stephanie attended kindergarten. That is how adults lay grown-up schedules on little girls. That is also how the state practices child abuse. It happens a lot in rural places when city people forget that life is different in the countryside.

In 1985 Vermont mandated kindergarten in all its schools. Weatherton, under this mandate, had started its kindergarten a year early. When this story (an all too typical one) was told to one of the supporters of the mandatory kindergarten bill, he was genuinely shocked. "But we didn't mandate that she attend," he said. "We only mandated that the town provide a kindergarten. She could have stayed home or gone to day care."

"But her mother is a poor working single woman," he was told. "What else can she do? Education is her only hope for Stephanie. Society has told her that for years. The better-off parents make other arrangements. They take their kids to kindergarten and pick them up afterward. Mrs. White knows this. She didn't want Stephanie to fall behind, to be deprived of still another advantage the better-off kids have. If people like Mrs. White don't get Stephanie to kindergarten, we've installed a headstart program for the better off!"

"Oh," said the legislator. He came from Burlington, Vermont's largest city.

"Look at it this way. Stephanie's life of schedules, and deadlines, and regimentation began when she was only five. She spends the waking hours of her childhood alone, without her parent, riding a bus nearly three hours a day, wondering why the big kids do what they do, waiting in Mrs. Livingston's kitchen, remembering the night her mother's car broke down and she was left, or the day the second bus didn't come and she cried because she didn't know where to stand in the other school while she waited."

The gentleman from Burlington, where the kids walk down the street to kindergarten in little groups in the daylight, said: "We didn't know about those transportation problems in the rural areas. Most of us live in the big towns." You could tell he was sorry. It was in his eyes. "I guess going to kindergarten is different in the country," he said.

Urban practices forced on the countryside hurt those least deserving to be hurt. It is still an old story, often told, and it's still sad. This is the kind of tragedy the shire system will be able to avoid. The shires will understand their own special needs. They will allow those of their communities that can use kindergartens to advantage to do so, and at the same time they will allow experiments with different forms of early education in those communities that cannot. A Vermont of shires will no longer force little girls through the suffering of Stephanie White.

•

In 1827 Vermont created its first centralized instrument of education, a state Board of Common School Commissioners. The board had only two duties. One was to compile a list of suitable textbooks; the other was to make recommendations for educational reform or improvement. In fulfilling its duty to make the textbook list, the board met with considerable local hostility. After all, said the townspeople, what did those people know about suitable textbooks? The board ruefully observed in its report to the legislature:

So generally diffused through the great mass of the community is

the sense of personal, as well as political independence, and so
sleepless is the jealousy of arbitrary power which is almost instinc-
tive in the popular mind, that the attempt, however well intended,
to dictate and prescribe the books to be used in our common
schools, is regarded by many as an invasion of the right of private
judgment, and, consequently, as incompatible with the genius of
our free institutions.

Six years after its creation, the Board of Common School Commissioners was ignominiously abolished, not to be resurrected for a quarter of a century.

But as the years passed, efforts to create a state, as opposed to a
purely local, school system gradually succeeded. In 1892 the legislature finally ordered the towns to consolidate their multifarious local
school districts into unified town school districts. This measure was
referred to well into the 1940s as "the vicious Act of '92," the death
knell of public education in Vermont.

In 1912, as the winds of the Progressive Era passed over Vermont,
the legislature took a major step toward conferring ultimate educational responsibility upon the state—it created the Commission to
Investigate the Educational System and Conditions of Vermont. The
commission, in an action then virtually unheard of, decided to contract the study of Vermont education to the Carnegie Foundation for
the Advancement of Teaching. Not surprisingly the Carnegie Report
excoriated the fragmented, locally controlled school system. It urged
the creation of a state-controlled system in the name of better supervision by expert educators. The most regrettable proximate result of
the Carnegie Report was the resignation of Vermont's experienced,
respected commissioner of education, Mason S. Stone, who refused
to serve under the hierarchical structure enacted by the legislature in
a fit of temporary insanity following presentation of the report. "Centralization," Stone remarked, "leads to bureaucracy, and bureaucracy
leads to paternalism." With Stone's departure the job went to the chief
architect of the report itself, a professor of education at Columbia.

Eight years later pressure from the towns forced repeal of much
of the Carnegie-recommended structure—an undoubtedly satisfying
result for Stone, who by that time had become lieutenant governor.
But by 1935, in the midst of the Depression, centralization was back
in the saddle. A legislative commission on education, concerned about
dangerous political movements and the threat to democracy, recommended a stronger role for the State Department of Education and

sought to mandate minimum school standards. In doing so, however, the commission appeared to shed a tear for the passing of the locally controlled school and questioned the economic efficiency of a more centralized system. The commission seemed to feel that centralization in education was the price that had to be paid to preserve democracy in troubled times. The commission's implicit belief that only dire necessity justified centralization made its report unique. Every other such effort, before or since, found centralization and consolidation to be a positive goal.

Following World War II the march toward centralization proceeded unabated. During the 1960s the door was opened to a wide variety of liberal social innovations in the spirit of the Great Society. Without fail every study or report on education in Vermont from 1962 on has urged the transfer of more power away from local districts, the consolidation of small schools, and a reduction in the power of local citizens.* A favorite idea has been to create regional school boards and reduce the number of superintendents. Numerous prestigious commissions and reports have invariably recommended drastic reduction in the number of supervisory unions in the state (to, variously, twenty-five, twelve, and eight) and consolidation of small school districts.

In 1987 Governor Kunin proposed the latest study of this hoary proposition and appointed as co-chairmen of the study committee State Senator (and former governor) Philip H. Hoff and State Treasurer (and former legislator) Emory Hebbard. The committee's findings were utterly predictable.

The governor hoped the committee would adopt an earlier report by a prestigious commission with strong ties to the business community. It advocated the elimination of nearly two-thirds of Vermont's school districts and the elected boards that went with them. But her committee, fearful of public outcry, decided to try the back door. It proposed the retention of the local boards while, under cover of language that can only be called duplicitous, it stripped the boards of their political power, beginning with their budgets. The inept title of the commission's final report was "Strengthening Local Control." Stuart Rosenfeld (see below), in the most thorough analysis of Vermont state

---

*Jonathan Sher, in an analysis of a consolidation plan by the North Carolina Division of School Planning, pointed out that: "since 1986 this Division has conducted twenty-two merger feasibility studies . . . they have never recommended anything other than merger."

educational policy ever published, practically predicted that title as early as 1976, when he pointed out with amusement that whenever the state made a raid on local education, it did so under the pretense of shoring up community power.

The findings of these many study groups (with the possible exception of the last one) have been automatically hailed by leading educators and the usual collection of centralists, notwithstanding the fact that in no instance has any objective evidence been presented that centralization offers any benefits to education other than the more efficient control by the Department of Education. As a department spokesman observed in 1975, "every previous major reorganization study started from the premise that reorganization was automatically necessary." Also every subsequent study, one might add.

The exception was Rosenfeld's wholly unofficial study, published in 1977. In it he recited the history of school-centralization efforts prior to 1976 (in considerably more detail than we have done here) and then examined the actual results of consolidation in a sample of Vermont high schools. This thorough and dispassionate study – utterly ignored by the Department of Education's centralizers and their legislative friends – is well worth reading in its entirety. Its conclusions, however, are summarized by the Rosenfeld as follows:

> The economics of scale [offered by fewer, larger schools] that, theoretically, could be obtained under ideal conditions are usually offset by the reality of added administrative costs found in larger, more bureaucratic organizations. The efficiency of the educational system may be increased by additional resources and professional business management, but ultimately it is reduced by the impersonality and alienation associated with larger size. Equality of access to educational resources may be improved through standardization, but true equality of opportunity is still a function of class background and environmental factors. Most research has shown that equal access to resources does very little to equalize outcomes. Removing the parents and the community from the process ignores the evidence that shows the importance of family and peer groups to achievement.

The board, the department, and its various commissioners have not found such evidence congenial. Indeed it is probably not unfair to say that none of them have even concerned themselves with the possibility that centralization might be a *mistake*. Their goal has been to centralize more control in themselves at the expense of local citizens and to reshape the overall system to make life easier for those administering it from the center. They do so simply because they are convinced that with their qualifications and experience they are better equipped to make decisions about local education than anybody else.

A remarkable manifestation of this attitude was the brief and tempestuous career of Vermont State Commissioner of Education Harvey Scribner (1969–71). Scribner's program will be quickly recognized by friends of community education everywhere. At that time a number of small high schools remained in the state, to the infinite disgust of those of Scribner's persuasion, a philosophy highly refined by immersion in the nation's most advanced educational thinking at the University of Massachusetts. Scribner had been taught somewhere that children learned because they were engulfed in "learning opportunities." Since small schools necessarily afforded fewer learning opportunities, their students learned less than students in consolidated schools. Therefore the correct policy was to force small schools to close.

Of course Scribner and his allies never bothered to actually look to see whether any data backed up this improbable theory. They just knew it had to be true, in the same way that Aristotle determined, by logic alone, that women must have fewer teeth than men. When one of the authors, then a legislator, persuaded Governor Deane Davis to seek federal funding for a study to find out whether small schools really were inferior to large schools, Scribner mobilized a veritable Grecian chorus of educators to block the effort. Their position was that it was not possible to agree on any standard against which students could be objectively measured, since every student had different capacities and interests. This "rubber-yardstick" theory of assessing student performance may well have been the high-water mark of educational imbecility in Montpelier.

Scribner bagged quite a few small schools in his drive to consolidate. In their place grew up large union high schools, with the fleets of shiny school buses and their unfamiliar names (including U–32 in East Montpelier, the only high school in America apparently named after a German submarine). It is a sad irony that at the same time these small high schools were forced to fall on their swords, research was beginning to appear that showed unequivocally that big was clearly not better in education.

In a thorough analysis of the effects of school size on education, published in 1964, Roger B. Barker gave unquestionable evidence that the smaller the school and the smaller the town it serves, the better the education it provides. Barker and his colleagues argued that the standard wisdom put forth by large-school advocates were "illusions." In small schools there are more "forces at work stimulating and compelling students to more active and responsible contributions" than in large schools. Even in such "extracurricular" activities as music, "education and experiences were more widely distributed among the small school than among the large school students."

Meantime more studies were turning up that could find no relationship between size and economy of scale in school expenditures. Kirkpatrick Sale points out that in a nationwide study of school districts economist Werner Z. Hirsch "was unable to find significant economies of scale in larger school systems." A major study by Jonathan Sher of North Carolina state University and Rachael B. Tompkins of the Citizens' Council for Ohio Schools completely reversed the established wisdom on size of schools. They found that by nearly every standard the small school in the small community ranked better than the large union school. Wrote Sher and Tompkins:

> ... despite the massive human and financial investments made on its behalf, consolidation has not dramatically alleviated the educational problems endemic to rural areas. And, perhaps most damning of all, consolidated units have not even been proven to be more successful than existing small schools and small districts – ones which have had to make do with relatively meager resources and only the scantiest professional attention. By consolidating, rural communities relinquished the advantages of smallness and received pitifully little in return.

As the 1970s turned into the 1980s an avalanche of scholarship appeared that buried the big-is-better thesis for education. The theory of "learning opportunities" silently vanished, and progressive educators rushed to recreate the virtues of the small school in the form of the mixed-level classroom. Even Scribner himself, who departed Vermont in 1970 for a higher-paying post in New York City just ahead of a mob with tar and feathers, has come around. He is now, in terms of his earlier positions, quite thoroughly reactionary, although his current views are presented with the breathless earnestness of one who has just discovered, once again, the Philosopher's Stone. Meanwhile the damage in Vermont has already been done.

Some of it is reflected in the passion of the Department of Education for new facilities. In the 1960s this took the form of promoting union high school education factories, complete with greenhouses, pools, and the inevitable acres of asphalt for parking the buses. By the 1980s, with about as much union-district consolidation accomplished as was likely, the department had begun to lean heavily on small towns once again, this time to construct new and larger school houses. The madness that accompanies these kinds of standards can be seen in the most recent round of mandates—such items as the ten-acre rule, which says that if a town is to build a new school house, it must be on at least ten acres of land. Picture that in a tiny rural village!

A major event in this history of state control of education occurred with little fanfare in 1982, when the legislature passed Act 151. Though not anywhere as near as controversial as the "vicious Act of '92," Act 151 confirmed ultimate state control of education. Prior to its enactment, the Department of Education certainly had assumed implicit power to bully school districts, but the power was never spelled out in so many words.

Under the new act, the Board of Education was given the power to "adopt . . . rules for public schools relating to instruction, faculty, curriculum, libraries, educational materials and physical facilities which are necessary to provide an acceptable educational opportunity." The act also conferred upon the board the power to "approve" any public school which exhibits the proper "minimum course of study" and "substantially complies with the Board's rules for approved public schools." This approval may be revoked for "substantial failure to comply." What happens when a school loses its approval? Its state aid is substantially reduced and its students are deemed truants (that is, outlaws).

A good recent example of Act 151's application is the town of Barnet. There may well be some residual animus toward the people of Barnet in the Department of Education, because when Barnet's McIndoes Academy was closed in 1969 the town did not vote to join a nearby union high school district. Instead its citizens decided to tuition their high schoolers out to any school found desirable by their parents, notably old and prestigious—and private—St. Johnsbury Academy. To department officials, who regard with horror the idea of public funds finding their way into the coffers of a private school, this was much to be regretted.

Barnet ran afoul of Public School Approval Standards, an enforceable wish list decreed by the department in 1984. The Barnet village school (grades 5–8) was held to be inadequate, and townspeople were instructed to get busy building another one. The new school, of course, had to be another architect's original, estimated to cost $2.1 million. (Among educationists it is considered very gauche to build a second school using plans already used elsewhere – just as Ymelda Marcos believed it gauche to wear the same pair of shoes twice, at least in public.) Barnet citizens were informed, darkly, that their failure to get with it would produce declarations of truancy and interruption of state aid. An agent from the Farmers Home Administration was even dispatched to Barnet to dangle low-interest federal funds in front of the townspeople to get them to cave in. And they finally did.

The powers conferred by the "vicious Act of '82," now give the Department of Education virtually complete power over public elementary and secondary education. The local folks can organize school boards, of course, and those boards can even quibble with the department, which has admittedly tried to be agreeable, much as one would try to maintain a reasonable demeanor in the face of ridiculous demands from a wrong-headed child. But when the crunch comes, the locals will do what the state decrees. Local control of education has increasingly come to mean little more than the determination of bus routes and lunchroom menus. Although the state is having trouble putting the new Public School Approval Standards in place, school systems are expending a lot of energy complying with some and figuring out ways to circumvent others.

Governance of Education in the Shires

At present, then, the extent of state control of local education in Vermont is staggering. The state controls teacher certification for all public-school teachers. The state maintains a list from which local school boards can choose superintendents, and woe unto the school board that desires some hard-headed practical citizen instead of a person who has all the right qualifications (and hasn't gotten crossways with the Department of Education in his previous job). The state controls teacher training. The state prescribes courses of study and number of days in school. The state establishes the school-leaving age. The state decrees the boundaries of superintendency districts and can change them without local approval. The state can, and does, forbid towns from seceding from union districts (as happened in Weathersfield). The state demands local compliance with its Public School Approval Standards, or else an erring local district will apparently be consigned to some sort of educational receivership.

The commissioner of education, as we noted earlier, is selected by the Board of Education, not the governor. The board is composed of seven members who serve terms of six years. They cannot be reappointed, so a governor's influence over them is reduced to jawboning. In living memory only one real critic of state control of education has ever been named to the board (Robert O'Brien, of Tunbridge), and he resigned in despair after a year of isolation, frustration, and hostility toward his decentralist views. In short, the Board of Education, and under it the commissioner and the Department of Education, comprise a separate empire unto themselves. While the members of the board may differ sharply on specific issues, it has long been clear that they are unanimously in favor of an ever-increasing state role in education and opposed to the idea that the local yokels might have any idea at all which is better than the ideas of the right-thinkers in Montpelier with their M.Ed. degrees.

This growing empire of educational centralists will be dismantled by the rise of the shires, and not a moment too soon.

Under the shire plan the power to control elementary and secondary education will be brought home to the people of the shire. How its schools will be governed will be decided, as in so many similar cases, by the shire-moot itself. In some shires a board of education might be popularly elected by districts within the shire. In others it might be elected by the shire-moot, with due accord to geographical balance within the shire. In yet others the shire board might be elected by the members of school-district boards within the shire, much the way members of a union high school district board are now elected. In some cases the shire might not have a board at all, the shire-moot instead setting educational policy and the shire manager delivering it through an education department in the same way he or she would manage the police department or fire department. In this case the shire manager, not a shire school board, would hire the superintendent of schools.

But under what we believe will be the dominant model, a shire school board will inherit all of the supervisory powers of the present State Board of Education. It will name the shire superintendent. The shire school board, and not the state, will make decisions about the necessity for teacher certification. The shire board, and not the state, will make decisions about academic requirements, textbooks, instruction methods, courses offered, basic competencies, and number of days of school. The shire board could decide to terminate mandatory schooling when a student mastered required material, whether or not he or she was sixteen years old.

Since the shires will begin with local (town and school district) powers kept exactly as they are until the people of the shire vote to change them, they will inherit a variety of ways of educational governance. One might have two union high school districts with their boards, each serving several K–8 or K–6 systems complete with their own elected boards. Another might have one union high school with its "sending" districts and a lot of high-school-age students who have traditionally been tuitioned to other high schools now outside the shire. What the shire does with these arrangements – from keeping them as they are (conceivably subdelegating all educational policy to districts within the shire) to abolishing them altogether and controlling everything at the shire level – will be up to the shire's citizens and subject only to the requirements of shire charter change in the new Vermont Constitution's home-rule provisions for shires.

Some will say that our proposal for education in the shires would mean the end of state control over public education. They would be precisely correct. It would mean the restoration of true community and parental control. And it would lead to a remarkable flowering of educational achievement.

For to bring education back to the shires would not be simply a recreation of the halcyon days. Today a much more compelling argument can be made that centralized control of public education leads to bureaucracy, regulation, paper shuffling, paternalism, special-interest aggrandizement, parent and student alienation, and wasted tax dollars. Worst of all it clearly leads to the stifling of the initiative and spirit of a free people. It is not coincidental that the nation which has epitomized freedom for six hundred years, Switzerland, has adamantly refused to allow the creation of any national education ministry and has jealously kept education power at the level of its communes.

We have argued that there is a strong case for small *sized* schools in educational theory. But there is also a growing store of evidence favoring locally *governed* schools, the kind of schools that will be found in the shires. Denis Doyle and Chester Finn Jr. have examined the trend toward more centralized control of education in recent years, as the states have increasingly displaced local school boards in the decision-making process. Their conclusions are that this trend threatens to be pernicious for three reasons. First, they say: "State education departments are notoriously sluggish and formalistic bureaucracies, hardly the kind of public agencies one would happily entrust with responsibility for sustaining a reform movement or for administering anything so unpredictable or so loosely coupled as a school system." Central regulation, in short, won't get good results. Or, as Theodore Sizer wrote in his book *Horace's Compromise*: "Once regulations, collective bargaining agreements, and licensure get installed, change comes hard. Every regulation, agreement and license spawns a lobby dedicated to keeping it in place. The larger and more complex the hierarchy, the more powerful the lobby becomes, ever more remote from frustrated classroom teachers, poorly served students, and angry parents."

Second, Doyle and Finn observe, central direction and control overlooks the importance of a "school ethos" or "shared moral order" that has proven to be indispensable in good education. This kind of spirit cannot be mandated from the center but must be painstakingly fabricated over long periods of time by educators, school boards, parents, and citizens of the community generally. Central control makes this spirit far more difficult to attain; indeed what often can be achieved is the work of local administrators who ignore or evade the formal rules.

Third, a "McSchool" system obliterates diversity, which may be a good thing if you are hungry for a reliable Big Mac in a remote place, but it does not favor good public education. The right to be different, to shape schools to a community's values and needs, to be distinguished in some way – all of these things encourage local support for schools and cohesion within the community.

To the observations of Doyle and Finn we would add that if one believes in the civic-humanist ideal of free citizens fulfilling themselves through joyous participation in self-government, then a prime locus of that activity will have to be the intensely important project of governing the education of one's own children. If that function is removed from the people's effective control by a horde of administrators and reams of regulations from some distant central power, then the whole civic-humanist vision becomes pretty much a bad joke.

•

Witness: It is 8:30 on Friday evening, January 27, 1959. Newbury, Vermont, population 1,437, is playing basketball with Groton, Vermont, population 738. It's a Newbury home game. The girls lost the opener 37 to 32. There were eleven girls on the team, six starters and five subs. The tallest was Pamela Dewey at 5 feet, 8 inches. Downstairs three members of the senior class are selling refreshments. Two other students are still taking tickets in case there are late comers. Outside the Newbury Town Hall the windows of three cars are clouded with steam. It is cold, and the couples making out in the cars between games are doing their best to keep warm.

The ten Newbury cheerleaders came on at 8:35. Eight had the "good" uniforms, and two had the "old" ones. At 8:40 the boys' game began. The tallest boy on Newbury's team was 5 feet, 10 inches. There were thirteen on the team. Ten wore the "good" uniforms. The town hall was so small that the basketball court's center circle intersected the top of the free-throw circles. Newbury won the toss and lost the game, 51 to 48. The crowd, on the stage, in the balcony, and sitting in chairs along the edges—where if they stretched out their legs, they would literally be "in play"—yelled their heads off. There was sweat, whistles, screams, passion, hatred, jealousy, suspense, disappointment, selfishness, and bravery in that little town hall that night. There were even two men in black-and-white-striped shirts who were alternately despised and adored for the most selfish of reasons, greed—in this case for more points and another victory. It was, in short, a typical high-school basketball game between two schools in the Hilldale League.

As basketball, what happened in Newbury that night would be called by most standards awful. But as high-school sports, it was most likely close to the best in America. If we estimate there were fifteen students at the game who participated only as spectators, that meant there were fifty-four students present in all (not counting the six out in the cars, who may have forgotten to come back in for the boys' game). This was 77 percent of the entire student body of Newbury High School. Fifty-five percent of the student body was actively involved. They had a *function*, they were part of the event. Even so, Newbury's participation was not quite as good as most of the schools in the Hilldale League, because Newbury High was one of the bigger schools.

The Hilldale League sponsored other events, like the annual one-act-play contest. On that evening the high-school drama club would involve at least half of the students. Besides the actors there were makeup people, prop people, ticket takers, and students who handled the lights, pulled the curtain, and prompted from the wings. There were girlfriends and boyfriends in the audience. There were students who made posters, and others who took them around. How was the acting? Better, perhaps, in relative terms than the basketball. One year little Newbury's drama club went on to defeat Montpelier (population

7,500) and Barre City (population 9,580) in dramatic competition. They performed Chekhov's *The Boor*. Even if the acting wasn't superlative, the participation was awfully good indeed.

By 1970 the Hilldale League had vanished. Only two of its seven hill town high schools, Danville and Concord, still hang on. The basketball is better in the bigger union high schools that have superseded the likes of Newbury High. The acting's about the same. But involvement by students and community – the heart of education in a democracy – has faded to a shadow of what it once was. In the area making up the former Hilldale League, the number of high-school students that have a chance to step before their parents as the *community's* representatives is now dramatically reduced. The linkage between school and town, and the value this linkage has in the rearing of citizens, has all but disappeared. Under the shires we have a chance to bring it back.

•

The State's Role

In the shire system the state will back out of public education almost completely. It will retain responsibility for the state university and state college system (although the Community College of Vermont might well be incorporated into shire adult-education programs). Since state aid for education would become unnecessary with the resource-equalizing plan described in Chapter 10, there would be no state education aid funds. The state would also handle relations with the federal government (Office of Federal Contracts). It would have some duties in the area of special education (Office of Technical Services), and educational statistics (Office of Shire Data). The state would also continue to supervise the teachers' retirement system.

Beyond this there would be one area in which the state's role could be enhanced. That is in developing measurements of educational performance. Over the past decade or so there has been increasing activity in this direction, much of it spurred by citizens and legislators concerned about how well our children are actually learning after their twelve-year immersion in public education.

The state's educational administrators have always been wary of demands for assessing results. The idea violated their deeply held precept that the schools should be left to the professionals and experts. If every farmer and shopkeeper knew what he was getting for his education tax dollar, and if he didn't like it, there could conceivably be

190

hell to pay for the school system. This is especially true if the farmer and shopkeeper were able to compare their school's performance with that of the school in the next town. It is not part of the educator's makeup to welcome competition among schools. Further, educators are quick to state that there is no consensus on what ought to be assessed, and thus tests of any kind would unfairly shut out important factors, particularly those not subject to precise measurement. Finally, the towns have feared the kind of rigid statewide exam that they presumed (quite understandably) would be forthcoming from the state educational hierarchy.

Over recent years the Department of Education has frequently launched various assessment devices, including the Basic Competencies Program that caused so much hilarity among students when it appeared in 1978. (One question, for high-school students: "Given a group of two-digit whole numbers, sort them in order.") There has always been a lingering suspicion that the department was not seriously interested in developing a workable system – its main object was to give the impression of serious activity to fend off irate legislators and citizens who, if they felt ignored, might demand some real results.

At the root of the problem, along with the educational administrators' reluctance to be rated, is the fact that the Department of Education is in control of the school system. If Vermont schools fared poorly on some assessment, it would necessarily reflect negatively on the department itself. After all, local schools must do what the state says through legislation and regulation. If they do, and the results are poor, a large share of blame would probably fall on the Department of Education itself.

Under the shire system there would be no Department of Education. The state would no longer be in charge of public elementary and secondary education. It would not be in danger of taking the heat for poor educational performance in the state's schools. This would open the door for the Office of Shire Policy to develop techniques for assessing educational performance. For those shires that requested it, the Office of Shire Policy would periodically assess a shire's schools and publish the results. The state would emphatically not have the power to require a shire to do any of the things in its schools now required by the state. Nor could it mandate a statewide evaluation. It would merely provide a service on demand and publish the results for interested citizens, without sharing in the responsibility for producing those results. What was to be measured would be decided by

191

individual shires in concert with the state officials and local citizen and teacher organizations. Individual shires could request that special tests be employed to assess their progress on programs unique to themselves.

This disinterested assessment of educational performance from outside the shire would be a useful starting point for the process of achieving true educational accountability at the shire level. Citizens of the shire would be more apt to insist that their local schools be measured or evaluated if they were certain that submitting to the process would not precipitate an avalanche of mandates from the state and subsequent loss of local control. Indeed the Office of Shire Policy, which will make the assessment, will be located in the Agency of Shire Support Services, where the *professional ethic* will be defined in terms of accurate measurement per se, and not in terms of supporting this or that educational philosophy.

Going about It: Education in the Shires

Good local education requires community agreement about an acceptable level of education. It requires a careful, experience-based analysis of the most efficient way, in terms of tax dollars spent on school resources, an acceptable level can be achieved. Then, after committing those resources, it is necessary to see if they did in fact produce the hoped-for results. If not, the reasons why must be identified, and methods of correcting the revealed problems must be determined.

If in a given shire results fall short of expectations, there are a number of things that might be to blame. The expectations might have been unrealistically high. The teachers might not have done a good job – perhaps because the pay scale was not enough to attract better teachers, or because the pupil-teacher ratio was too high. The students might have simply come to school hungry or have suffered from classroom conditions not conducive to learning. Perhaps the parents have dropped the ball, showing too little interest in their children and their education.

Once analysis has shown the nature of the problem, a shire can take steps to solve it. One of the solutions might well be increasing school expenditures, but there are numerous other things that might be done. It may be found, for instance, that the unique problems of one local K–8 district are inadequately addressed, and therefore their students are going to the union high school inadequately prepared. It might be learned that a union high school is too big and too distant from several of the local sending towns, and two smaller high schools would be more desirable. It might be discovered that with simple adjustments in school governance, communication between the union high school and the local grade schools could be improved and agreement on basic common curricula reached. The shire community might even decide to eliminate local districts altogether and create one unified district. This would, of course, take a shire charter change, which, it will be remembered, requires a two-thirds vote of the shire-moot and a two-thirds vote of the people in a majority of the towns in the shire. It is reasonable that these kinds of changes ought to have the strong support of the shire community, because they so profoundly affect it.

Unfortunately a systematic educational-accountability process of the sort we envision is rare. Ordinarily school-board budget decisions are made with little or no reference to educational output. There are so many teachers to pay, so many administrators, so many bus drivers, so much athletic equipment, so much to pay on the construction bonds. The important choices about education – as distinguished from merely running schools – have been largely pre-empted by the state.

The shires might well look to the state for technical assistance in such areas as facilities construction, new educational techniques, textbook selection, and the like. With the state relieved of the responsibility for the product, it should become a useful service agency to the shires. With the state government organized to help measure results rather than policy control, local education should improve. Instead of the state pressing the towns to build more and bigger school buildings (in what has appeared to some to be a pathological desire to enrich architects and construction firms), under the shire federation the state will go into business as a vendor of educational technical-assistance services, in competition with other private-sector vendors and even with other school districts. Under the present system, a local school district accepts technical assistance from the Department of Education for two reasons: it's free (to it), and if the district went elsewhere at its own expense the department might consider it an insult, with unknown consequences for the offending district.

With freedom to decide how to educate its children, and with resources equalized through the revenue plan proposed in Chapter 10, the people of the shires would become a lot more involved with their children's education. For instance if a citizens' group wanted some change made in shire school policy, it would have a realistic opportunity for a fair hearing from the shire school board, many of whose members would probably be known personally to members of the citizens' group. Even more important, the shire school board would actually have the power to make the changes if a majority saw fit. Local hearings on local issues are a vastly different proposition from public hearings of the Department of Education or legislative committees, which ordinarily concern themselves with statewide policy changes, uniformly applied. There are few things more discouraging than realizing that one has to create a public furor throughout the entire state merely to get some local school policy changed.

Freed at last from the shackles of state and "expert" control, shire school boards would begin to experiment with ideas that shire people thought useful. Some of the experiments undoubtedly would fizzle, but that fact alone is worth something. A shire which hit upon a nifty idea would soon be visited by school board members from other shires, who would take the idea back and give it a try. The Office of Shire Data (located in the Agency of Shire Support Services) might facilitate this process by regularly publishing an informative newsletter and resource guide.

Some shires might well become interested in performance contracting to improve educational outcomes. This involves a contract between school and contractor, whereby the contractor is paid to the extent that children approach agreed performance norms. The contractor might be a private firm, as such a firm specializing in computer-aided instruction. Or it might be a group of teachers within the system itself. This practice has been applied at the federal level through what is known as the OMB A-76 bidding process. The Federal Office of Personnel Management recently proposed an imaginative process whereby federal civil servants could form employee-owned companies to bid for a wide range of jobs, and if successful could reap the capital gains on their stock holdings.

Other shires might decide to institute an educational-choice system, commonly known as a "voucher system" (although actual vouchers need not be used). In such a system the shire would provide the equivalent of educational food stamps to parents to buy the education of their choice from a wide range of education providers. The great virtue of the voucher system, or its variants, is that it gives parents the power to choose in their child's best interests, instead of accepting the services of a monopoly provider (the shire). In doing so it creates a marketplace discipline for education. Those schools which are doing a good job in the parents' eyes will gain students, while the poorer schools will lose them.

Vermont is nationally known for having had a smoothly working educational choice system for over a hundred years. There are ninety-five Vermont towns today which do not have public high schools and do not belong to union high school districts. The high-school children in these towns, comprising 24 percent of Vermont's high-school (grades 9–12) population, have the right to attend any approved non-parochial school, within or outside the state. By law, their town governments will pay the full tuition cost of any public school chosen, and at least the union high school average tuition ($4,338 in 1988–89) to any private school chosen.

Under this plan students in Londonderry, for instance, attend private schools such as Northfield Mt. Hermon, Taft School, Stratton Mountain, Suffield Academy, and East Hill School, as well as Green Mountain Union or Leland and Gray, nearby union high schools. Students in Barnet and Peacham have the choice of private St. Johnsbury Academy, public Danville High School, or Blue Mountain Union. Students in Barre Town can choose among nearby Barre Spaulding, Montpelier, U–32, Twinfield, and Williamstown, all public high schools, without having to board away from home. The same scheme is in effect for grades K–6 in some thirty-five towns which do not have any public schools at all, or which do not offer all six grades. Educators may disapprove, but from all accounts parents love it. In some cases parents have chosen to move into a town simply because it gives them the right to choose their children's school.

Yet the interest in a parental choice system may wane with improvements in the educational product that will occur when the shire system is put in place. In fact it is the evils associated with distant control of education that have led parents to seek alternatives to the present system. One important reason to keep education in the hands of local public schools is that the building of shire communities over the years will depend in part on the community-enhancing properties of public schools. Nevertheless some shires will undoubtedly explore various plans to increase parental choice in education. There is increasing reason to believe, from recent U.S. Supreme Court trends, that if the parental-choice scheme were applied generally to all parents within a district, tuition could be paid to parochial schools as well as to secular public and private schools. This suggests that the idea would be popular in such towns as Burlington and Rutland, which have Catholic high schools, and in the eastern suburbs of Burlington, where there is a strong Baptist private high school in Williston.

Other shires might try the community education idea, pioneered in this country by the Mott Foundation in Flint, Michigan. The community education philosophy views a broadly defined educational process as central to the success of the community itself. It focuses on involving school children in community activities and in involving the general public in the schools, both as volunteers in instruction and as participants in adult education programs. Community education builds upon the community's schools but goes far beyond the school itself to interweave education into all facets of community life. It stresses civic involvement, volunteer service, leadership skills, and the mingling of all ages in a varied learning process. Though the idea has been well received in New Hampshire for many years, it has never caught on as such in Vermont, for reasons we are unable to fathom, although an informal approximation has been going on for quite a while in the small town of Rochester.

The Danish folk school, which reconstructed Danish society in its nineteenth-century renaissance, is another concept that might spark shire interest. The folk school was dedicated to the proposition that students were part of something much larger than themselves – the Danish nation. Their duty was to equip themselves with knowledge, self-reliance, and motivation so as to make their country prosper. The folk high school was, in American terms, a program of residential adult education in practical skills needed in a rural society, conducted with a strong spirit of cooperation and community service. With a new spirit of local patriotism resulting from the rise of the shires, the folk school idea might well become more attractive than conventional adult-level vocational education or community college courses.

"Education with Production" (EWP) is the new name for an old concept: the school where students work. Many of the Danish folk schools operated in this mode, as have several well-known American colleges, such as Berea, Warren Wilson, and College of the Ozarks. East Hill School, a private K–12 school in Andover, Vermont, exemplifies the idea. At East Hill education is interwoven with productive work on an operating farm. At College of the Ozarks students operate some twenty-one diversified enterprises, including a radio station and airport as well as the usual college-support services. Vermont's

Sterling College, in Craftsbury, is a place where students learn how to harness a horse and skid logs, as well as appreciate the tales of Chaucer. At many Vermont high schools, diversified occupations and distributive education programs offer students the chance to earn an income while working part time in a local business. Under EWP students are more than employees; they have responsibility for the work they do, and they play a major role in managing it.

Trying an EWP program in a public Vermont high school today would probably be difficult. The laws of the state are designed with classroom attendance in mind, and public-school administrators see their schools as nonprofit eleemosynary institutions which have pupils in custody, not as enterprises accomplishing productive tasks. With the shire free to set its own rules, including the school-leaving age, it seems likely that EWP would soon make an appearance. So would school-based student enterprises, pioneered in Vermont at Hazen Union in Hardwick.

This, of course, is the fundamental point of this chapter. The shires, unshackled from control by an oppressive state, will be able to experiment, change, readjust, and consolidate in a never-ending pattern of innovation. With effective measuring devices on line, failures will be short-lived. The alternative is for local districts to expend most of their creative energies (as they do now) establishing methods of outwitting state standards.

Another innovation that would almost certainly appear in the shires would be the use of unconventional teachers in the classroom. For years it has been education gospel that only someone properly trained in methods of instruction and certified by some government body can transfer knowledge to children – a proposition notable for its palpable foolishness. Too often the result has been the imparting of flawed knowledge by teachers who really don't know much about what they are teaching.

There is now a noticeable trend nationally toward the use of non-certified instructors at the high-school level. New Jersey has pioneered in this direction, despite the hostility of traditional teachers' organizations (so powerful, in fact, that Rutgers, the state university, declined to offer a course to equip such "alternative-route" teachers with fundamental classroom-management skills). These teachers are, however, obliged to take professional education courses and eventually to qualify for state certification. A Vermont shire could, absent the present state rules, recruit a retired master machinist to teach vocational education, or a registered nurse to teach hygiene, or a retired college professor to teach philosophy or economics, or a local entrepreneur to teach business management. Other innovations that shire schools might find attractive are merit pay and community-service sabbaticals for teachers, character-education courses, magnet schools, diplomas for mastery instead of longevity of attendance, and a new emphasis on civic consciousness, shire history, and community participation.

The most exciting new avenue of experimentation holding out promise to local schools might be the use of new educational technology. In the past few years advances in this field have been breathtaking. With products already on the market even the most isolated rural school can have access to the best instructional materials and programs in the world for its pupils. If the old idea of a multiplicity of learning experiences had any merit at all, that objective can now be achieved without school consolidation. In fact it can in large measure be achieved without students' going to a school at all.

In a small house huddled on the edge of the Arctic Ocean, a young Eskimo girl is completing her work for a business-management course. The course comes to her via satellite from LearnAlaska, the world's most technologically advanced and geographically extensive electronic educational system. When the girl finishes a lesson, she takes a quiz, which is scored in seconds from LearnAlaska's computer eight hundred miles away in Anchorage. When she needs library resources, she calls up the card catalog at the University of Alaska library and puts in her request over the line. She can also download the text of current articles to her home computer. Alaska, not surprisingly, has the largest ratio of computers to pupils of any state.

In several counties in rural Virginia, high-school students are taking a college-level calculus course via an Apple computer and attached video player. The course is interactively programmed, and the teacher is trained especially for presenting it over television. The video includes actual footage of calculus applications in business and science as well as the teacher and the blackboard. Wicat Systems, in Orem, Utah, has pioneered in its own company school with similar interactive programs using computer-driven laser-disk technology. Dozens of suppliers are now flooding the market with interactive hardware and instructional materials. One hundred and seventy course offerings are now available through the TeleLearning "electronic university" based in San Francisco. Another program, at the University of Maryland, uses live two-way satellite transmission to allow Spanish students to speak with Spanish-speaking people in Florida on an "electronic field trip." The Army at Ft. Knox, Kentucky, has developed an extraordinary computerized simulator for training tank crews without firing $1,000 shells all over the countryside, and the Air Force has a jet engine mechanic training program that displays the precise steps to take even as the mechanic works on the actual engine.

In a rural area much like Vermont, Kirkwood Community College, in Iowa, has put in place a dedicated microwave network that allows its teachers to teach classes simultaneously at centers in eight Iowa communities (plus the state prison), with the students able to pose questions and be seen by all other students on the network. A similar system is in use on the campus of Chico State University in northern California.

As information transmission and data accessing become cheaper and cheaper, it is not hard to imagine an educational system of the not-too-distant future as follows. A student, relaxing at home in an easy chair, turns on a multimedia instructional machine driven by a computer. He selects a course and a lesson. Then he sits back while a three-dimensional holographic image of a nationally known master teacher begins a lecture. The teacher makes a point the student doesn't grasp, so he punches another button, finds an approximation of his question on the flat, multicolored video terminal, and asks for an answer. The laser disk whirs, and the teacher goes back over the material in response to the student's confusion. Interspersed with the holographic teacher are video-disk segments showing appropriate film clips or ingenious Star-Wars-type computer graphics. At the end of the session there is a review and a quiz to determine the student's level of mastery. He can also call up practice problems and prerecorded classroom discussions, and he can have access to the university library for quick transmission of text materials to his computer and printer. The cost of the course is deducted from his bank account (or from that of whoever is paying for his education) through electronic funds transfer.

There is nothing about this that is beyond the capability of today's technology. Although the cost today would be prohibitive, no one doubts that that cost will continue to go down. Our grandchildren will have access in their homes to learning resources and techniques that we today can scarcely imagine, at a cost that everyone can afford.

To those interested in human-scale education, the holographic teacher may seem too impersonal to be taken seriously. One may also wonder how citizenship and community awareness are learned by students sitting alone at home in their living rooms. We offer these images with the full expectation that new educational technologies will be turned to humanistic and communal purposes under the shire system, much as breakthroughs in communications technology, if we have the will to insist on it, can be turned toward democratic goals. We present these images to reemphasize a central point of this book: technology can be a force for decentralization. Rural places no longer need be blackmailed into centralizing schemes by the assertion that educational funds and choices will be lost if they don't fall into line.

As the shires begin to master the possibilities in this new education age, freed from the constraints of the past, astonishing advances will become possible. But key to it all is the principle of restoring the power over education to parents and local educators responsive to the desires of the people of their own communities. With that power and freedom, all things are possible.

Chapter 12

THE COMPASSIONATE COMMUNITY

The major difficulty in this centralization [of welfare] is that it tends to destroy a sense of local responsibility for the well being of the local townspeople; when the state pays relief costs there is a feeling that there is no need to worry about the matter.

— Andrew Nuquist

EVERY society must face squarely the problem of the chronic poor. Over the centuries two kinds of policies have emerged in the Western world: a policy of managing the poor, and a policy of emancipating the poor. The former is just the sort of thing one would expect from a society controlled through a welfare mega-system operated by distant bureaucrats armed with categories and cohorts, forms and formulas. The latter is a policy that can only be applied at a level where neighbors have a genuine concern for the less fortunate and share a community ethic which strives to help the needy achieve economic and social independence.

In a Vermont organized into shires, human services will be decentralized to the shire level, and the shire welfare organization will have the responsibility to mobilize private and public resources in support of the needs of all citizens. This will include both the poor and the nonpoor with special problems, such as alcoholism, child abuse, and the like. It will also include the handicapped and the elderly. In what follows, however, the emphasis will be on the needs of the dependent poor, particularly their life-support needs.

A foremost objective of the shire welfare system will be the reintegration of the poor into a caring community – to free them from the cold hallways of bureaucracy and try to retrieve what Gerald Suttler and David Street call the "irretrievable social loss" that occurs with "the transfer of responsibility for caring for others to a bureaucracy." Instead of viewing the poor as mere consumers of resources extracted from others, their fellow citizens will come to see them as neighbors suffering under misfortunes and worthy of help at least until proven otherwise. Those who receive aid will accept an obligation to do in return whatever they can to enhance the well-being of the people of the shire as a whole.

A shire welfare system will integrate a panoply of social services, public and private, into a single framework. As it is, the social welfare system is divided into segments – one for income support, one for probation administration, one for rehabilitation, and so on – with little linkage to the voluntary sector. While administrators from each segment may attempt some coordination locally, they are prisoners of their funding sources and chains of command.

In the shire community people will come to view welfare as a temporary phenomenon. Because welfare "officers" will be part of the community, they will know better the churches, families, schools, employers, and voluntary groups that can be mobilized to get the welfare recipient on the road to self-sufficiency as quickly as possible. Conversely the recipient will be more aware of his or her responsibility for getting off welfare at the earliest opportunity.

Families of welfare recipients will likewise be more attuned to the obligation to proffer assistance within their means. And when welfare recipients graduate to self-sufficiency, they will continue to feel an obligation to reach back and help others who are experiencing similar problems. These are the kinds of attitudes and perspectives that develop in communities of human scale.

All this means that shire welfare officials must have very broad administrative discretion to decide how much, and in what form, community assistance should be given. This implies fairly radical legal changes and an abandonment of the principle that all persons in broad categories must be treated equally. It recognizes instead that each welfare recipient is an individual and that aid must be tailored to the key objective of lifting that person out of need.

And finally such a system implies work. Not just work by the able-bodied who do not have preschool children; work by everyone. The forms of work in our society are so numerous and varied that almost no one, however feeble or disabled, can successfully argue a case for total indolence.

Welfare in Vermont

Such a sweeping reorganization of the welfare system requires a survey of its evolution. Like the rest of New England, Vermont adopted its early welfare concepts from the Elizabethan Poor Law of 1601. While caring for the helpless was considered an act of Christian charity, the English Poor Law dealt harshly with the "able-bodied poor." Every parish was required to put its poor to work, in a workhouse maintained for that purpose. Beggary was severely punished; vagrancy, when repeated, was a capital offense. To prevent migration of the poor to parishes where conditions were better, Parliament in 1662 passed the Act of Settlement and Removal, which allowed parishes to expel a man from another parish, even though he was employed and self-supporting. The danger that he might someday have need of relief was too grave to be accepted.

These features were carried over into early Vermont. Each town was required to care for its poor at its own expense. As early as 1797 the legislature decreed that towns might "build, purchase or hire a house of correction or workhouse, in which to confine and set their poor to work . . . and such house may and shall be used for keeping, correcting, and setting to work vagrants, common beggars, lewd, idle and disorderly persons." There were sections in the law which permitted officials to "fetter, shackle or whip, not exceeding twenty stripes, any person confined therein who does not perform the labor designed to him or her, or is refractory or disobedient to lawful commands." The conditions in such poorhouses, peopled with the idle, the criminal, the insane, the senile, and the helpless, remind one of the horrors of *Oliver Twist*.

Another poverty program from that era was the putting out of the poor to bid, an early example of privatization of government functions. On bidding days the poor were marshaled upon the town common and auctioned off to the lowest bidder. The successful bidder, in return for much-prized cash, accepted the obligation to take care of the victims according to humane standards. There was, however, little policing, and frequently a new bidder would approach the town authorities to bid the unfortunates away from their current guardians at a lower price, which usually presaged more severe privation.

Vermont found it necessary to enact its own settlement laws to prevent the welfare population from moving into towns which had made overly generous provision for their poor. If a man moved into a new community, he had a three-year probation period before becoming a bona fide resident. If during those three years he accepted public relief, his residency status reverted to zero, and the expense was charged to his town of origin if at all possible. For a pauper who had once received relief, the opportunity and motivation to achieve self-sufficiency shrank. The publication of the names of aid-receiving paupers in town reports was not finally laid to rest until 1961.

The Vermont system was built around a town officer called the overseer of the poor. The law charged the overseer with the care of all poor persons so long as they might remain within the town. The overseer was authorized to bind poor persons over to work for private employers and charged with preventing the town's indigenous poor from "strolling" into other towns where they might become public charges. He could lawfully warn newcomers to move on, or go back where they came from, or otherwise vanish from public view. The office was not ardently sought after at town meeting, but occasionally someone could be found to take it who delighted in minimizing public expenditure and thus basking in the approbation of tight-fisted taxpayers. Stories about a relative handful of such overseers eventually, in more enlightened times, gave the office a bad name, and it was essentially abolished in 1966 when the state took over the welfare system.

This old, town-based historic system seems harsh and uncivilized to modern readers, but it should be emphasized that Vermont was not alone in borrowing its harsh welfare practices from England. In early New England, dominated by God-fearing Protestants, there was a loathing of those who chose idleness and dissipation over industry. By their indolence it appeared to townspeople that the able-bodied poor had abandoned the road to salvation and succumbed to the wiles of Old Scratch. There was little sympathy in such a community for these exhibits of the Devil's work, nor was there any opprobrium attached to their harsh treatment.

On the other hand Vermonters were, for residents of a poor state, remarkably compassionate toward those whose penury was involuntary. Many a town history offers examples of a genuine civic concern for the less fortunate, and many an overseer worked long hours seeing to the needs of those placed in his charge. Although the centralizers of the 1960s were fond of pointing to examples of local mean-spiritedness as a rationale for stripping the towns of their responsibilities, the needy fared better in Vermont than in most other places. The reason, of course, was that welfare had not become a great system but remained a human responsibility in a small community. Reorganizing Vermont into human-scale shires will create an opportunity to restore that responsibility.

Modern Welfare Programs

The towns began to lose their role in welfare with the New Deal. In 1945 New Deal public-assistance programs were consolidated into the Vermont Public Welfare Department. Two years later the State Department of Institutions and Corrections was created, leaving a new Department of Social Welfare to handle the newer federal relief programs. Chief among these were the Old Age Assistance Program, medical assistance to the blind, disabled, and medically indigent, and Aid to Dependent Children (now Aid to Needy Families with Children, or ANFC). In recent years federal categorical programs have multiplied, and they now include the Food Stamp Program, WIC (food assistance for needy women, infants, and children), and the Community Work Experience Program, along with a Job Training Partnership Act administered jointly by the Department of Social Welfare and the Department of Employment and Training. There are also federal programs under the Social Security Act designed to support the permanently needy (elderly, blind, and disabled). All these programs have their own chains of command and funding authority. The package is beyond the comprehension of any citizen not holding a graduate degree in social work. As such it is also beyond democratic control.

The most controversial program is ANFC–UP, which provides cash payments to needy families with children. UP stands for "unemployed parent." This option allows payments to two-parent households if the breadwinner has been employed and earned at least $50 in six of the preceding thirteen quarters. ANFC is what is most commonly thought of as "welfare." ANFC recipients also are entitled to receive food stamps, Medicaid, and, where available, public-housing assistance. At the close of 1988, some 6,917 Vermont families received ANFC payments, and 14,916 received food stamps (which have less stringent income standards).

There also remains a program called "general assistance," which unlike the others is wholly state-funded. It is an emergency short-term-relief program available to those who, for example, have been burned or flooded out of their homes. Most general assistance recipients qualify for categorical assistance and depart the general assistance rolls as soon as processing can be completed. Since the 1970s general assistance has not been available to able-bodied single persons, who must be referred to private charities for assistance.

The policy of the state toward its ANFC-food-stamp population is to help the recipients move toward self-sufficiency, a task easier defined than accomplished. The Reach Up program, announced by Governor Kunin in 1986, tries to get welfare recipients (those without preschool dependent children) to accept more education, prepare themselves for entry-level employment, take specialized training where appropriate, arrange day care, and work themselves into regular employment as soon as possible. Reach Up offers incentives for going off the welfare rolls: continued eligibility for Medicaid for fifteen months, extended day-care benefits for the children, and a $100 cash bonus.

In spite of incentives like those in Reach Up, however, there are good reasons not to go off welfare. Vermont offers eligible recipients one of the highest benefit levels in the country. In 1985 a single mother with two small children could receive ANFC and food stamps alone sufficient to bring her income to 97 percent of the state poverty level. Only Alaska offered more generous benefits, and only California equaled Vermont's. Neighboring New Hampshire offered just 82 percent of the poverty level, leading many there to suspect that a short trip across the river might result in more wholesome living conditions. The ANFC program in Vermont has an annual budget of about $40 million.

In 1987 in Vermont a mother with two children (one in school) and no significant assets was entitled by law to $544 a month in ANFC and $103 a month in food stamps, for a net tax-free cash income of $7,764 a year. By contrast, the same woman, working as a retail clerk for $4.86 an hour for fifty weeks a year, would earn a gross income of $9,718. When Social Security taxes, earned-income tax credits, work-related expenses, and child-care costs are taken into account, the working woman enjoys a usable income of $6,281 a year, almost 20 percent less than she can get from welfare alone – not even counting school-lunch and Medicaid benefits. Even if this woman got food stamps while working ($951), her usable income would still be less than if she refused work altogether and remained on welfare. It is a rare spirit who will work forty hours a week to be able to enjoy only 80 percent of what he or she can get for not working at all.

The effects of the present welfare system are not unique to Vermont but seem to be endemic to welfare populations everywhere. They threaten to create a permanent poverty class which has abandoned any intention of becoming self-sufficient. It is true that, nationally, only 15 percent of the welfare case load remains on welfare for as long as eight years – but it is also true that that 15 percent consumes half of the entire welfare budget in any given month. How to address the problem of the permanent welfare family has become a major national debate.

Defects of the Welfare System

The current state-federal welfare system is not an example of a community extending assistance to its own who are no longer able to provide for their needs. It is an example of a system which vests rights in certain eligible beneficiaries. Once the applicant can establish that he or she is eligible, then the benefits are delivered by the state welfare agency. Eligibility is determined solely by testing the applicant's income and assets. Other potential sources of aid – parents, children, siblings, voluntary agencies, etc. – are not a part of the calculation. The recipient is dealing with an impersonal government bureaucracy, receiving monies which came from who knows where – certainly not in any meaningful sense from the recipient's neighbors. The result is a welfare system that insults the poor and nonpoor alike by isolating one from the other and dismissing their sense of a shared humanity.

It also has adverse effects on the family – making separation of husband and wife more likely by offering support for the single mother. By the same token it discourages fathers from marrying the mother of their children. The Unemployed Parent option of ANFC is a partial corrective to this, but many men, otherwise eligible, would rather consign their wives or mistresses to welfare than join them on the dole. Proving that the father worked the required six quarters of the past thirteen may also be difficult, particularly if the man has worked for cash on an irregular basis. Employers who pay "off the books" are not enthusiastic about certifying to amounts paid.

Again, the availability of welfare is a substantial economic disincentive to work. Since there is no effective work requirement associated with ANFC or food stamps, idleness can be an easy choice. The apparent indolence among those on welfare is a chronic cause of resentment, not so much among the well-to-do, but among the working families who live next door and who are only marginally better off.

Perhaps the most fatal flaw in the state welfare system is its breaking of the reciprocity between recipient and community. In a humane society a community would ensure a decent and humane level of subsistence for those who were unable to attain that level through their own efforts. In return those assisted would do whatever they reasonably could to get off welfare; or if that were unlikely because of their age and condition, to make some reciprocal contribution to the well-being of the community.

The flaws in the present system are not correctable so long as welfare is centrally organized and managed. What is required is a truly compassionate community which accepts the responsibility for dealing with its own unfortunates. Where the community is relatively autonomous, where its members view themselves as in control of their own community destiny, and where there are few outside sources of either aid or control – in short, in a democratic shire – a humane welfare system is far more likely to evolve.

But where a higher power has removed responsibility from the community on the grounds that community-based welfare would result in inadequacy or inequality of treatment, that spirit of responsibility and autonomy is stifled. Income support for the poor is no longer the problem of the locality, although sporadic charitable efforts may continue, such as emergency food shelves and church rummage corners. The higher power – the state and federal governments – sets up its own administrative apparatus. Bureaucrats hand down rules and regulations. Auditors police the critical "error rate." Instead of a compassionate community caring for its poor, we have a bureaucratic apparatus delivering benefits according to strict rules and regulations – and we have recipients bringing lawsuits when it appears to them (or to Legal Aid) that their rights have been violated. The welfare poor become a class apart from the rest of society, in opposition to the rest of society. This situation can only be described as an American tragedy. It is hard to see how it can be cured short of returning to the kind of governmental structure resembling the shire.

At first blush restoring the responsibility for welfare to the shires would result in inequalities around the state. Some shires would have substantial resources and few welfare families, and thus they would operate exemplary programs. Others would have few resources and many welfare families, and the benefits would be inadequate for decent subsistence. If state or federal monies are bestowed on the poorer shires to help them meet their needs, some distribution formula must be arrived at, relating the need to the payments. Deciding who is needy, how many of the needy there are, and what each of them should get is precisely the problem currently answered by the vast compendium of rules and regulations.

There are really only two ways of allocating funds for the poor which preserve local autonomy in welfare. One of them is to equalize the resource bases of the shires as suggested in Chapter 10. Then the shires would have enough in the way of resources to meet their legitimate overall needs, however defined in the formula. A shire might, however, choose to have excellent roads and schools but very low welfare benefits. This assures inequities of treatment, which the modern mind has found so loathsome. And here the emigration problem arises again: the poor will surely be tempted to migrate to a more generous shire. Then the call would arise for a resurrection of the old settlement laws, so that the shire of origin would have to foot the welfare bills for its emigrants. It is not likely that this kind of system will find favor.

The other way out is much more difficult. It is to create a community ethic which redefines the status of the poor and the responsibilities and perceptions of the shire society as a whole. Its goal is to maximize the sum of economic and psychological benefits. Though the beneficiaries in one shire might not get as much in benefits as those in another, their overall well-being might well be greater: instead of merely receiving, they would belong. Instead of merely accepting, they would gain self-respect from being able to give. Instead of relying on government aid, they would benefit from a wide range of assistance offered by caring neighbors. With such a system in place, a shire will in all likelihood not choose to starve its poor to pay for roads or schools, and thus a resource-equalizing strategy could be attempted with considerably more confidence.

Welfare in Switzerland

It is worthwhile to examine the workings of two welfare systems which have long been in place and which have long been viewed as extremely successful. Both illustrate the way in which a shire welfare program will operate.

The welfare system of the Swiss cantons is unique in the Western world. It begins to operate long before a person seeks welfare aid – in the schools. The goal of Swiss education is to prepare its young people for economic self-sufficiency, literacy, and civic responsibility. If a student falters, that fact becomes the concern of the whole community: teachers, parents, pastors, police, youth workers, and friends of the family.

The Swiss national government maintains a comprehensive program of social insurance to protect its people against unemployment and illness. In addition it has a program comparable to our Supplemental Security Income (SSI), which provides in effect a guaranteed income for the needy elderly and disabled. Unlike welfare systems in most other countries, the Swiss program features wide administrative discretion in place of hard-and-fast eligibility rules. These programs, taken together in conjunction with individual savings and voluntary assistance, provide for the needs of those who are aged, sick, or seriously handicapped.

For those who do not fall into these categories, there is a cantonal system of means-tested welfare comparable to our ANFC-food-stamp programs. This system is funded entirely by the cantons, so it behooves the cantons to invest in prevention of pauperism. Indeed, as in the old days in Vermont, a welfare recipient's canton is responsible for his benefits for five years after he relocates to another canton.

The overriding goal of Swiss cantonal welfare policy is to help the poor achieve self-sufficiency at the earliest possible moment. The canton welfare authorities offer advice, counseling, information, and social services including, if necessary, financial and material aid. Unlike the American system, the Swiss provides that the amounts of financial aid granted are not prescribed in law but are left to the case worker's discretion. As a grantee progresses toward self-sufficiency, the amount of the grant is reduced.

The cantonal welfare office also has no hesitation about calling on families to help provide for a needy relative. Parents and even grandparents are required to contribute in line with their own resources, and adult children are required to help their parents and grandparents if they can. Where divorced fathers refuse to provide adequate child support, the welfare agency makes the payments and then pursues the father for reimbursement. Wealth and income are reported annually by every citizen, and the records are open for public inspection, so there is little doubt about any particular father's resources.

Welfare clients who decline to cooperate with the case worker may find that their grant has been changed, or that it is dribbled out by an appointed guardian, or that it is limited to materials and vouchers. The case worker may also call in family, friends, former employers, and teachers of the client's children to contribute toward designing a solution—a way out—for the client. Swiss welfare administrators believe that their job is to help clients see how they have to change their lives so as to cease being a burden on the canton—a far cry from "delivering benefits to which the client is entitled."

Switzerland also exhibits unusual societal controls promoting self-sufficiency. Family, church, and school cooperate to mold young people into conscientious, self-sufficient citizens. The *Jugendamt* (the public youth-recreation, character-building, and career-preparation program in each village) reinforces positive and community-supportive attitudes. Grassroots democracy is a hallowed Swiss tradition, and informal mutual aid is the norm. For an able-bodied man to accept welfare would have a disastrous effect on his valued reputation in his community, and in his militia unit.

According to one student of the Swiss welfare system, Ralph Segalman, there are two lessons to be learned from the Swiss experience. One is the vital importance of individual family and local community responsibility, reinforced by social and educational institutions and especially by public opinion. The other is best expressed in Segalman's own words:

> In the United States, federal power has grown enormously. The American picture is one of huge social, fiscal and governmental problems which cannot be resolved by the participation of its local citizens, and these problems become unmanageable even with the involvement of the best minds and leaders.
>
> The Swiss scene is far different. The recognitions of problems is first made at a strictly local level, then representatives of other nearby localities who may be affected by the same problems are consulted. Many area problems are solved by intercommunal compacts.
>
> At the local level it is possible for everyone to know each other. It is also possible at this level to ask questions and to receive clear answers, to understand the issues and the people affected. At the local level, the citizen either gets involved or suffers the results of

someone else's activity.

It would probably be impossible for other Western nations to decentralize to the degree the Swiss have. But probably the first lesson from the Swiss experience would be to relegate as many problems and tax bases as possible to smaller local units of government where the citizenry can get involved. The apathetic or dormant local American community would soon awaken when it finds that it holds both the responsibility and assets related to the issues.

The Mormon Welfare System

Another remarkable welfare system is that of the Church of Jesus Christ of Latter-day Saints (the Mormons), founded by Vermont-born Joseph Smith and Brigham Young. The Mormon system is also community based, but the community is one of religious co-believers, not a geographical area like a Swiss canton.

The doctrinal basis of the Mormon welfare system lies in the church's Doctrine and Covenants, in which the Lord says, "If any man shall take of the abundance which I have made, and impart not his portion, according to the law of my gospel, unto the poor and needy, he shall, with the wicked, lift up his eyes in hell, being in torment." From its inception in 1830, the Mormon church has encouraged its members to achieve economic independence, to save and avoid debts, to create industries that afford jobs for church members, and to actively participate in caring for the church's needy.

The Mormon welfare system, however, did not appear until 1936, called into being by the Depression. In announcing the new plan, the first president of the church remarked that "Our primary purpose was to set up, insofar as might be possible, a system under which the curse of idleness would be done away, the evils of a dole abolished, and independence, industry, thrift and self-respect once more established amongst our people. The aim of the Church is to help people to help themselves. Work is to be re-enthroned as the ruling principle in the lives of our Church membership." Each Mormon is expected to act in accordance with the principle that "the strong, who have been blessed with greater gifts, are under special obligation to the community. . . . Those who have must give to those who have not. Thereby the strong become stronger."

The central figure of the Mormon welfare system is the bishop of each ward, or congregation, who acts as chairman of the ward welfare services committee. Each year the bishop estimates the welfare needs of his ward and prepares a "production budget." Mormon farms and enterprises across the country then contribute their share of this budget, which is coordinated through the bishops' central storehouse in Salt Lake City. Each local ward also maintains a storehouse – it may be as informal as an area set aside in the bishop's barn or basement. In addition each Mormon makes a cash offering of the equivalent of two meals a month, which is used for cash expenses in support of the poor.

The provision of cash and materials to the needy is only the economic manifestation of the ward welfare program. Even more important is the role of the bishop and church leaders in counseling families that are heading for trouble. The church features a host of home teachers, visiting teachers, and lay assistants who stand ready to step in to assist families in difficulty. The availability of peer support is a key ingredient in minimizing problems of dependency.

Where there is a concentration of Mormons in a community, as in Utah, the church also operates sheltered workshops, the most famous of which is Deseret Industries. Founded in 1938, Deseret offers job opportunities to those church members who for one reason or another – at least for the moment – cannot be expected to compete in the regular labor market. It salvages and recycles all sorts of household items for distribution or sale and has become a self-sustaining operation. Interestingly retirees and others who are financially independent come to Deseret to work alongside those who have no alternative; the factory is not solely given over to the poor.

The Mormon system recognizes the importance of welfare recipients' making a contribution to the community. In that vein one of our favorite anecdotes relates to Moosehaven, the retirement home operated in Florida by the Loyal Order of Moose. At Moosehaven every retiree is expected to perform some form of useful work in the operation of the home, whether it be kitchen work, lawn mowing, or bookkeeping. When residents get too old and feeble to do even minor tasks, they become "sunshiners." Their job is to sit on a park bench for two hours a day and greet every passer-by with a smile and friendly hello. Even so small a gesture toward community betterment as that preserves the principle of contributing in return for benefits.

Some Examples

It is easy enough to declare the objectives of a welfare system but quite another matter to design a working model. There are, however, numerous real-life examples that illustrate many of the ingredients of a welfare system which might be created in a shire.

The Sheldon Home: One of the real successes in humane care for the poor in Vermont was The Sheldon Home (originally The Sheldon Poorhouse). The Sheldon Home offered decent subsistence and humane care to the needy from as many as ten towns in Franklin County, until it finally closed its doors in 1958 after 125 years of operation.

Most of those in The Sheldon Home were either orphans, who would graduate when old enough to go into farming or a trade, or elderly people with no prospects for outside employment. The home attempted to be as self-sufficient as possible to minimize taxpayer costs. In the 1930s it boasted a seventy-five-head dairy farm, over a hundred pigs, and extensive gardens. Residents performed much of the work themselves. The Home Association assessed the grand lists of the towns of origin to meet its cash needs. The association was governed by a board composed equally of the overseers of the poor of the participating towns and other citizens.

The Sheldon Home was a forerunner of the various senior-citizen residential and congregate eating centers now common around the state. With Social Security and Old Age Assistance (OAA) to cover costs, the modern centers are on a relatively sound financial footing. The modern centers do not, however, mix seniors with orphans or other needy persons, and they do not offer any prospect of returning their inhabitants to economic self-sufficiency.

Community Improvement Corporation: The idea of the community improvement corporation (CIC) has reappeared periodically in recent years. One version, inspired by the work of Brandeis University Professor Shimon Gottschalk, appeared in the *Congressional Record* in 1973. It would operate within the framework of the existing ANFC and food-stamp programs.

The goals of the CIC plan are to give the needy a real opportunity to achieve identity and self-respect as well as a decent standard of living; to strengthen the work ethic of contribution in return for reward; to eliminate the uncaring hand of the welfare bureaucracy; and to help produce a stronger human community in which each citizen can feel he or she has a place.

In a Vermont of shires the members of a shire CIC would be persons entitled to receive welfare assistance under existing criteria within the shire. The CIC would contract with the shire Office of Social Welfare for the total support of its members, for which it would receive periodic cash payments equal to the members' cash benefits and their share of the department's social-work and administrative costs. Each welfare recipient would become a shareholder of the shire CIC and also an employee, at a salary equal to his or her welfare entitlement. The CIC would hire such administrative and social-service staff as it saw fit, or it would contract with a private firm for those services.

From the beginning the principle would be clearly established that child-rearing and caring for the sick and aged are highly valued and important types of work for which the basic salary would be paid. Other types of work might include neighborhood cleanup, manning the shire recycling center and skills exchange, beautification, school tutoring, serving as health-care aides, crime watch, and housekeeping assistance to the elderly or disabled.

Aged and handicapped persons would be offered duties conforming to their interests and capabilities. Some might answer telephones and visit or call on shut-ins. Some might clip newspapers for community scrapbooks, or, as at Moosehaven, just sit on park benches, smile at passers-by, and keep an eye on children at play.

If participants in a shire CIC received only the base salary equal to their previous welfare entitlement, the arguments for the CIC plan would be its removal of the stigma of being welfare-dependent, a strengthening of local community life, and the empowerment of recipients to decide how the social-services budget should be spent. The CIC would, however, offer one additional incentive.

In any community there are many services for which there is some demand but for which no public or private employer can afford to hire additional personnel at prevailing wage rates. Since all CIC members have a guaranteed base salary, the CIC could contract to provide the services of any of its employees desiring a supplementary income, and it could charge the other party (school, parks department, grocery store, etc.) only the difference between the CIC salary and the prevailing market wages. Thus a grocery might hire a disabled young adult to provide security services the store could not otherwise afford, or a neighbor might pay for additional child care. Beyond some level the CIC member would have to share income with the CIC. The more successful, of course, would graduate to private-sector employment.

CICs would be a first step in breaking the social isolation of dependent individuals, in restoring their sense of personal worth, in

215

generating motivation to overcome obstacles, in giving them practical work experience, and in reintegrating them into the larger community. It would reinforce the work ethic and decentralize the administration of government services while removing the stigma of welfare dependency. It would not enlarge the current welfare budget.

CICs would give the poor a new sense of control over their destinies instead of perpetuating their subjection to a welfare bureaucracy. They would introduce free market elements into the provision of social services, allowing themselves and their members to choose vendors instead of taking whatever the government dictates. They would open opportunities for supplementing incomes through additional work, and thus start welfare recipients on the path toward regular employment.

The Relief Corporations of the Thirties: Except for its relationship to the established welfare system, the CIC idea is far from being as radical as it might sound. For in the early days of the Depression scores of "unemployed leagues" sprang up from coast to coast, many of them wholly private, others aided by grants from local governments and, later, by the New Deal relief agencies.

It must be pointed out that the participants in these leagues were not the aged, disabled, or retarded, but almost entirely able-bodied working-age people whose only misfortune was to have been thrown out of work. Nonetheless in the absence of an effective national welfare program (which did not start until 1935, and then only for the elderly), the unemployed leagues achieved remarkable results.

A Vermont-scale example was the Unemployed Relief Club of Waterloo, Iowa. In September 1932 rumors reached Waterloo that potatoes and onions were being left to rot in the fields on Minnesota farms because farmers could not hire help to harvest them. When the story was confirmed, 174 unemployed men left Waterloo for Hollandale, Minnesota, in trucks donated by local businessmen. In three days the men harvested enough vegetables to "earn" two boxcar loads of potatoes, onions, carrots, and cabbage, which were transported back to Waterloo free of charge by the Rock Island Railroad. Thus was formed the Unemployed Relief Club.

Within six weeks club membership had expanded to more than a thousand, and a four-story office building was leased at nominal rates for the club headquarters. The members set up an auto-recycling garage, which constructed several trucks out of parts scavenged from disabled vehicles. By mid-October club members arranged to trade their labor for seventy-two hundred pounds of corn meal and a half-ton of pork from Grundy County farmers. By December the organization had received fifty tons of shelled corn.

During the same period other club members were harvesting nineteen hundred cords of firewood on shares, which went to heat members' homes. Over a hundred older members began a project of recycling over a thousand toys for underprivileged children at an average cost of a dollar each. A similar project recycled donated clothing and made thirty-seven hundred pairs of mittens from old garments. The club also sponsored a barber- and beauty shop for members and a carpentry and painting shop for furniture repair. A canning and surplus-food-recycling project was launched, and arrangements were made to barter goods with Waterloo's doctors and dentists in return for medical and dental care.

The club inaugurated a system of barter-and-trade certificates, denominated in hours worked, to reward members for work performed. The local business community and charities cooperated fully, and although there was never much hope for providing full sustenance for the club's members, the activity was judged to be a great success.

Other examples abounded in the 1930s. The Dayton, Ohio, Mutual Exchange grew out of the need for a market for clothing being made by a group of unemployed workers. The operation aimed at giving the unemployed an opportunity to exchange their labor for food, clothing, and shelter, and at creating a substitute for money as a local medium of exchange.

Scrip issued by the exchange was traded for goods produced by farmers, craftsmen, and local firms, some of whom then used the scrip for their purchases in the community. The exchange was, in effect, a multiple barter system, and it kept nine families off of welfare while aiding hundreds of others.

The Unemployed Cooperative Relief Association of Los Angeles was another noteworthy example. It began when an enterprising but unemployed man ventured out into farm country where he swapped his labor for a sack of vegetables to take home. Within a year after its inception in 1932 the association boasted forty-five separate units all over Los Angeles County.

A major activity of the association was the recycling of foodstuffs which would otherwise have gone to waste. In one month the association distributed 4.7 million pounds of food to over a hundred thousand persons, at a total cost (gas and oil) of only $2,588. The distribution program was aided by a local traffic court, which directed violators to work off their fines by trucking produce for the association. The local associations also served as shoe- and clothing-recycling centers. The right to receive benefits was measured by the amount of work contributed to the association's programs, customarily two days a week.

The self-help groups of the 1930s proved to be a temporary phenomenon. Some disintegrated from internal quarrels and incompetent management, and all disappeared as new federal welfare programs came on-stream and as the national economy eventually recovered at the end of the decade. But for a few brief years they illustrated an astounding variety of self-help efforts, almost always launched on a shoestring by the unemployed themselves. In light of their well-documented experiences, is it visionary to believe that the small-scale human community of the Vermont shire might see as creative and fulfilling an effort?

Transfer-Payment Reinvestment: Another innovation in assisting the able-bodied poor emerged in France in 1979. Called *Chômeurs Createurs*, the plan offered unemployed workers a lump-sum unemployment benefit grant to get started in an entrepreneurial small business. If the business failed, the entrepreneur had no obligation to repay. Within a year and a half of offering this option, 80 percent of the participants were still in business, and perhaps three fourths of those were reasonably well established.

In 1984 the French government revised the program, funding it from general revenues so that higher-paid workers (with higher unemployment benefits) did not get an advantage. Any unemployed person could apply for a grant under the program, not just those covered by unemployment compensation. Also the government made more effort to review business plans.

Great Britain launched a similar program in 1982, called the Enterprise Allowance Scheme. Enthusiasm has been great; some 160,000 people enrolled as of 1987. The scheme gives a grant of £1,000 pounds for investment, and pays a stipend of £40 a week for the first fifty-two weeks. Workers receiving grants must work full time, survive a "scaring session" (to alert them to possible pitfalls), and take part in management-training programs. Belgium and the Netherlands have created programs like France's; Ireland and Australia, like Great Britain's.

Such schemes cannot, as yet, be implemented in the United States because the moment a person eligible for unemployment compensation starts his or her own venture, he or she is no longer considered to be "looking for work" and benefits cease. Efforts are underway to persuade Congress to authorize several demonstration projects in which this rule is waived.

Conclusion

None of the foregoing examples illustrates all of the ingredients of a sound shire welfare system. The programs described have arisen in different places to meet widely differing problems. And yet the fundamental principles of reintegration into the community, movement toward self-sufficiency, mutual aid, community support, and contribution in return for benefit appear throughout. Taken together, many of these ideas could well be adapted to the Vermont shires. And best of all they can be even more easily expanded to other fields of public compassion: to rescue the elderly from the warehouses to which they have been condemned. To let communities work imaginatively at human-scale means of reintegrating the elderly and handicapped into the community – to do more than reserve them a parking space or build them an access ramp and then say (as we are apt to do under federal megastandards), "There, we've done our part." Indeed the instinct of multi-town cooperation for relief of the elderly is already visible in pre-shire form in the nascent Rochester Community Care Home, a joint effort of five tiny towns deep in the Green Mountains of central Vermont. The citizens there designed the home to make it "no longer necessary for seniors to leave their community when they could no longer take care of themselves."

What is crucial, as always, is that responsibility be decentralized from remote governmental bodies to local communities, and that the people of those communities rediscover the spirit of autonomy and mutual aid which are indispensable to any human society worthy of the name. Creating a Vermont of shires will make that rediscovery possible.

Chapter 13

PEOPLE AND THE LAND

Breathes there the man, with soul so dead,
Who never to himself hath said,
"This is my own, my native land!"
Whose heart hath ne'er within him burn'd
As home his footsteps he hath turn'd. . . .

– Sir Walter Scott

EVERY society is shaped and molded by its relation to the land and environment. It is true of the Inuit along the frozen shores of the Arctic Sea, of the Bushmen in the desert of Kalahari, of the Quechua in the shadows of the Andes. And it is true as well of Vermont and Vermonters.

Yet the forces of giantism and centralization are cutting deeply at the bond between Vermonters, their communities, and their land, much as they have elsewhere in the country. Federating Vermont into self-governing shires, little citadels of democracy fashioned to the contours of the living earth, offers a stout defense against those destructive forces.

At the center of the attack against the linkage between the people and their land is the systems axiom, which reads: democracy and a clean environment are incompatible. In a discussion of the beliefs that define the "Vermont mystique" Donald Nagel lays this view out to perfection. One belief, he says, "holds that the state's strength is the survival of small-town virtues: town meeting, local government, respect for one's neighbors and community. Another holds that the state's glory is its natural splendor: unpolluted streams, clean air, open pasture land. Unfortunately the two beliefs are incompatible." Because of development pressures from out of state, says Nagel, "the first belief could, within a decade, destroy the second."

Does the writer really believe that respect for one's neighbors and community are incompatible with unpolluted streams and clean air? That town meeting and open pasture land cannot coexist? Indeed he does, and it is this very kind of blackmail that must be vociferously rejected by those who dream of a Vermont where democracy and ecology can work out the natural union they so clearly share.

This Land Vermont

Many states of the American Union exhibit a vast variety of land forms. New Jersey has its rolling hills and its pine barrens. Illinois has its Deep South cotton fields, its grain-laden prairies, and its hardwood forests. Montana has the high plains and the Rocky Mountains. Mississippi has its delta and its piney woods. Vermont is different. Few states, indeed, can boast such a uniform landscape as Vermont. Or one so steadfastly inspiring. Or one more economically important. Or one more redolent of a people's ancient struggle for liberty.

Vermont – covering only 9,609 square miles, an area smaller than five counties in Arizona alone – is really little more than one old, two-hundred-mile-long mountain range flanked by two long valleys. There are probably few places in the state where one cannot see a crest of mountains marching off on the horizon or be too far from a quiet village, a placid pond, or a dairy farm. From the hall of the House of Representatives in Montpelier one may occasionally see deer nibbling brush along the hillsides of Hubbard Park.

For centuries the Vermont landscape has evoked strong emotions, from the rhapsodies of the artist and poet to the exuberant joys of the vacationer and skier. But more important than these outbursts has been the quiet but deep-seated attachment of the Vermonter to his native soil. The Vermonter's attachment to his land has recognized its aesthetic and productive and sometimes its market values, but more commonly it has been an attachment of the soul. It sprang not only from the soul's affinity for a place, but also from its need to possess, protect, and pass on improved.

Indeed the history of the land in early Vermont is unique. For Vermont, as it happened, began as a no man's land between two vastly different systems of land tenure. To the south and east, in the other states of New England, land was owned by individuals in freehold.

Any man who gained title to land was free to use it as he saw fit, exchange it as he saw fit, bequeath it as he saw fit, and deny its use to others for any reason, or for no reason at all. The only real limitation was embodied in the ancient maxim of Anglo–Saxon law, *sic utere tuo, ut alienum non laedas*: loosely, "you may use your own as you please, so long as you do not invade the equal rights of others." In addition one could not create perpetuities in land ownership, or seek to control ("entail") land once conveyed or bequeathed. And of course one was obliged to pay annual property taxes. But that was about it. The name "freehold" was aptly chosen.

To the west in the colony of New York the land-tenure system was diametrically opposite. There, on the great estates of the Hudson Valley, the patroons held the land as a Plantagenet duke might have – as feudal lords. On the vast estates of the Van Rensselaers and Livingstons thousands of farm families dwelt in poverty and hopelessness on land they could never own. Each year the lord exacted a quitrent. No farmer could pass on his land and improvements to his heirs, for neither belonged to him, but to the lord. Each year the farmer was summoned to work a week or two at the lord's sawmill – and if he needed sawed lumber, he could have it only from the lord, at the lord's price. He might not cut down a tree near his own dwelling or buy goods anywhere but at the lord's store. Farmers who balked at such onerous terms found themselves in the law courts, facing distraint and ejectment at the hands of the lord's hand-picked judges, sheriffs, and juries (on which no tenant farmer could serve). The lord did not approve of tenants' reading – they might get unruly ideas – so there were no schools. The idea of democracy, so cherished by Anglo-Saxon freemen from time immemorial, was utterly unknown on the Yorker estates.

Reverend John Taylor, a Mohawk Valley missionary of 1802, aptly characterized life on these great estates: "The same evil operates here, as in many parts of the country – the lands are leased. This must necessarily operate to debase the minds and destroy the enterprise of the settlers. If men do not possess the right of sale, they never will or can feel independent. The Americans can never flourish when on leased lands; they have too much enterprise to work for others or to remain tenants. I find that they are greatly depressed in mind and are losing their animation." A group of petitioning Livingston tenants in 1795 had put it more directly: "[The leasehold regulations] are oppressive and burthensome to the last degree, unfriendly to all great exertions of Industry, and tending to degrade your Petitioners from the Rank the God of Nature destined all Mankind to move in, to be Slaves and Vassals."

To the men like the bold young Allen brothers who filtered into Vermont when it was the wilderness frontier of New England, this Yorker land system was anathema. More: it was hell on earth. Never, they were convinced, was a people so accursed as those who lived under the feudal yoke of an arrogant Hudson Valley patroon surrounded by luxury, served by slaves, and prospering from the unpaid labors of landless serfs whose rightful gains were systematically expropriated by the power of monopoly and corruption. The Vermont settlers' loathing of the Yorker system was so pronounced that, on the Yorker side, Lieutenant Governor Cadwallader Colden nervously observed (in 1763) that unless New York's jurisdiction were pushed aggressively to the east, the dreaded "republican principles of New England would be extended." The "republican" and "feudal" systems overlapped in Vermont, and the settlers clashed.

The Yorker tenant farmers had risen up before against the feudal lords, in Prendergast's Rebellion of 1766 and in countless encounters along the Massachusetts border. But the rebellion in disputed Vermont was led not by tenants groaning under the feudal yoke on land owned by the lord and protected by the lord's sheriffs, but by freeborn settlers determined to own their land free and clear, under a republican form of government of their own choosing. The Vermonters fully grasped the importance of freehold land ownership – not only to their own economic fortunes but to the future of the nascent Green Mountain republic. "These bloody [Yorker] lawgivers know we are necessitated to oppose their execution of the law, where it points directly at our property, or give up the same," bellowed Ethan Allen. "That person or country of persons are cowards indeed, if they cannot as manfully fight for their liberty, property and life as villains can do to deprive them thereof."

When Vermont's constitution writers cribbed from George Mason's Virginia Declaration of Rights and Thomas Jefferson's Declaration of Independence (in force since 1777) to begin their handiwork, their first borrowing was this powerful affirmation of human rights: "That all men are born equally free and independent, and have certain natural, inherent and unalienable rights, amongst which are the enjoying and defending life and liberty, acquiring, possessing and protecting property, and pursuing and obtaining happiness and safety. . . ." The Vermont Constitution went on to banish slavery and servitude (of the

223

sort so notorious in New York to the west), require compensation to the owner when private land was taken for public use, protect liberty of conscience, and guarantee equal protection, due process of law, and the historic rights of Englishmen.

This fundamental issue of the importance of freehold property ownership (and its corollary – widespread distribution of that ownership among the people) cannot be overemphasized. Throughout the two centuries since Vermont's land system was decided in favor of freehold, Vermonters have revered the ownership of land and property. They have done so not to hoard it and gloat over it, like some Ottoman sultan or Plantagenet king, but because they well understood that secure and widely distributed property ownership in fee simple was essential to the economic independence of the free citizen and militiaman and to the preservation of a free republic. And they understood too that a true community could not be established if property were controlled by a distant sovereign, whether he were an arrogant and ignorant Hanover king or, in modern transmutation, an equally arrogant and ignorant central planner.

Speaking approvingly of newcomers to Vermont during the 1930s, Governor George D. Aiken said, "They own land that they can call their own. They have realized that desire to own land which is in the hearts of almost all people. Being home owners makes citizens more loyal to their country. They feel they have a stake in their community and their government, and that they themselves are part of it. Over 82 percent of the farmers of Vermont own their homes and farms. That is a good reason why it is so difficult to interest them in overthrowing the American form of government." In that testimony is the reverberating echo of Ethan Allen and the appeals of the Yorker tenant farmers for a chance to become freeholders.

The Vermont tradition, rooted in freehold property ownership, persisted undimmed throughout the years. Rules might be created, to be sure, restricting some uses of property noxious to a community. Even zoning might be (just barely) tolerated, so long as it did not encroach too far on a landowner's legitimate rights, and so long as it remained subject to the collective conscience of a local community. Zoning, for all its faults, was a local matter, and it was unlikely that any local board would persist in working a real injustice on a landowner, at least for any length of time.

For almost two centuries there was little in the way of conflict over issues of land use and ownership in Vermont. Then in 1969 came a major assault on the ancient and essential tradition of the freehold. The driving force of change was a demand for all-season recreation in Vermont's clean and unspoiled environment. Suddenly Vermonters once again knew the intoxication of a land-speculation boom, a boom scarcely dreamed of since the end of the sheep era a century before. This development boom was something new, and Vermont was not at all prepared to cope with it. State laws allowed local town governments to use police-power controls to guide growth, but most rural towns had never had much to do with zoning, since there was so little development pressure. The cause célèbre that launched one of the bitterest political battles in Vermont history was the report that the International Paper Company intended to build 20,000 cheap vacation homes on a rocky hillside in the town of Dover.

In May 1969 Governor Deane C. Davis, a quintessential Vermonter, judge, and business leader elected at age sixty-eight to cap his career of civic service, appointed a blue-ribbon commission chaired by retired navy officer Arthur Gibb (not a native Vermonter) to think up a way to address the problem of rapid growth in certain areas of the state. The commission could have relied upon the traditional Vermont practice of local regulation of development. Indeed as of mid-1968 the legislature had upgraded the state's Municipal Planning and Development Act to authorize towns to impose stringent zoning and subdivision regulations, including such features as site-plan approval, design-control districts, performance standards, and planned-unit-development regulations. Under other statutes towns had considerable power over roads, power to seek injunctive relief for nuisance, and sweeping powers in sewage disposal and other health-related matters.

With some modest augmentation and technical assistance from state experts and lawyers, these town powers were enough to have dealt with almost any conceivable development. Relying on the towns to guide their growth, however, would have required a local will to act. The Gibb Commission did not believe local people would act to implement sufficiently stringent local rules to control large-scale development. And so the commission opted to recommend state control of development through a sweeping scheme of permit requirements. In 1970 the legislature, by an overwhelming margin, enacted Act 250, the now-famous (or notorious) development-control act. It has become one of the most studied and emulated land-control laws in U.S. history.

In a gesture toward local control, Act 250 created district environmental commissions to issue development permits. Detailed criteria for the permits were written into state law, governing everything from air and water pollution by a development, to its impact on schools and municipal services, to its effects on "aesthetics" and "rare and irreplaceable natural areas." A state Environmental Board was created to prepare guidelines for the permit process and act as an appeals board. Such inconvenient concepts as democracy were avoided by having the governor appoint the members of these boards and commissions. Finally two important plans governing development in Vermont were to be prepared for subsequent legislative approval: the capability and development plan and the land use plan.

Initially it was anticipated that the capability and development plan would be a technical plan for the state, indicating which sorts of development were best suited for which areas in light of their environmental carrying capacity and numerous other policy considerations. It was to have been followed by a legislatively approved land use plan, which would declare what activities could be conducted in which areas – in other words a statewide zoning scheme. In November 1972 the Environmental Board made public its first versions of the two plans. Their sweeping statements alarmed opponents of centralized land use controls, while the plans' lack of detail and general vagueness dismayed the state's vociferous and well-funded environmental movement (largely a creation of immigrants to Vermont who feared that ignorant or greedy Vermonters might let their state turn into something resembling the places the new arrivals had left behind).

The history of the ensuing three-year battle over state land use planning has been told elsewhere and need not be recounted in detail here. Suffice it to say that the advocates' policy of choice was, simply, state government control over the use and exchange of all land in Vermont.

To the acute distress of the national environmental movement, which had vigorously touted Act 250 as the leading model for the nation (it became Exhibit A for the Udall–Jackson National Land Use Planning Act voted down in the House in 1974), Vermonters overwhelmingly rejected the policy of centralized control implicit in the state land use plans. They rejected it for a host of reasons. Some had to do with the arrogance and "furrin" origins of the most prominent land use-control advocates, some with the cooling of the economic and real estate boom in the early 1970s, some with a growing shortage of affordable housing, some with the havoc state zoning would have played with local property-tax bases. But the main reason that a state land use plan was beaten down (three times, in successively weaker versions) was because Vermonters came to realize that implicit in the plans was a threat even more serious than the "no-growth" philosophy which would cost them jobs, housing, and retirement income. For the land use plan carried within it the premise that privately owned freehold property was to be no more. Henceforth all property was to be "social property," "held" rather than owned by individuals for the greater good of society at large, i.e., the state. And the land use plan was the epitome of managerial centralism as well as a threat to Vermonters' human rights.

This "social property" theory, openly espoused by a few honest advocates of the original land use plan but vigorously denied by others, meant that the state would, where it saw fit, enforce regulations to the very limit of its constitutional power without paying compensation to the landowner. It meant that the power over the sale and exchange of all land in the state would ultimately be centralized in a board of bureaucrats at the state capital. It meant a restoration, in modern guise, of the Hudson Valley feudalism that early Vermonters found so abhorrent. And thus it was not surprising that Vermonters saw state land use planning as a mortal threat to their cherished tradition of individual liberty and a republican form of government. At one point the land use plan opponents aired a radio spot featuring the ghost of Ethan Allen raging against feudal tyranny. It did no historical injustice.

•

Witness: Hub and Mary were not in the habit of going to public meetings, maybe because they were almost always held at 7:30 P.M., which was before Hub had chores finished. But this night they had asked his son Charley and his wife to come over and do chores so they could find out what the government had in mind for their land.

Hub and Mary's land was vital to them, not only in the emotional way that farmers feel about land, but also in a more practical sense. Since Charley got the job at the machine shop, it was pretty clear that he was not going to take over the farm in a few years when Hub hoped to retire. The land was probably worth almost a million dollars now — that's what those real estate brokers had said — and that meant a happy retirement for Hub and Mary, maybe in Sarasota where two other couples from town had moved.

When Hub entered the high-school meeting room that night, he noticed the maps on easels along the side wall. It didn't take him long to locate his farm. It was in a light-green area marked Resource Conservation Area. Hub wondered what that meant.

When the meeting began, an enthusiastic young man with a blow-dry hairdo talked for a while about "saving Vermont" from various threats. He said the state land use plan would do that by stopping development on prime agricultural lands. "In these Resource Conservation Areas," the speaker said, "farming will go on as always."

"Don't speak up, Hub, you don't know enough about this," whispered Mary. But it was too late. Hub was on his feet. "Mister, I don't know much about this sort of thing, but what I think I hear you saying is that my farm here will have to remain a farm forever. Is that right?" The speaker acknowledged that this was a great virtue of the land use plan.

"Who's gonna be farmin' it?" asked Hub.

"Why I suppose you are, aren't you?" was the reply.

"Well, I ain't gonna last forever, and my son's found other work, and I don't think you folks in Montpelier ought to count on me to keep on farming into the next century."

"Well surely you can find another farmer to buy it from you when you reach retirement age," replied the presenter, an employee of the state's Environmental Board.

"Not so durn easy," replied Hub. "We're already at the end of the dairy route, the land ain't real level for the machinery, and there ain't a whole hell of a lot of people starting up in the dairy business these days, with the blend price down. I 'spect we'll probably take up somebody on an offer who has something else in mind, like putting in vacation homes. Is that all right?"

The man from Montpelier looked nervous. "Actually, no," he replied. "Putting homes on your fine farm would damage the public interest, and I'm afraid that wouldn't be allowed."

Mary, always timid, had heard enough. "You mean to tell us the state is going to keep us from selling our land when we get ready? That's all the retirement a farmer has, his land. If we can't sell when the time comes, how're we gonna ever retire?"

The man from Montpelier felt a hundred pairs of eyes turn from Mary to him, the eyes of landowners who were rapidly coming to understand that the land use plan would be for many a one-way ticket to a penurious old age. "You have to understand," he said, "that your personal finances and retirement plans are not taken into account under this plan. It is for the preservation of Vermont itself."

"Like hell we do," said Luther Harmon, who was never one to mince words. "You can't save Vermont by robbing its people."

When Hub and Mary walked out to the Chevy later, they knew Luther had it right. "Ma," said Hub softly, "would you look up our representative's home phone number? I've got some calls to make."

Bear in mind Hub and Mary have worked together for forty years, seven days a week, keeping intact the postcard scenery that the state land grabbers like so much. They are growing old now, and they are tired. Day in, day out, they have gone to the barn, cut hay, and mended fence. While there were many that liked to look at their place from a distance, there were few who were willing to do the work to keep it going.

The great cultural contradiction that turned the rape of Vermont landholders like Hub and Mary into a social as well as an economic crime is that those so interested in keeping Vermont cosmetically rural don't *like* farmers or farms. In only one week in the fall of 1988 the Vermont press carried two stories that hammer this fact home. An innkeeper in Craftsbury Common tried to use Act 250 to stop the students of Sterling College from building a barn because it didn't "fit" the view from his inn. And a team sent by the state to inspect the school in Grand Isle opined that the smell of cow manure on a nearby farm was "not conducive to learning." This, remember, when all of Vermont is committed to "saving the family farm" – especially the planners. The trouble is the planners want farms, but they have sensitive noses. Nor do they like the feisty independence and often unkempt political behavior engendered by the hardscrabble life as a steward of the land.

⋅

One by one the versions of the state's land use plans were defeated in the legislature, along with several of the key legislators who had favored them. With the final defeat of the land use plan in 1976 the pendulum swung back, much to the dismay of the environmental movement. Vermonters of all stripes want a clean and healthy environment. They want irresponsible development curbed, adequate roads constructed, adequate sewage disposal, and reasonable provision for public services necessitated by growth. They will not, however, accept the argument for turning their land over to the state, or for bringing the police power of the state to bear on even the most minute land use decisions. Had they done so, Vermont and the Vermont tradition would have entered a wholly new phase – one in which there would be little point writing a book such as this. A spiritual obituary would have been sufficient. Instead even the requirement that the state have a land use plan was quietly removed from state law in 1984.

But as so often happens, the advocates of social property and state control of land use and ownership came back strong, only three short years after their official defeat. In September 1987 Governor Madeleine Kunin named a Commission on Vermont's Future, chaired by the former head of President Carter's Environmental Protection Agency, who had arrived in Vermont earlier that same year. The commission's report resurrected the state land use plan idea of 1972, this time disguised as a collection of regional plans to be coordinated by a council of regional commissions. A long list of "goals" were advanced for the plan, and woe unto the town which failed to "address" the goals correctly (their plan would not be "acknowledged," a quaint term borrowed from Oregon to avoid use of the plain but dangerous word "approved"). The commission also recommended a statewide property tax on new industrial and commercial properties ostensibly to discourage municipal efforts to attract new enterprises, but also to fatten state revenues.

Governor Kunin assiduously promoted the adoption of legislation to carry out the commission's recommendations (except for the statewide property tax, which she favored but the legislature clearly did not). The basic premise of her proposal was to move Vermont into a "new planning era," where nothing of consequence would happen unless provided for in the state's new regional land use plan. The plan was to be "uniform in standards, specific in requirements, and tough on delinquents." Despite the usual lip service to "citizen" participation, it would be stitched together by the usual planners, experts, bureaucrats, and environmental lobbyists in Montpelier. The result was Act 200, described by one conservative critic as "one of the most misbegotten pieces of legislation in the post-Ice Age Era," and by Vermont's fledgling Green movement as "a complete mockery of Montpelier's claims to respect our precious municipal liberties," a plan which would make Vermont "the most centralized state in the country." Even State Senator Harvey Carter, an early and enthusiastic advocate of state growth controls, ruefully described Act 200 as "a citizen's nightmare, a lawyer's dream, a selectmen's confusion, and a bureaucrat's delight."

Act 200 sets forth an amazing collection of goals. *Sample:* "Development shall be planned [i.e., controlled] so as to maintain the historic settlement pattern of compact village and urban centers separated by rural countryside." (*Translation:* "Nobody builds in the country. It screws up the pretty views.") *Sample:* "Significant scenic roads, waterways and views, particularly along the Interstate network and other scenic corridors," shall be preserved and protected. (*Translation:* "Your hayfield will always remain a hayfield, whether you like it or not. Especially if it can be seen from the Interstate.")

State agencies are required to withhold grants from towns whose officials share an insufficient enthusiasm for the state's interpretation of these sweeping goals. In the version of Act 200 which finally (and narrowly) passed in 1988, towns are not required to have approved plans, but if they do not, they get no state funds for planning, and their town plan will be banned from Act 250 proceedings. (Their selectmen will probably not be invited to state-sponsored conferences, either – a dubious penalty.) The regional planning commissions mandated in Act 200, whose members are appointed by local governments, will become powerful unelected regional governments, beyond the reach of voters at town meeting, and, of course, principally funded from Montpelier to do the state's bidding. A more drastic contrast with our democratic, autonomous shires can scarcely be imagined.

In short Act 200 establishes a state-dominated land-use-control system no different in principle from the feudalism of the Hudson Valley manors of old. If a farmer owns a pretty pasture (a "scenic vista") along the Interstate, he will be prohibited from converting that pasture to homesites – this despite Act 200's continual nagging about the need for "affordable housing."* The act directs the towns to plan in accordance with state "goals" of astonishing breadth and imprecision, or suffer the pain of noncompliance. Act 200 is the Final Solution dreamed up by the Pretty People determined to decree the Perfect Little State – oblivious to the outcries of cantankerous human beings, dull-witted local governments, and misguided citizens who still believe in liberty, community, and participatory democracy.

---

*Which, ironically but poignantly, is most often found in towns that have no plans and no zoning. The schemes of the centrist land use planners always call for low-income housing, but it is a shallow demand which always ignores the fundamental truth that the rural poor don't fit the idealized landscape any more than does a high-rise billboard advertising lite beer.

231

Liberty? Curtailed in the "public interest" by a gang of zealous planners who are convinced they know what is better for you – and for the state – than you do. Democracy? A nuisance to be celebrated in rhetoric but avoided wherever possible in practice. Participation? Wonderful, so long as those who participate concur in the vital importance of The Plan. It is significant that in some eleven public hearings held on Act 200 during 1988 not once were its advocates even close to a majority, and in at least two cases every single person in the room expressed opposition to it. These sham public hearings, glorified as "citizen participation" in a "continuing planning process," are viewed by the managerial centralists as tedious and meaningless exercises to be endured while the experts make decisions about "scenic vistas" in the planning warrens of Montpelier. When legislators proposed that the voters be given a chance to express themselves in a referendum on the desirability of this expert-hatched scheme, the friends of "growth control" in the legislature thunderously voted that proposition down. It is almost unimaginable that any such system would ever be invented within a shire.

Throughout the battle between social-property feudalism and freehold ownership a number of imaginative proposals were brought forward for resolving real land-use and environmental problems. These alternative proposals were fully conformable to the freehold theory of property ownership. They avoided the fatal idea of using the coercive power of the state to confiscate the property rights of landowners pursuing innocent enjoyment of their property, without at the very least requiring the public to give something of equivalent value to the landowner for his coerced cooperation – something of real economic value in addition to whatever warm, rosy glow might result from his giving up his rights in land for the benefit of the public.

All these nonstatist proposals were ignored by the central planners and their political allies. They were ignored deliberately, because the planners' true agenda was not merely to stop pollution or guide growth. The evils of pollution and unchecked growth merely served as convenient rationales. Their real goal was and is to put an end to the nuisance of freehold property ownership, vest all control over the use and exchange of land in the state, and make sure that they would control the state.

Environment, Land, and the Shires

Before describing, however briefly, the various techniques available to a shire for guiding land use in ways consistent with the principle of freehold ownership, it is necessary to describe how the existing environmental-protection system would be changed in a Vermont of shires. We reaffirm the rightful power of the state government to protect the natural environment – the air, water, and soil of the state. No shire should have the power to allow such things as combined sewage overflows into Lake Champlain (something which Burlington, whose legislators almost invariably vote for strict environmental laws, has been doing for over half a century). The state may and should delegate responsibility for much strictly environmental protection to the shires, but it should retain residual jurisdiction to force an end to unacceptable pollution. Nor should a shire be allowed to pollute itself, even in the (unlikely) circumstance in which its doing so would not affect another shire. Indeed this is a key component of the conceptual framework of this book: let real environmental protection be the responsibility of the central power.

Much of the environmental-protection game in Vermont has little to do with the actual prevention of environmental pollution, however. In other matters under the Act 250 rubric – things like municipal impact, adequate water supply, transportation, parking, and aesthetics – the shire will have primary authority. To deal with these concerns each shire will have the responsibility of creating its own environmental commission, replacing the nine existing district environmental commissions that now cover the state. Unlike the present commissioners, who are appointed by the governor (often at the behest of environmental organizations), the shire environmental commissioners will be selected in a manner to be determined by the shire-moot. They could be appointed by the shire council and ratified by the shire-moot, elected by the shire-moot, or elected popularly at town meetings or in general elections. The people of each shire will be free to decide.

The shire environmental board (if the use of a board were the manner in which the shire decided to approach these matters) would take over the responsibility for issuing permits now issued by the State Health Department, involving such things as sewage disposal and water supplies, and those now issued by the State Environmental Conservation Department that deal with issues such as shoreland protection. Shire environmental boards would be free to contract with the state, or with private concerns, for technical assistance needed for effective administration of the permit process, or they could even choose (foolishly, in our opinion) to opt out and leave the matter in the state's hands. To the extent that a shire wanted planning and zoning, the shire environmental board would supervise that process.

We have watched, with interest, environmental protectionists battling to protect various lakes' shorelines as well as wetlands in Vermont. We are convinced of one thing: no one cherishes these entities more than those who live near them. If the latter were *empowered* to protect them, they would. There will be more natural-area protection going on in a Vermont of shires than there is now. Those who doubt such a judgment should talk to neighborhood groups struggling to protect natural areas in what will become Burlingshire, groups that have been continually handcuffed by the process set in place by those who favor centrally planned standards over human-scale standards.

Whenever a specific development was of a size or impact exceeding a single shire, the state could be given review or appeal authority or the power to mediate (but not mandate settlements of) disputes among adjacent shires. Applicants could appeal denials of permits for projects within the jurisdiction of a single shire environmental board to the shire court, and ultimately to the supreme court. On less important matters involving the border areas between shires, the adjacent shires would be free to combine their environmental boards on an ad hoc basis.

What sorts of tools might shires adopt to deal with land use, environmental protection, and growth, without at the same time destroying the vital human right of freehold property ownership? There are many such techniques. Sad to say, most have not been implemented because it is always more attractive to land regulators and growth controllers simply to use the police power of the state to impose uncompensated restrictions on property owners. Nevertheless a few methods deserve mention.

Environmental Mediation

Of considerable importance in our restructuring of Vermont's environmental-protection system will be a provision for mediation of environmental disputes. One of the great defects in Vermont's environmental-control system has been the role of the district environmental commissions as prosecutor, judge, and jury. Applicants for permits frequently feel that the commission exists simply to put a stop to their projects, while clothing their antigrowth prejudices with various legal findings. One notable case was the denial of a permit for a conference center in Winhall on the grounds that, at a certain time of day and in a certain time of year, sunlight reflected off the proposed center's windows might distract motorists on Route 30 several miles away. Another notorious case was the proposed Pyramid Mall in Williston, the permit for which was denied for the political reason that the mall's success might have a negative effect on the profits of downtown Burlington merchants some seven miles away.

Environmental mediation, pioneered a decade ago in Seattle and now practiced (and taught as a profession) by Woodbury College in Montpelier, brings the disputing parties together with a skilled mediator. Instead of marching the applicant before a legal firing squad, mediation brings him into a process where a responsible balance can be struck among competing claims – a process symbolic of the practical adjustments that make local democracy work. Mediation cannot always work – some claims are simply irreconcilable – but the vast difference in attitudes it engenders among opposed parties has made it successful in many contentious cases. Interestingly when one of the authors first proposed environmental mediation in Vermont in 1973, the suggestion was arrogantly rejected by the then-chairwoman of the Environmental Board, on the grounds that mediation was utterly unnecessary in view of the board's concern for environmental protection.

Capital Investment Planning

The foremost determinant of future land use may well be the availability of public services. These include, most obviously, roads, schools, water and sewers, police and fire protection, and such quasi-public services as electricity and telephone. It is possible, of course, for a private developer to supply many if not all of such services – Walt Disney World is an extreme example – and thus be independent of public facilities. This is not common, however. As every city planner knows, the location of highway routes and interchanges, water- and sewer lines, and power-distribution lines can be enormously influential in the shaping of growth. All of these factors are under the complete control of the public, and public control of them can be implemented without any danger at all to anyone's property. Capital investment decisions do, admittedly, create winners and losers, but the public is under no requirement that its legitimate activities in these areas produce equal windfalls or wipeouts for all.

Individual Action Techniques

Another category of land-use-protection tools are those techniques for efficiently enforcing the common law of nuisance. This body of law, developed over hundreds of years, has a lot of problems and uncertainties. A rationalization of the system has been developed, however, by Robert Ellickson of the University of Southern California School of Law. His institutionalization of nuisance law would place the risk of loss from external harm on the landowner carrying out the damaging activity. Once a plaintiff established that a nuisance has harmed him – when an activity is deemed "unneighborly" by contemporary community standards – he may seek judicial relief. The court might decide among four possibilities: injunctive relief; damages without injunctive relief; neither damages nor injunctive relief (judgment for defendant); or injunctive relief with compensation to the defendant. Where injuries are pervasive but individually insubstantial – the soot that slightly dirties everyone's wash – the court would levy a fine on behalf of the public generally. The Ellickson system offers a rational, flexible framework of resolving conflicts caused by the action of property owners, while generally avoiding police-power regulation. It is the sort of approach that a shire might well want to experiment with.

Compensated Regulation

Another creative idea for guiding land use without inflicting the costs on a hapless landowner is the idea of compensated regulation, offered by Jan Krasnowiecki and James Paul of the University of Pennsylvania Law School. Under this plan, land in question would first be valued as in eminent-domain proceedings. The shire would guarantee this value to the owner and would-be developer. Then zoning-type regulations would be applied to guide the future use of the land. If these regulations prohibited an existing use, the owner could draw upon the guarantee for damages. If they prohibited a possible future use, the owner might ask for a shire-supervised sale of his property. If the proceeds of the sale were less than the guaranteed value, the shire would be obliged to make up the difference.

A similar idea is "inverse condemnation" of land whose use the government seeks to restrict. When, for instance, a government land regulation (other than a regulation controlling harmful or noxious use) destroyed more than half of the unrestricted fair market value of the property in question, such a law would allow the owner to require the government to condemn the property and pay just compensation.

To some, half may seem a very large amount of value to lose before the government could be required to pay for what it confiscates, but in many zoning cases far more than half of the unrestricted value is wiped out by regulation without any compensation whatever. This proposal would put a brake on the appetite of government for imposing public costs on private landowners whose lands happen to be in a strategic location. It was defeated in the Vermont House of Representatives in 1988 but will certainly reappear.

Transferable Development Rights

A land use scheme gaining in favor nationally is that of transferable development rights (TDRs). To oversimplify somewhat, under a TDR scheme an overall limit is placed on the intensity of development of an area. TDRs are assigned to all land in the area on a per-acre basis. The government also publishes a schedule showing the number of TDRs required to carry out various development projects – so many for a shopping mall, so many for a high-rise, etc. A landowner wishing to develop must then acquire sufficient TDRs to satisfy the schedule for the kind of development he proposes. He does this by buying TDRs from other landowners at a market-determined price, after which the sellers will be unable to develop their property (unless they buy TDRs from someone else). There are some caveats about this kind of approach – the TDRs, for instance, must have real economic value and must be applicable over a relatively large area – but the scheme does eliminate microdecision making about individual developments, and the corruption that often accompanies the zoning process.

The town of Warren, Vermont, in 1983 was reportedly the first in the state to try out a TDR scheme. Warren allows owners of scenic meadowlands to sell the development rights covering those lands to owners of parcels adjacent to ski areas. In one of the two instances in which the plan was used, the town itself acquired the development rights to a farm to reduce the price to a farmer who wanted to buy it and keep it in operation. The town has not resold the rights to developers, however. The idea is also being actively pursued in Rutland Town. A related idea, the leasing of farmland development rights by a Vermont land trust, is described in the next chapter.

Public Land Banking

Many of the problems of rapid growth can be effectively dealt with by having the government itself buy the crucial pieces of land and thus force development to occur on the government's terms. While this approach will not satisfy free-market purists who prefer no governmental role in the land market, it does have the great advantage that it avoids the uncompensated confiscation of private land rights.

Perhaps the leading example of astute public land banking is that of Edmonton, Alberta, Canada. Back in the 1930s the city came into possession of a large number of land parcels within and around the settled part of Edmonton, as a result of tax foreclosures. Soon after World War II oil was discovered nearby, and Edmonton became a boom town. Since the city owned so much land, interspersed with private parcels, and since it also owned the electric utility system, no significant development could occur without city participation.

The city made an unusual proposal to landowners: combine your small parcels along with the city-owned parcels to make a parcel large enough for a planned development. The city would do the planning, make the street and utility investments, reserve land for schools and parks, and convey lots back to the original parcel owners in proportion to their contributed land. The city would put the remaining lots on the market, to be developed in accordance with the overall plan.

At first the private parcel owners were reluctant to get involved, but as they considered the comparative value of the planned-unit-development lots versus an uncoordinated development of what land they already owned, they began to come around. The first parcel to go on the market was a howling economic (and aesthetic) success. When the city opened the second parcel, landowners were waiting in line at city hall to take part.

Edmonton may have inherited particularly fortuitous circumstances, but the technique it used is sound and workable – and it avoids regulation of private land. It is something of a model for the Burlington waterfront-development project, which would combine city-owned and private land into a planned commercial development. (The Burlington proposal was voted down by the electorate in 1986 but is likely to return in some form.)

The foregoing is only a bare smattering of proposals for guiding land use and growth, and is offered only for the heuristic value of the methods described. The important point is that Vermont's priceless environment can be protected, and growth can be made to occur responsibly, by techniques which respect the vital human right of freehold property ownership so essential to the existence of a true democratic community. With the room for experimentation afforded by the existence of forty shires, many of the techniques described may well get a fair test at last. The environment, freehold property, and grass roots democracy will undoubtedly benefit.

Chapter 14

VERMONT'S AGRICULTURAL FUTURE

When tillage begins, other acts follow.
The farmers therefore are the founders
of human civilization.

– Daniel Webster

ERMONT cares deeply about its farms. In 1988 it became
the only state in the union to replace a cut in the federal milk
subsidy with a 50-cent-per-hundredweight subsidy of its
own. A Vermont without farmers is hardly imaginable. Yet there are
clouds on the horizon of American agriculture that cast their shadows
over Vermont and the nation.

We are told, for instance, that Vermont dairying cannot survive
without a regional price-support system, and that such a system is
impossible to attain from a Congress that dances to the tune of national,
not regional, interests. The law of increasing size and mediocre policy
explains why America cannot act to keep its agricultural sector decentralized and thereby healthier – both economically and ecologically.

A Vermont of shires can do little to redress national problems, and
shires will hardly make the cows give more milk or encourage the bees
to make more honey. Yet the shires will have important indirect advantages for Vermont agriculture which may prove valuable in the battle
to save the farms.

The decentralist *tone* of the new shire federation will invigorate
efforts to experiment in ways to make dairy farming more profitable

and to establish innovative agricultural enterprises. The Vermont Department of Agriculture has actively sought diversification, but it suffers from all the problems of centralized institutions, most notably the incapacity to resist the influence of the single interest that dominates the whole, in this case milk cows. After the shires are in place, nearly every agricultural interest in Vermont will be within hand's reach of a government that can help it and one that has its interests at heart.

Most of the shires in what is now Franklin County, for instance, will be heavily influenced by dairy farming. But in some shires along Lake Champlain apple growers will have access to a government much more interested in apples than the State of Vermont *as a whole* can ever be. The apple might become the agricultural symbol of such shires. A shire's name might be used in marketing apples. In other shires maple syrup producers will become a dominant agricultural interest, while in still others it might be Christmas tree growers. Since the shires will take shape in terms of bioregional uniqueness, they will become natural cocoons for distinctive agricultural enterprises: in a shire of mountain lakes and streams, brook trout; in a valley shire of second-growth pastureland, fallow deer; in a shire along the fertile flatlands of the Connecticut River, vegetable farms.

Some shire governments might become directly active in agriculture, owning and operating a shire farm, like the county farms of old, perhaps in connection with welfare or corrections or educational programs or some combinations of these. Still another shire might have a shire flock of sheep that would be shepherded in the summer by high school students to graze pastures for private landowners. Other shires might vote subsidies for farmers in trouble, much as Vermont towns have often relieved farmers of property taxes when a barn burns down and a new one must be built.

It would be silly to suggest that the shires can make agriculture work in Vermont in ways it was not meant to or in places where it was not meant to be. But governments built to a human scale, governments located not in the distant halls of Montpelier but nearby and in touch with local prospects and problems – these kinds of governments can have a strong catalytic influence. Not only will shire governments be more able to encourage innovations that show promise, they will also be more likely to detect enterprises that are off the wall. In short all the advantages of small government will act to the benefit of those who work the land. A Vermont of shires can demonstrate how to bring farming and governance together in ways beneficial to both.

Dairying in Vermont

Agriculture now ranks third to manufacturing and tourism as an income generator for Vermont, but its importance, both economic and symbolic, is far greater than its statistical significance. It is not by accident that the statue crowning the Vermont State House is that of Ceres, the patroness of agriculture, rather than Vulcan, the patron of manufacturing, or Mercury, who can be loosely identified as the patron of tourism.

One need not go as far as Thomas Jefferson, who wrote that "those who labor in the earth are the chosen people of God," in whose "breasts He has made His peculiar deposit for substantial and genuine virtue." And yet one cannot gainsay that farming has left a deep mark upon the character of Vermont, and that the values of the agriculturist remain the values for which Vermont has so justly been celebrated.

For of all Vermonters it is the farmer (along with logger and quarryman) who produces closest to the land. Historically, during the centuries when agricultural life gave form and substance to Vermont, the farmer was not a party to the manipulation of paper values and the realization of windfall gains, or to a life without hard physical work in such conditions as the changing seasons would provide. His was the world of the genuine, the natural, the God-given. He arose before dawn, conformable to the needs of his livestock. He savored the pungent aroma of the cow barn, the fragrance of the apple blossoms in May, the smell of the new-mown hay. He and his farm wife planned their life together to do what had to be done, cutting wood for the winter and the sugaring, fixing fence, seeing the milk safely to the dairy, guiding their son's hands as for the first time he steered the team or tractor, putting up food for the long winters. Affluent the farmer was not, but strong in mind and spirit, an essential working part of a beautiful though sometimes severe world which made sense – and was profoundly satisfying – to those who dwelt within it.

"Nearness to nature, nearness to God, a truer philosophy, a keener human sympathy, higher ideals, greater individuality, will ever be stamped upon the life and character of the country home," observed Robert La Follette. He might have added that the farmer and his wife usually formed the bedrock of civic leadership in rural towns, devoting long and uncompensated hours in the service of their community.

If its agriculture were to wither away to a memory, Vermont would in time cease to be anything unique. It would become just a distant suburb of Boston, its character defined by tourist restaurants and shopping malls. Not only does a living agriculture contribute so much to the character of Vermont, but it is absolutely indispensable to preserving the landscape which in our time has become so vital a component of the state's economic attractions.

As recently as 1953 Vermont could boast 10,527 operating dairy farms, producing 1.9 billion pounds of milk a year. In the early 1960s, however, drastic changes in the federal milk-marketing order accelerated the exodus from dairy farming. Thousands of small farms were faced with the choice of borrowing serious money to install newly required concrete floors, stainless-steel bulk tanks–and twice the number of cows to pay for the improved equipment. It was too staggering a choice for most–they sold out. By 1988 only some 2,592 of Vermont's 6,400 farms were still shipping milk. They produced 2.4 billion pounds of milk–52 percent of New England's total. Vermont's dairy farms are getting fewer but larger, and their future is strongly dependent upon the federal dairy price support program.

That program, unfortunately for Vermont dairymen, has been under long and powerful attack since 1980. To explain its complex workings in detail would require a large book. Suffice it to say that the federal government fixes a minimum price which any dairy must pay to a farmer. That price is a "blend price," a weighted average per hundredweight of the market price for manufacturing (Class II) milk and the higher market price for fluid milk (Class I) for the Boston milkshed. In recent years these prices have been most often the federal government's Class II support price, and that price plus the USDA-set "Class I differential" for the milkshed.

A federal support price far above the market price for manufacturing milk through the late 1970s, coupled with the ready availability of cheap government credit to marginally efficient producers and tax laws which invited nonfarmers to enter dairy farming, resulted in a nation awash in milk. Since consumers would not consume all that milk at the store prices resulting from the government's price fixing, the federal Commodity Credit Corporation (CCC) found itself with billions of pounds of surplus butter, cheese, and nonfat dry milk, produced and stored at substantial cost to the taxpayer. True, the bulk of the government's surplus stocks came to it from regions other than New England, notably California, where many processing plants exist only to convert milk into government surplus stocks; but to adjust milk-price supports among regions would require protection against inter-regional milk shipments, something Congress seems highly unlikely to approve.

Beginning in 1981 Congress, over the furious opposition of many in the dairy industry, began to prescribe reductions in the CCC support price. Milk that was supported at $13.10 per hundred weight in 1981 was supported at $10.60 in 1988. The result was considerable shrinkage in producers (but not a lot in production, since the survivors often made more milk to gain back the income to meet their fixed costs). The future impact of federal dairy support price reductions is never wholly clear, but it does seem clear that Vermont dairymen have little choice but to face competition in a very strong marketplace, without government support for their product at an attractive price. Thus there has come to be a premium on efficient farm management, strong breeding programs, modern equipment, advanced technology, and economies of scale. Where well within living memory herds of ten or fifteen cows were commonplace in Vermont, there are probably no dairy herds left in the state today with less than thirty cows, and the state average is sixty-five. The annual production per cow has advanced from under 7,000 pounds per year in 1953 to 13,575 today (1986).

To make things worse average production per cow is likely to increase by as much as 20 percent in the next few years, as more and more farmers begin to use bovine growth hormone (BGH) and iso-acid feed additives. BGH, injected into a cow's blood stream, prolongs the period of full milk production after calving and has been shown to increase annual production by as much as 40 percent in controlled experiments. The iso-acid additive helps a cow to extract the maximum nutrition from feed, which also converts into more milk. David Call, dean of the College of Agriculture at Cornell, has predicted that 30 percent of the dairy farmers in New York State will disappear when these products are in widespread use. Alice Hooper, of the University of Vermont's animal science faculty, says that even a 25-percent production increase per cow will cause "severe economic dislocation" in Vermont. In late 1985 the UVM College of Agriculture launched a task force to seek ways of helping surplus farmers make a transition to other occupations.

And techniques for making cows more productive are probably not the final step. Dr. Sanford Miller, director of the FDA's Center for Food Safety and Applied Nutrition, recently described startling progress in fixed-bed enzyme synthesis, in which raw natural materials are converted into food by chemically recreating animal metabolic processes. This creates the specter of a 30-foot tall plastic supercow, ingesting a hay-feed mix from a conveyor belt at the top, while a white-coated technician opens a faucet to pour off fresh milk at the bottom. The final step, presumably, will be to produce a synthetic feed through bacterial or fungal action on old rubber tires or recycled newspapers.

Aside from the growth of a milk-consuming population within reach of Vermont's dairy farms, there is not a lot of hope for any significant expansion of Vermont dairying in terms of the number of people to whom it affords a livelihood. The combination of faster inter-regional transportation, a declining federal support program, technological advances, changing consumer preferences (toward diet drinks and low-fat substitutes), development pressure on farmland, and the high cost of capital does not make for enthusiasm among farmers. If these forces remain in place, it is probably safe to say that the number of dairy farms in Vermont will steadily decline – at least to a plateau of about 2,000 – and those that remain will tend toward becoming large, highly capitalized operations like the huge Doug Nelson farm in Derby.

New England dairy farmers are battling back with an organization called RCMA (Regional Cooperative Marketing Association). The farmer-members of this proposed regional milk cartel refuse to ship milk to handlers unwilling to pay a specified "overorder" price (a price higher than the federal milk-marketing order minimum). The RCMA territory includes all of New England plus much of New York, New Jersey, and Pennsylvania; therefore transportation costs (say, from Ohio) would be so high that New England handlers would not be able to get milk delivered below the RCMA price. RCMA requires that practically all of the producers in the region participate, and the percentage is now over 98 percent.

One may be permitted some sympathy for hard-pressed dairy farmers desperate for higher milk prices, but it is not likely that the RCMA cartel will remain effective over the years unless rigorously enforced by government. There will always be a few producers eager to increase their market share by undercutting the higher RCMA price, and there will always be handlers (notably Farmland Dairy in New Jersey) who will truck milk in from a non-RCMA state like Ohio. Milk will move into the border areas of the RCMA region, in New York and Pennsylvania, and unless RCMA is prepared to buy the output of its members who would otherwise ship to those handlers, the effort will start to unravel. Finally consumers cannot be forced to buy milk at an above-market price. They can switch to other products. A can of diet soda plus a calcium pill is a poor substitute for Grade A Vermont milk, but there is no way the government can ban such a choice. It learned that during the dairyman's war against oleomargarine, which was thoroughly lost. Over the long run a RCMA-type cartel is not likely to succeed in keeping every producer in business. And if dairy prices continue to drop, the least-efficient producers will continue to go under. This is not a happy scenario for a state whose character and traditions have been so throughly shaped by the family farm.

Other Alternatives

What, then, can be done to sustain agriculture in Vermont? We suggest a ten-point program for Vermont agriculture.

First: Vermont agriculture can obviously seek out more opportunities for diversification, a thesis endlessly preached at agricultural extension meetings and farm conferences. In recent years an astonishing amount of diversification has taken place, sometimes to the disgust of old-line dairy farmers. Maple sugar, Christmas trees, firewood, pulpwood, wood chips, sawlogs, nursery stock, and honey have always been second crops for Vermont farms. New ones are now beginning to appear. Southern Vermont valleys are suitable for such crops as peppers, eggplants, melons, and tomatoes, while in the colder north, broccoli, cauliflower, cabbage, and carrots can be grown. The Champlain Valley, with its midsummer dryness in the rain shadow of the Adirondacks, is ideal for beans and grains. Wild chanterelle mushrooms have become a major speciality crop in Nova Scotia, from where they are flown to Europe, and frozen fiddleheads are an increasingly popular gourmet food item in Manhattan stores. A hill farm in Barre Town is marketing ginseng root to Asia.

Farmers in Hartford and Andover are succeeding with naturally raised pork, marketed through the Vermont Natural Pork Farmers Cooperative. Turkeys are making a comeback, and an enterprising (Harvard-educated!) young farmer in Lincolnville, Maine, has become a national success story for marketing smoked fish — trout grown in his own ponds, plus salmon flown in from the Northwest and various Maine seafood products. Sheep, once the mainstay of Vermont's rural economy, are making a notable comeback. Don Mitchell, a leading sheep raiser in New Haven, Vermont, observes that the new wave of sheep breeders are far more innovative than most dairy farmers, many of whom seem to be "prisoners of old technology."

Deer farming is a growth industry in upstate New York. Venison is only 3-percent fat, low in cholesterol, and in great demand in metropolitan restaurants. Deer require practically no maintenance and average one-seventh the feed requirements of steers. Forageland that cattle would find rather desperate looks like the Promised Land to deer—and to beefalo, a creature which is three-eighths buffalo, needs no special feed, and resists disorders and the elements. (Beefalo look like the ideal farm animal, if only they can be kept fenced in.)

Another exotic farm crop is tourists—some of them very exotic indeed. An increasing number of working Vermont farms advertise for short- and long-term summer guests, who live with the family and sometimes help with the farm work. Farms in Enosburg Falls, Rochester, Bradford, South Newbury, and West Glover are now actively promoting farm vacations as a second-income program. David Russell, a national-award-winning dairy farmer in Starksboro, keeps draft horses. When he sells Christmas trees in December to augment his income, the buyer's family rides into the woods behind the team to cut the tree as if in the nineteenth century. Says Dave with a grin, "Value added has taken on new meaning."

David and Lucy Marvin have been widely celebrated as successful tree farmers who earn a complete living from six hundred acres of tree products without growing garden crops, raising livestock, or earning off-farm income. Their efforts brought them recognition as National Outstanding Tree Farmers of the Year in 1983. Their Butternut Mountain Farm, in Johnson, produces each year 3,600 gallons of maple syrup, 150 cords of firewood, 75 cords of pulp, 25–50,000 board feet of sawlogs, and 1,500 Christmas trees. Much of the Marvins' success is due to a shrewd knowledge of equipment and where to buy components cheap, homegrown ingenuity, an informed flexibility in meeting market opportunities, long hours and a great deal of hard work.

Perhaps the star example of a balanced, diversified Vermont farm is the Steven James farm in Weybridge. James is, first of all, an integrated dairy producer-handler with 175–200 milking cows. He sells 250 gallons of milk per day, plus butter, cheese, and yogurt to Middlebury College. About three quarters of James' $1 million a year in sales come from dairy products. The remainder comes from apples, potatoes, plums, squash, and Angus–Simmental beef cattle.

Another notable example of ingenious modern farming is Wright's Dairy Farm in North Smithfield, Rhode Island. Here Ed Wright markets all of the output of 125 Holsteins to 3,000 customers a week in a retail store on the farm premises. Looking for a market for heavy cream, Wright hit upon the idea of cream-filled pastries, which became an immediate hit in the French-speaking community in Rhode Island. Originally Mrs. Wright made the pastries in the farm kitchen, but demand has increased to the point where they are made in a commercial bakery from Wright's cream. Along the same lines, in Greenfield, Massachusetts, the Western Massachusetts Food Industry Association is exploring a wide variety of new products and processing technology to assist in diversification.

Second: Farmers must continue to aggressively study and make use of emerging technology. Otherwise they will be left behind, along with the low-ceilinged, dirt floor, hand-milked dairy farms of yesteryear. Computerized technology is now in place at Vermont Technical College in Randolph which identifies each cow as it enters the milking parlor (by sending a signal to a transponder hanging on a collar around the cow's neck), computes the correct feed ration based on that cow's milking history, and triggers release of the right amount through a chute to the feed trough. The computer also keeps track of insemination, milk production, butterfat content, mastitis treatment, and almost everything else a herdsman would wish to know. Similar kinds of systems are already in place on farms all over Vermont. The American Farm Bureau Federation is now in the process of establishing a satellite-based video- and data-transmission system which will offer training programs for farmers along with market information. In the Midwest, farmers who grow wheat, soybeans, pork, and feed grains for the world market can receive market reports over phone lines via on-farm computers. Other specialized programs help them plan such things as crop allocation, credit management, and herbicide- and pesticide-application programs.

New reverse-osmosis technology on the Herbert Venheim farm in Lunenburg has made it possible to remove 20–30 gallons of water from 40 gallons of 2-percent maple sap, cutting subsequent evaporator-fuel consumption by up to 75 percent while increasing threefold the number of taps an evaporator can handle. Venheim's system, made in Quebec, uses only one gallon of oil for every gallon of manufactured syrup, less than one fourth the normal amount.

Another new process in development is a combination of on-farm ultrafiltration (UF) of milk and aseptic packaging. The high-temperature UF process yields a whole-milk concentrate to which the consumer adds water, just as one does now with frozen orange juice. The aseptic packaging–a sealed pouch–allows this concentrate to be stored without refrigeration for as long as six months. Taken together, this combination of technologies would allow a farm to market reconstitutable fresh milk over a far larger market area, due to the three-fourths reduction in transportation and refrigeration costs. (The appearance of this technology will probably be accelerated as handlers seek lower-cost milk supplies from the Midwest in competition with cartel-priced New England milk under the RCMA described above. Almost certainly federal regulation will be sought to prevent this.)

Third: New products from conventional crops must be aggressively developed. A major step in this direction is the creation of a New England Dairy Products Center at the University of Vermont, which will eventually be funded in part by royalties on the new products and processes it develops. UVM dairy scientists have already been instrumental in the development of boruga, a yogurt-based beverage very popular among Caribbean immigrants to the United States. Boruga is being manufactured by the La Vida Corporation in Hardwick. Another early success has been American Brie and Camembert cheeses, developed in cooperaton with the Guilford Cheese Company in Guilford.

Fourth: Vermont dairymen in particular have always sold their product "over the farm gate" to a handler. They have rarely profited from the downstream activities of processing, distributing, and retailing what they produce on the farm. Now that is beginning to change.

The seventy-year-old Cabot Cooperative Creamery, in Cabot, has set an excellent example of forward integration in the dairy industry. Until 1984 Cabot, like most rural dairy co-ops, simply collected, processed, and sold the milk produced by its five hundred farmer-owners. In addition to fluid milk, Cabot sold butter, cheese, sour cream, and yogurt under its own label. In that year, under the leadership of new general manager Bill Davis, Cabot plunged heavily into direct retail marketing, shifting its products to meet stronger market demand. It has produced new gourmet products and sliced butter for restaurants. Most important it has aggressively entered the retail markets in southern New England and metropolitan New York, promoting Cabot products with consumer coupons and sweepstakes tickets.

As a result revenues and profits have soared. In 1987 Cabot earned $927,556 on sales of $61.8 million, up from a profit of only $85,000 on $53 million of sales in 1984. The average profit allocation per member rose from $31 to $2,000. Cabot's farmer-owners whose equity is paid up split $281,712 in cash dividends. By 1988 over 80 percent of Cabot's members will have all of their equity shares paid up from reinvestment of dividends. The cooperative also has a profit-sharing plan for its employees and recently opened the first company-sponsored day-care center in Vermont. It does not operate its own retail outlets but earns revenues from every other stage of dairy production and marketing.

Another example of forward integration in the dairy industry is Agrimark. This dairy cooperative was created in 1981 at the initiative of Agway, a diverse, 102,000-member, $1.7-billion farm co-op which serves agriculture in twelve northern states. Agrimark was created to take advantage of an opportunity for the purchase by dairymen of the H. P. Hood Company, an established handler and distributor of dairy products in the New England region. With Agway's leadership, some 3,500 New England dairymen became Agrimark co-operators. With a major investment from Agway plus its own farmer-generated capital, Agrimark acquired all the capital assets of Hood. Those assets (mainly plant and equipment) were then leased back to Hood for a fee which Hood pays Agrimark.

Through its own tanker-truck fleet and transfer stations, Agrimark collects milk from its farmer-members at prices prescribed in federal milk-marketing orders and sells it to Hood for processing and distribution. (Agrimark also sells milk to other handlers.) Hood's earnings are split between Agrimark and Agway on the basis of their respective investments in Hood. If Agrimark's investments from lease payments, Hood's profits, and profits from its own operations produce a surplus, dividends are paid to Agrimark's farmer-owners. In 1987 Agrimark's 2,500 members were paid $1.5 million in cooperative dividends, representing 6 cents per hundredweight of milk delivered.

Both Cabot and Agrimark are designed to allow farmers to gain a share of the profits from downstream processing and sales of their products. While there are complaints by farmers about having to supply additional capital to the cooperative from time to time, they are undoubtedly better off for being able to earn the cooperative dividend in addition to the price received for their milk.

Interestingly this trend toward forward integration was foreseen and urged by Governor George D. Aiken, who observed in his classic *Speaking from Vermont* (1938): "The only safety for dairymen of our New England states lies in looking forward and planning for the time when they, by themselves or in cooperation with consumers, will distribute a far greater percentage of their own product in the city market than they are doing today." Now, half a century later, Vermont dairymen seem to be responding.

Another, smaller-scale example of farm integration – this time, backward integration – is the Windsor County Feed and Supply Company in South Royalton. In 1984, faced with the prospect of the last independent feed mill in Vermont going out of business, thirty Windsor County farmers put up $60,000 in equity to purchase the company. Now the farmers buy (from themselves, at competitive prices) a feed-grain mix which, unlike the mix sold by national feed corporations, is constant in component proportions regardless of fluctuation in the national feed-grain markets. By 1987 feed production had increased more than 25 percent, a $30,000 loan from the state had been paid off, and farmers had received their first small dividends.

Fifth: Whatever the source of the product, aggressive marketing has become essential to its success. A major part of the state's agricultural-development strategy is its strong emphasis on marketing. The strategy includes greater use of the Vermont Seal of Quality, technical marketing assistance for small food-processing businesses, promotional campaigns and themes, agricultural processing facilities, export-market penetration, and support of local farmer's markets and pick-your-own operations. In due course shire brands will gain market acceptance, much as Vidalia (Georgia) onions and Deaf Smith County (Texas) wheat have done.

Sixth: Farmers' cooperatives have proven merit as ways of increasing returns to individual farmers. The dairy cooperatives in Vermont are large and highly capitalized, but co-ops in other areas often need organizational, management, and financial support.

Vermont Northern Growers Cooperative (VNGC), based in East Hardwick, is a good example of a young cooperative struggling to gain a foothold in a specialized market – in this case, carrots, cabbages, squash, radishes, and beets. These crops are customarily grown by hand on an acre or so – an enlarged family garden. As a result harvesting is labor-intensive, and it takes a lot of farmers to produce the volume of vegetables to make the marketing cooperative feasible. So

VNGC raised new capital to purchase a Swiss-made carrot-harvesting machine – for lease to members – to harvest carrots from the co-op's own seven-acre field.

Another growing cooperative is the Deep Root Cooperative in Westminster, which sends organically grown Vermont produce to Boston twice a week for sale at natural-foods and speciality stores. The Vermont Natural Pork Farmers Cooperative and the Yankee Shepherd Cooperative (lamb) are others. A key consideration for such co-ops is the complexity of marketing their equity shares, which can consume vast amounts of time and legal fees. Making the process of share issuance quick and simple would be a real aid to smaller cooperatives. Again, despite considerable progress in recent years, small cooperatives often face serious lack of interest at conventional lending institutions, a problem which the old-line Farm Credit System's Banks for Cooperatives have been slow to confront. The private Cooperative Fund of New England, based in Randolph, has tried to fill the gap, with promising results but limited capital.

Seventh: Vermont needs an active strategy for import replacement in food. According to a report on "The Vermont Food System: Toward a Traditional Self-Reliance" (written by Richard Tarlov of Plainfield for the Rodale Press' Cornucopia Project in 1984), Vermonters import 73 percent of their food from out of state. The value of this imported food is $370 million, of which $19 million represents trucking costs. The study showed that Vermont imports 98 percent of its beef, 91 percent of its carrots, 95 percent of its onions, 64 percent of its potatoes, and even 43 percent of its apples, though it is a major apple-producing state. These imports are in spite of the fact that all these products and more could be reasonably well produced in Vermont.

Now there is obviously a danger in going overboard to create an autarkic, inward-looking food economy, as Japan has done for rice and Switzerland for dairy. There is no point trying to coax oranges, avocadoes, and coffee beans out of Vermont's soil and climate, or in competing with efficient Midwestern grain producers on rocky Vermont hill farms. Even so, however, there is considerable room for strengthening the Vermont agricultural economy, and the Vermont economy generally, by getting Vermonters to consume more home-grown products.

A major obstacle to this has been consumers' insistence, spawned by national advertising, on "perfect," uniform vegetables. While such vegetables, puréed into baby food, would be indistinguishable in nutrition and flavor from irregular vegetables, consumers have developed the habit of thinking of them as inferior. Thus vegetables grown by major agribusiness corporations on broad, flat, well-drained farmland (such as the federally-subsidized irrigated areas in California) appear on Vermont shelves, while locally grown vegetables are confined to the farmer's market.

Another obstacle to developing a market for Vermont produce has been the relative absence of local canning facilities, where local produce can be put into cans for store sale. Efforts to fill this gap—in Shelburne, Berlin, and Barton—have either collapsed, been limited to the Mason-jar, home-use market, or turned toward high-priced gourmet items. Without a strong consumer market for locally grown food, canneries will not flourish, and without canneries consumers will rarely see locally grown canned (or frozen) foods where they shop. This is a chicken-and-egg dilemma badly in need of a creative solution.

Vermont is a major customer for Midwestern feed grain. In recent years the possibility of partially escaping that dependency has opened up with the development of low-alkaloid lupin. Unlike the high-alkaloid wild lupin seen along New England roadsides, low-alkaloid lupin can be processed directly into cattle feed simply by grinding. It has a relatively high protein content (35 percent, compared to 49 percent for soybean mash) but costs about half the price of soybean mash delivered to New England. The ground lupin can be used to replace soybean mash for 20 percent of a dairy-feed ration and can be fed directly to poultry and maybe pigs. Lupin grows well in a cool climate and slightly acidic soil, making it very attractive for New England. It also returns nitrogen to the soil, which makes it a good rotation crop for corn and potatoes.

In 1986 a biochemist in Illinois developed a process for converting chopped cornstalks and wheat straw to animal feed. The process dissolves the lignin in the plant fibers to allow animals to digest high-carbohydrate cellulose. The main ingredient in the process is hydrogen peroxide, which is manufactured commercially through electrolysis. While the economics of the conversion are not yet fully determined, such a process ought to open the door for greater production of animal feed within the state and region.

Eighth: The Vermont dairy industry should consider becoming an energy producer as well as a milk producer. The Foster Farm, in East Middlebury, has been the prototype. There manure from its 600 cows is dumped into a tennis-court-sized concrete digester which generates methane gas. The gas is drawn off to power a 150-kilowatt electric generator which sells power to the Central Vermont grid. The remaining sludge is separated into dry, odorless solids which are used for cattle bedding, and a nitrogen-rich liquid which is piped out to the cornfields. Bob Foster reports that so far the system has more than paid for itself ($300,000 at 14-percent interest) when the avoided cost of handling manure in other ways, and the fertilizer value of the effluent, are taken into account.

A similar but much larger (750-kilowatt) plant was proposed for the town of Addison in 1983 by Vermont BioElectric Corporation, which had designed the Foster plant. This plant was designed to accept manure from 7,000 cows. An additional feature was the proposal to use the waste heat from the methane digester and engine to heat an agroponic greenhouse for growing market vegetables year-round. Unfortunately the project foundered on a dispute over the price Vermont utilities would have to pay for the power under federal law. The obvious way to avoid this problem is to make use of either the methane heat energy or the generated electricity right on the farm.

One way of doing that would be to link the methane system with an ethanol-production system. Such a system has been put in place at a farm in Granton, Wisconsin. There the methane is burned to distill corn mash into grain alcohol, which is then used as tractor- and truck fuel. Like the dried sludge from the methane process, which makes animal bedding, the residue from the ethanol distillation (DDG: "distiller's dried grains") is of real value as an excellent animal feed. It can also be made into 40-percent-protein "renewed wheat" for human consumption, in a process developed by two Lambert, Montana, housewives over their kitchen stoves. The ethanol-production process also yields carbon dioxide, which would be a welcome addition to a methane-heated agroponic greenhouse. Other high-tech breakthroughs include room-temperature superconductivity storage for electricity, advanced flywheel storage, and high-capacity rechargeable-battery-powered farm equipment. These would allow an energy-producing farmer to market his product directly to nearby farmers and consumers without having to deal with the electric-power companies.

To implement these processes on a scale large enough to make a substantial difference in the incomes of Vermont dairy farmers, a number of obstacles will have to be overcome. The engineering and economics of the most efficient processes must be reduced to a cookbook for farmers, updated periodically as more experience is gained. A cooperative for buying needed equipment in large quantities at volume-discount prices ought to be considered. The development of automated, computerized control systems, which would minimize the farmer's management time, is important. The removal of the usual regulatory barriers—or an agreement on the price of farm-generated electricity to the utility—would also help matters along. The result would be that farmers would both replace costly imports (electricity, tractor- and truck fuel, fertilizer) and produce new export crops (gasohol and electricity).

Ninth: A major new effort should be made, through the University of Vermont and its research stations, to promote the benefits of "low-input" agriculture. A growing body of experience on the farm shows that while low-fertilizer, low-herbicide, no-till cropping may result in lower gross sales per acre, the net revenue per acre is significantly higher—and often is produced with a lot less time and labor. The epitome of low-input farming is the Pennsylvania Amish. They traditionally operate well-diversified farms with horse- or mule-drawn implements. Amish farms average seventy-five acres and produce milk, alfalfa, hay, wheat, feed corn, vegetables, fruits, and sometimes tobacco. The Amish use tested methods for crop rotation, manuring, and erosion control and add a large dose of mutual aid. They produce as much corn per acre as large Iowa farms, and as much milk per cow as Wisconsin dairy farms. Typical gross sales are $125,000, with a family netting from $25–40,000 a year. Widespread farming in this way would obviously require a lot of cultural changes, a lot of commitment, and a critical mass of farmers for mutual support, but the Amish have proven it can be done successfully.

Publisher Robert Rodale has been the prophet of "regenerative agriculture," an agriculture based on working with nature instead of trying to overpower it. In the pages of Rodale's *New Farm* magazine are innumerable success stories of farm flexibility, minimizing the use of nonrenewable inputs, new crops (notably amaranth), soil improvement, and local agricultural self-sufficiency. Over 70,000 people now belong to Rodale's Regenerative Agriculture Association. Under legislation championed by Vermont Senator Patrick Leahy (now chairman of the Senate Agriculture Committee), USDA, traditionally hostile to organic and low-input agriculture, will have to commit some significant research resources away from designing massive mechanical pickers for ethylene-gassed, baseball-hard, pink tomatoes and toward intelligent application of low-input, efficient agriculture. The University of Nebraska has reported enormous enthusiasm among conventional farmers for information about low-input farming. At UVM, a new B.S.A.A. (Bachelor of Science in Alternative Agriculture) degree curriculum has been launched under the direction of Professor Bill Murphy. It includes special courses in organic agriculture, small-woodland management, ecology, energy alternatives, small-business management, sustainable agriculture, and "alternatives for Vermont agriculture."

Tenth: As farmland becomes more desirable for nonfarm development, its fair market value increases, even though its value as a farm, measured by the cash return on farming, remains relatively constant. This means that farmers in developing areas will face steadily increasing rates of property taxation without being able to generate the income required to pay their higher taxes. Ultimately such farmers will almost certainly have to sell for development. Of course when they do so they will reap a very large windfall cash return – but they will be out of farming, and so will their land.

From the standpoint of protecting Vermont farming, some way needs to be found to counter this problem. To be economically sound it should advance income to meet the property-tax payments while the farmland is increasing in value, and recover the income advanced when and if that increased value is realized at the sale of the farm for development. As early as 1970, when a development boom was driving up land prices for farmers (and others), legislators were beginning to address this question.

Programs for relieving the property-tax pressure on operating farms should be consolidated and improved. There are now four such programs in Vermont, overlapping in terms and conditions. The creation of a single state land trust – proposed by State Representative McClaughry in 1972 – would make for a cleaner, more understandable program. (That bill was later published in the *Harvard Journal on Legislation* as a model bill for the nation.)

The various tax-relief programs adopted by the Vermont legislature since 1972 generally allow the owners of qualifying farm- and forestland to elect to have their land taxed on the basis of "use value" by their towns. The state then reimburses the town for the difference between the use-value taxation and the higher fair market value taxation that would have been imposed absent the program. While this approach is economically correct, the use-value-subsidy idea has a number of problems. The most obvious is that it puts the state and town at odds over the amount the state must pay on behalf of the farm. The town naturally wants as much as it can get, and there is thus a temptation for it to inflate the fair market value of the property. The state wants to pay as little as it can get away with and thus has an incentive to contest the fair market value appraisal and also to overvalue the use value to minimize the difference. The lien provision in one of the state programs shows up on the farmer's net-worth statement as an offsetting debt to the value of his land, and, psychologically, causes him to resent the state's having a string on something he regards as wholly his. Finally the program is only funded to the extent the legislature chooses from year to year, which can make for uncertainty in times of budget deficits.

Our proposed State Land Trust Act achieves the same ends in a more effective way. Under it the trust (a state-created corporation) is funded by the assignment of receipts from the general property-transfer tax (we proposed 1 percent of the sale price in excess of $10,000). Thus in periods of active land sales – the periods in which property taxes on farmland will be rising sharply – the revenues will accumulate to finance the land trust program.

In operation the state land trust offers to lease (not buy) the development rights on qualifying farmland. The price of the lease is the product of the local tax rate and the value of the development rights, as determined by rural land appraisal commissions. The farmer pays full taxes to the town on the fair market value of the farm. The lease payment to the farmer from the land trust covers the amount due for the development-rights portion, and the farmer himself supplies the remainder, representing the tax due on the use value. If the land trust should default on its lease-payment obligation, the farmer would regain the development rights without penalty.

If the farmer wishes to recover the development rights – for instance, to be able to sell his land for nonfarm uses – he may do so by paying a lease-termination price equal to half the capital gain enjoyed by the property while under lease, to a maximum of five years' lease payments with interest.

While the economic effect of the plan described is not materially different from the existing Vermont programs, the proposed land trust has several advantages. The trust is an institutionalized program with a permanent source of funding. While a town could impose taxes on the development rights at a value higher than that determined by the

257

independent rural land appraisal commissions, it would be the farmer, not the trust, who would have to pay the difference; thus it remains in the interest of the local taxpayer to resist overvaluation, and the state (i.e., the land trust) does not find itself in confrontation with town appraisers. Also the leasing of development rights by the trust makes those rights into income-producing property for the farmer. Finally there is no lien on the farmer's balance sheet. (The balance sheet, however, ought to reflect the value of the development rights only after the lease-termination price is paid.)

The draft legislation also proposed that the state land trust provide technical assistance to community land trusts throughout the state. Since the bill was first proposed, the private Ottauquechee Land Trust, based in Woodstock, has evolved into a Vermont land trust, and has become a major land-holding organization. The small town of Goshen has created its own municipal land trust. Others are bound to appear.

The legislature failed to give serious consideration to the Vermont Land Trust Act in 1972, and failed again when it was reintroduced in 1973 and 1975, for four major reasons. The state land trust was built upon the relatively unfamiliar idea of separating farmland development rights from the underlying land, and Vermont farmers, unlike their counterparts in Connecticut and on Long Island, had never contemplated that possibility. In addition the state Farm Bureau during that period was championing a competing proposal which would have provided that taxes on farmland could not be increased more than 5 percent a year (a foolish idea, which failed of passage). The environmental organizations, which were strong on farmland protection, preferred to achieve that goal by their usual technique of imposing police-power controls. The fact that such police-power approaches as zoning for farm use simply extinguished a large portion of the farmer's capital value, his borrowing power, and his retirement security was not of great importance to them. Finally the land trust's premise that development rights ought not to be extinguished by government fiat, but rather should be treated as a possession of economic value, ran counter to the environmentalists' thinking that state confiscation of the right to develop had nothing to do with any "taking" of property values.

The provision for state purchase of farm development rights adopted in 1988 finally recognizes that development rights are property interests with economic value.

There is probably no objective reason why a private land-investment corporation could not enter into a similar arrangement with a farmland owner. Such an agreement would provide in effect for an annual option payment by the corporation to the farmer, approximately equal to the taxes on the land's development value, in return for an option to buy the farm at some time certain at a specified price. The farmer would be relieved of tax pressure, and the corporation would take possession of the farm at the end of the term. The final buy-out price could be paid in the form of a retirement annuity for life. This might be particularly attractive to an older farmer planning to retire. On the other hand a Vermont farmer might view this as a Faustian bargain, and the corporation might be reluctant to enter into an agreement which puts the risk of changing land-market conditions and price levels on the corporation for a lengthy period into the future. The corporation might end up with choice development property at a low price, or an overpriced piece of land in a location of low demand.

These ten points may not add up to a complete plan for the promotion of Vermont agriculture, but they would certainly go a long way to ensure that the spirit of agriculture so long associated with Vermont will have its best chance to survive as a living force in the lives of Vermont's people.

Chapter 15

No State
Is an Island

*But even as we emphasize the importance of
the small, human scale community, we must
continually recognize and affirm that we are
citizens of the planet, with responsibilities
to others throughout the world.*

— Transformation Platform,
New World Alliance

VERMONT is not burdened with the baggage of an older
period — massive urban-industrial sectors with their calcified
institutions, attitudes, and vested interests. As a result Vermonters are magnificently situated to participate in a seething movement of subnational networks which can transform relationships
between peoples everywhere.

As Vermont shows the world how liberty and community can be
achieved in its shires, towns, and villages, its example will flow to the
four corners of the globe, and Punjabis and Bantu and Quechua and
Azerbaijanis will take inspiration from our achievements. They will
see, nestled in the Green Mountains of North America, a small, proud
state which has made the yearned-for ideals of decentralization,
democracy, human scale, citizen responsibility, and true human liberty come to life. And, with our help, all people will take new heart
in their age-old struggle to achieve those same goals.

That is why the shires must *not* become what Richard Sennett calls
"communities against the world." The search for human scale is not

the search for the barricade; it is not the us-against-them communalism that typified many attempts to build new societal enterprises in the 1960s. Indeed all over America little governments are stepping out into the world as part of a growing awareness of the need for a profound reduction in the size of the institutions of global relations. Vermont can take the lead in this process.

What is needed are small polities that can democratize foreign policy, that is, bring global questions to the level of human scale. What is needed are internationally involved governments that are closer to the people and that have, nevertheless, enough structural credibility to give their long-term policies political clout. What is needed is something like a little American state that has the self-confidence to entrust its localities with day-to-day governance so it has the time and energy to take world affairs seriously. What is needed is what Vermont will be as a federation of shires.

Vermont has been remarkably active beyond its own borders ever since its beginning. During the Revolutionary War a British agent approached Ethan Allen on the main street of Arlington, inviting him to enter into negotiations with Sir Henry Clinton pointing toward a separate peace with the king. At that moment the Republic of Vermont began to develop its own foreign policy.

What happened between the Allens (Ethan's brother Ira led the negotiations) and General Frederic Haldimand, commander of British forces in Canada, is of little practical importance, for the American victory at Yorktown settled the matter. But in the course of these then-secret talks, Ethan penned one of his celebrated letters to the president of the Continental Congress. He did not admit that negotiations with the British were actually underway, but he made clear the right of Vermont to pursue its best course:

> I do not hesitate to say I am fully grounded in opinion that Vermont had an indubitable right to agree on terms of cessation of hostilities with Great Britain, provided that the United States persist in rejecting her application for union with them; for Vermont, of all people, would be the most miserable were it obliged to defend the independence of united claiming states; and they, at the same time, in full liberty to overturn and ruin the independence of Vermont.

In that declaration one can find an early signal of Vermont's independent action which has never been fully extinguished. It reappeared when Vermonters openly disobeyed the Embargo Act of 1807 and passed resolutions against it in their town meetings that caused President Jefferson to write years later that he had "felt the foundations of government shaken" in a manner that could "overrule the Union." It flashed again when Vermont Supreme Court Justice Theophilus Harrington refused to hand over runaway slaves under the Fugitive Slave Act, demanding a "bill of sale from the Almighty," and again when in 1856 the Vermont legislature appropriated $20,000 for the free-state forces in Kansas and sent southward resolutions condemning slavery. The Georgia legislature was outraged:

> Resolved, by the General Assembly of the State of Georgia, that His Excellency, the Governor, be and is hereby requested to transmit the Vermont resolutions to the deep, dank and fetid sink of social and political iniquity from whence they emanated, with the following unequivocal declaration inscribed thereon:
> Resolved, that Georgia, standing on her constitutional palladium, needs not the maniac ravings of hellborn fanaticism, nor stoops from her lofty position to hold terms with perjured traitors.

Later in the century when the United States sent marshals to prevent an Irish army from organizing in Vermont for an attack on Canada, Vermont ignored the marshals. In 1870 two thousand Irish Fenians charged across the border into Canada from Vermont soil.* In 1917 the Vermont legislature appropriated $1 million to do battle against Germany – before the United States had declared war. The state's largest newspaper, the Burlington *Free Press*, editorialized that if Vermont did insist on financing a war against Germany independent of the United States, it should at least provide the money by raising taxes, not by floating a bond. In 1941 Vermont acted much in the same way in what has been interpreted as a declaration of war far in advance of Pearl Harbor.

In more recent years Vermont has demonstrated a remarkable inclination to think outwardly on both a subnational and international plane. It pioneered the first interstate school district, helped create

---

*At one point during an earlier eruption of the Irish issue in Vermont, President Van Buren found it necessary to send General Winfield Scott to end the uprising. He arrived at St. Albans during a meeting of the "Patriots" (as anti-British forces were called). Historian Ralph Nading Hill reports that Scott "cautioned the citizens not to flout the neutrality laws. Ignoring the general, an irate assembly recorded 'that as friends of liberty and human rights we cannot restrain the expression of our sympathy when we behold an oppressed and heroic people unfurl the banner of freedom.' "

the TriState Lottery (Maine, New Hampshire, and Vermont),* supported the Connecticut River Basin Commission, joined with New York to protect Lake Champlain, and negotiated with Canada for electrical power.

On the nongovernmental level Vermonters created the annual Burlington International Games (with Burlington, Ontario) and their own small-scale Vermont analog to the Peace Corps. The School for International Training (Brattleboro), the St. Michael's College program for language training (Winooski), and Middlebury College's Breadloaf Institute programs for advanced foreign-language instruction (Ripton) have won national attention. The Japan Society of Vermont has worked aggressively to generate Japan–Vermont business and cultural exchanges.

And Vermont's private sector is increasingly involved in international trade. Many of Vermont's leading firms are now owned by foreign investors, chief among them Tsubaki (Bennington), EHV Weidmann (St. Johnsbury), and even the venerable Vermont Marble Company (Proctor), once the spawning ground of governors and the citadel of Republican political power. Obviously Vermont's industrial giants, General Electric (Burlington and Rutland) and IBM (Essex Junction), are very much attuned to conditions in the world marketplace.

The most recent expression of Vermont's world-mindedness was the nuclear-freeze-resolution movement of the early 1980s. For several years Vermont town meetings debated various calls for an end to the nuclear-arms race. Then in 1982 over 180 Vermont town meetings passed nuclear-freeze resolutions. It is hard to name a wider, more coherent, yet basically localized expression of global awareness by an American state in this century. The importance of the votes was exaggerated, although the nation did pay attention for a time. But the point is that the soil of cosmopolitanism was rich enough in Vermont to allow a network of activists to persuade the people of 180 towns to speak out on an issue of current international importance.

Vermont's tradition of world involvement will find support in the movement for subnational activity that is bubbling up all over America. By 1985 Michael Shuman of the Center of Innovative Diplomacy in California was writing a handbook called *Building Municipal For-*

---

*A program which openly and with pride impoverishes the many to enrich a few.

eign Politics. New Options reported on Shuman as follows:

> Shuman's practical side is real, but it is fueled by an animating vision
> that entirely transcends present-day politics . . . the vision may be
> transcendent, but the logic is pure *realpolitik:* "By transforming rigid
> nation-against-nation conflicts into fluid alliances of cities, where
> cities will ally on some issues and disagree on others, there is a better
> chance of creating more complex global politics where no one dis-
> agreement can lead to war between large geographic blocs of nation-
> states. . . . By making communities a basic building bloc of inter-
> national diplomacy, we may be unmasking thousands of new poten-
> tial transnational alliances that current nation-state cleavages hide."

A single issue of *Municipal Foreign Policy* in 1987 reported that San
Francisco was voting on an ordinance to turn the city into a nuclear-
free zone, that Tucson, Arizona, had passed a resolution condemning
"the cruel and inhumane policies of Angola," that several states (including Vermont) were suing to prevent their National Guard units from
training in Honduras, that Jacksonville, Florida, had declared an Apar-
theid Awareness Day, that Detroit had "solidified" its sister-city relationship with Minsk in the Soviet Union, and that Duluth, Minnesota,
was moving to establish a sister-city relationship with Petrozavodsk,
also in the USSR. Indeed, Vermonters were in the vanguard in 1983
when they moved to associate the town of Brattleboro with a sister
city, Cherkessk, in the Soviet Union.

The movement to promote foreign policy at the municipal level
is not totally dominated by the Left. Soon after the city of Seattle created
its own Office of International Affairs, the city voters, by a margin of
fifty-five to forty-five, rescinded a city ordinance that declared Seattle a "city of refuge" for illegal immigrants from El Salvador and Guat-
emala. Ron Bemis wrote in the Washington *Times* that the vote was
a "remarkable example of the 'electorate speaking to its elected.'"

The Structure of Wider Involvement

In order to give expression to Vermont's own impulses and to take
advantage of the climate for global experimentation that exists outside Vermont, some state governmental structure is desirable even in
a shire federation. One function of the state will be to provide guidance and assistance to local initiatives, and under the shire federation the state will be empowered to take the leading role. The state's

activities will also be more focused on creative state-to-state interaction and bioregional efforts. Thus as the federal government bypassed the states in its urban policies of the 1960s and 1970s, Vermont will pioneer an interstate effort to bypass Washington in the 1990s and beyond.

Global and subnational activities will be handled by the Agency of Vermont Affairs, which will house the offices of Global Involvement, National Affairs, and Subnational Affairs.

The Office of Global Involvement

The OGI will be the catalyst and guiding hand behind a wide array of actions designed to involve Vermonters in an expanded global role. A prime responsibility will be the management and expansion of programs like Vermont's people-to-people project with Honduras, begun many years ago. It might also generate new linkages between Vermont (and its cities and shires) and states or regions of countries on other continents, from Swiss cantons to Liberian states to *voivods* in the Soviet Union. For example a shire council might come to the OGI to get help in creating a sister shire program with a Scottish county or a mountain valley in Tibet or an island in the Philippines. Burlington already has a sister city in Puerto Cabezas, Nicaragua, and Yaroslavl, in the Soviet Union. The mayor of Burlington, Bernard Sanders, led a delegation to Yaroslavl in the spring of 1988. At the state level perhaps Vermont should become a sister state with one of the USSR's "republics" (sic), like Estonia, perhaps the Soviet republic most similar to Vermont.*

The OGI might also administer or contract for the administration of the Vermont Service Corps, begun in 1983 to parallel the federal government's Peace Corps. It could facilitate and encourage a wide range of citizen-exchange projects, such as Vermont high-school trips to the Soviet Union. It could publish a monthly newspaper to keep the shires and interested citizens and organizations abreast of news and opportunities.

---

*As this book was going to press two events occurred which accent our argument. The Communist governing body of Estonia, a formerly independent Baltic republic, passed a resolution defying the authority of the Politburo in Moscow to issue directives opposed by the Estonian people. Now there's a republic Vermonters can understand! Not long after that, Governor Madeleine Kunin went off to visit the Soviet Union and declared that Vermont would become a sister state with the Karelian A.S.S.R., a sub-republic north of Leningrad, half of which was stolen from Finland by the Red Army in 1941. Who authorized her to make this choice in the name of Vermonters we don't know, but certainly the people of Vermont had nothing to say about it.

An example of a special project that OGI might want to support or emulate is the Transnational Network for Appropriate/Alternative Technologies. TRANET was started some years ago by William N. Ellis, a one-time World Bank consultant who now manages the organization out of the house where he was born in Rangeley, Maine. Initially its goal was to spread the word about useful small-scale technologies in Third World economies, such as an easily made low-tech machine to turn out a modest number of egg cartons, or water pumps, solar grain dryers, and methane digesters. Over the years TRANET has developed into a full-fledged information-exchange network for grassroots development groups on six continents. TRANET has been particularly effective in calling into question huge foreign-aid projects whose side effects are destroying the people supposed to be helped.

The OGI might be the agency for supporting a citizen involvement program modeled after Senator Mark Hatfield's World Peace Tax Fund Act. Under the analogous Vermont Global Involvement Act, income-tax payers could claim a credit of, for instance, 80 percent of the funds they contributed to any of a long list of eligible organizations active in world affairs. For every dollar contributed by a tax payer to his or her favorite organization, the state would in effect contribute 80 cents in forgone revenues, up to a ceiling determined by the legislature.

The list of eligible organizations would be composed by OGI, as urged by citizens wishing to donate, and would be approved by the legislature. Organizations that come to mind include: any global-involvement program adopted by a shire, and programs sponsored by OGI, Friends of the Americas (Honduras), Vermont Service Corps, CARE, Catholic Relief Services, Friends of Solidarity (Poland), Appropriate Technology International, Quest for Peace, Democratic Nicaragua Fund, Volunteers in Technical Assistance (VITA), Pan American Development Foundation, Inter-American Foundation, Ground Zero Pairing Project, United Towns Organization (France), Middle East Peace Project, International Foundation for Youth Exchange (IFYE), International Red Cross, International Organization of Consumer Unions (Malaysia), Amnesty International, Habitat for Humanity, and Pueblo to People.

As will quickly be seen, this representative list covers the entire political spectrum, plus an equally broad range of nonpolitical self-help and relief projects. The requirements for eligibility would be that the organization actually exist and that it not merely be a conduit for some other cause. Additionally it must work with real people in foreign countries as opposed to being a research, study, or propaganda organization. It must not be a political party, guerrilla movement, or purely religious body (although religious relief agencies would qualify). The list of eligible organizations would be included in the tax forms. A model might be the list of over five hundred organizations distributed to federal employees for the federal government's United Way campaign.

One of the consequences of such a tax-credit opportunity is the whirlwind of activity it would cause among the friends of the eligible organizations. The program would provide a motivation to organizations to canvass in search of support. In the course of such activity the organizations would doubtless discover large numbers of potential supporters and activists, and the competition might well spill over into healthy public debates on the merits of various organizations.

A final activity of the OGI could be the sponsorship of an annual Vermont Prize, an equivalent of a Nobel Prize for that person or organization in the world who has done the most to exemplify the ideals of Vermont: liberty, community, democracy, and human empowerment. The winner would be chosen by the legislature. There is already a similar prize, called the Alternative Nobel Prize, for people who have done worthwhile things along similar lines. It is administered from the Isle of Man and bears a sizable stipend. The city of Salzburg, Austria, to cite another example, presents its Golden Ring Award to citizens or natives who have made great contributions to Salzburg or to humanity at large – most notable among them the scholar and philosopher of human scale, Leopold Kohr, a Salzburg native. The Vermont Prize would be accompanied by a stipend to be used for the prizewinner's continuing activities. It should be slightly larger than the stipend for a Nobel Prize. The worldwide renown earned by such an award would make the expenditure well worthwhile.

The Office of National Affairs

The ONA, located parallel to the OGI in the Agency of Vermont Affairs, would function to make clear what the consequences of national policies will be on Vermont and to mobilize opinion in Vermont and nationally on behalf of the state's interest. It would gather information about the implementation of national policies – actual or expected – on Vermonters, and if necessary use that information to push other state governments and the Congress in a more desirable direction.

•

Witness: In 1974 in the wake of the 1973 OPEC oil-price increase, the U.S. Congress imposed the 55-m.p.h. speed limit on the states. The law was accompanied by a "cross-over sanction" (that is, "if you don't perform as told on *x*, we'll withhold money for *y*"): if a state failed to enforce the 55-m.p.h. limit to federal standards, an increasing percentage of federal highway funds would be withheld as a penalty. In 1984 and 1985 Vermont was assessed enormous fines by the federal government because over half of the vehicles on the state's major highways were traveling in excess of 55 m.p.h.

Let us pass over the shaky economics of the speed-limit theory and look at the actual effect on Vermont. Threatened with the loss of millions of dollars in federal highway funds – actually funds paid in gasoline taxes by motorists – the Vermont State Police were forced to move their cruisers up onto the interstates, and even on one occasion to hire a plane to improve their enforcement performance. Unfortunately the most serious policing problem in Vermont, according to the legislature, local officials, state police, and citizens alike, was not catching people doing 65 m.p.h. on the interstates, but catching drunks driving at any speed through villages and towns. (Another pressing need was for police patrolling on back roads, where summer camp break-ins are a chronic problem.)

Thanks to this federal edict Vermont could not deploy its law-enforcement resources to deal with the problems thought most serious by its people. It had to fit into a straitjacket engineered in Washington. The story is the familiar one of applying systems solutions to human problems. When the requirement was finally repealed in 1986, the legislature, with a better appreciation of Vermont priorities, promptly and overwhelmingly changed the interstate speed limit back to 65 m.p.h., and the troopers went back where they were most needed.

Another case: in 1943 the federal government, at the urging of certain garment workers' unions, established regulations which prohibited the making of various products at home for sale to a manufacturer. In the 1970s such firms as CB Sports (Bennington) and Stowe Woolens (Stowe) had organized extramural manufacturing programs in which Vermonters made ski caps in their homes. This was a happy arrangement, particularly for mothers of young children and senior citizens who could produce the caps on their kitchen tables at their convenience without incurring the costs of day care, transportation, and work clothing. Unfortunately the Vermont practice violated the 1943 regulations, and in 1980 the Labor Department took action to put a stop to it.

But the knitters, led by an articulate young mother from East Calais, Audrey Pudvah, fought back. The issue vaulted into the national news, igniting a wave of indignation at a heartless government which would deny these women the chance to work at home. Senator Patrick Leahy and Vermont Attorney General John Easton, and volunteers Tom and Mary Evslin of Montpelier, took up the knitters' cause. In Washington Reagan's secretary of labor, Raymond Donovan, and one of the authors, then on the White House staff, worked from the inside. After some setbacks in federal courts, Bill Brock, the new secretary of labor, was finally able to "free the knitters" in 1985.

•

In the new Vermont the Office of National Affairs will watch for just such travesties as they are concocted by Congress, the national bureaucracy, and interest groups in Washington. Under the direction of the legislature, the ONA will ascertain the preferences of Vermonters and the interests of the shires, back those preferences with sound data and hard argument, and set out to prevent or undo foolishness. Its methods will include working with Vermont's congressional delegation, sponsoring public-education campaigns, and promoting town, shire, and state resolutions and memorials. The ONA will be a genuine tribune for the people, and for the governments of the people. The idea is to use Vermont's size and clout (such as they are) not to preclude variety in domestic affairs *within* Vermont, but to insist on it *outside* Vermont, among the states.

Here, however, we come to a sticky wicket: how to draw the boundaries of the ONA's concerns? We are not proposing a state-funded lobbying effort for or against whatever policies happen to be desirable or repugnant to a majority of the legislature. Certainly nuclear war would have an adverse effect upon Vermont. So would the rampant spread of AIDS. Taking a position on issues such as national gun control or universal health insurance or the Strategic Defense Initiative would be highly controversial.

The primary role of the ONA will be action on behalf of the state in cases where real or proposed national policies would have a specific and disproportionate impact on Vermont (or northern New England). The home knitters targeted for extinction happened to be in

Vermont (and later, North Carolina), but not, so far as anyone knew, in forty-eight other states. The 55-m.p.h. speed limit was a little closer call – all the western states, for example, were up in arms about it – but Vermont did have a disproportionate amount of uncongested rural interstates where a higher speed limit was much more reasonable.

The ONA would doubtless be vigorously active in opposition to a Vermont nuclear-waste dump, but it would have no particular role in overall federal licensing of nuclear plants. Admittedly it will be difficult to draw a clear boundary line between Vermont-specific issues and national issues of interest to Vermonters, but with judicious legislative oversight a good effort can be made. On general philosophical issues the key is to allow Vermont to react when there is strong agreement within the state but to keep narrow majorities from representing the state when consensus simply does not exist.

The Office of Subnational Affairs

The OSNA will be composed of two bureaus, the Bureau of Bioregional Policy and the Bureau of State Relations. The first will deal with the growing need to tie state policy to regions that transcend state boundaries. Bioregionalism permeates the smallest community and the grandest nation. At a time when vision based on ecological union is needed, Vermont, like other states, is hamstrung by political jurisdictions. It must lead the way in doing something about that.

Vermont's greatest concern (at least for starters) is the two ecosystems that define its borders, the Lake Champlain Basin, which joins Vermont, northern New York, and Canada, and the Connecticut River Valley, which extends from the peaks of New Hampshire's White Mountains to Vermont's Green Mountains and feeds New England's principal waterway. Other regional linkages are the Hoosic River system tying Vermont to New York and Massachusetts, and a portion of northeastern Vermont (caught wonderfully by the title of Howard Mosher's book of short stories, *Where the Rivers Flow North*) marked by a quilt of forest, bog, and lake extending into Canada.

All textbooks on state and local government contain the requisite chapter on regional cooperation among the states. From the seaports of the east to the great river systems of the west, there are models of state cooperation. But the capacity to build bioregional policy has not kept up with the planet's need for it. A state bureau to coordinate and promote bioregional policies with other state and national jurisdictions will not only bring a sense of direction and purpose to what are now widely disparate efforts, it will provide bioregionalism with the authority and visibility it needs to break into major policy arenas in the United States and Canada.

The second bureau in the Office of Subnational Affairs is the Bureau of State Relations. It will deal with individual state governments on matters that are not defined by contiguous bioregional concerns. It might sponsor negotiations directly with New Hampshire to iron out difficulties involving weight limits for logging and cattle trucks, or open direct negotiations with Ohio on the issue of acid rain, or handle questions with New York involving transportation across Lake Champlain. We see this bureau as not only an arm of state policy but as a research-and-development group. Vermont works at these things now but usually on a hit-or-miss basis. We need more of it, much more, and we need efforts planned, co-ordinated, and funded through the kind of permanent structure only the state can provide.

Another function of the Bureau of State Relations will be to dramatically increase and improve the practice of innovation exchange between Vermont and other states. It has long been understood that the primary source of program innovation in any given state is the experiences of other states. But it is still amazing to behold the lack of information exchange that exists among the fifty states. It would be the role of the BSR, under directives from the legislature, to make sure that Vermont has access to America's experimental laboratories, the other forty-nine state governments. In this network would be organizations such as the Center for Federalism, the Council of State Governments, and the Advisory Commission on Intergovernmental Relations. Vermont's activities would go far beyond current practices—limited to networking bureaus of government research or policy institutes usually located in the university system. The BSR would be a strong and visible governmental office reporting directly to the governor on matters specified by the legislature.

These three offices—Global Involvement, National Affairs, and Subnational Affairs—which together make up the Agency of Vermont Affairs, will be a major component of the state government of the new Vermont. We see Vermont's expanded role in the world as an energetic, expansive, even aggressive one, committed to carrying Vermont's ideals of liberty, community, and decentralization across America and around the world. The new Vermont will exert a powerful force in the minds of men and women everywhere. Its energy to do this depends on giving the shires most of the responsibilities that the state now has.

271

It will be yet another salutary result of the creation of the shire federation.

What Role for America?

The extension of this book's thesis from Vermont to the United States as a whole calls for a new national order upheld and served by a strong central government. The model that drives Vermont must be applied to the nation. Vermont could never accommodate the internal revolution we are suggesting if it were not the strongest polity in America. Likewise the American polity must be strengthened, not weakened, so that over the next century it (like Vermont) can decentralize domestic functions while it concentrates on those activities peculiar to itself as a nation state.

It will take a strong America to stand aside and let Vermont do what none of the states has ever done. America will have to trust Vermonters as Vermonters trust themselves. Strong parents let their children experiment, learn, and develop. Weak ones oversee each and every activity – not, we suspect, to protect their children as much as to soothe their own fears and doubts.

If America will give us the running room we need, much will be gained. From the beginning we have argued that Vermont can serve as a demonstration project for the future. Rot in the trunk of governance spreads from lack of democracy at the roots. What the United States needs most of all is citizens – people trained in democracy on a human scale who can understand and judge the workings of a representative republic.

But there is another reward. Only by strengthening democracy at the periphery can America sustain it at the center. No one now seriously believes that Washington can fine-tune domestic policy the way it has attempted throughout most of this century. The reason to abandon centralism, however, is not only to make government programs work better, nor is it only to create real citizens from democracy's raw material at the local level. Decentralization is also needed to save the center. The national government needs to simplify and delegate and divest in order to rescue America's sense of *national* citizenship. It must return to what it does best – governing the nation, not the nation's parts.

In a brilliant essay written in 1973 entitled "The Decline of the American National Government," a leading student of federalism, Robert J. Pranger, argues that as truly national functions have waned, "the redemptive nature of broad national politics has been replaced by localism writ large or, better stated, by the nationalization of local politics." Pranger is concerned with "the disintegration of a nationhood capable of providing a base for the broad general will." It will be impossible to forge citizens in the politics of human-scale democracy if there is no object of national citizenship protecting that movement from above.

What is that object? What are the elements of the "broad general will"? Pranger puts the answer succinctly: "The purpose of the federal system of national unity in the United States has been to couple liberty and safety." We agree. A strong central apparatus is needed to guarantee fundamental human rights (i.e., preserve our liberty) and protect us from foreign attack and environmental meltdown (i.e., keep us safe). The single best thing Americans can do to make liberty and safety possible is to abandon what Barry Karl calls "the myth of the New Deal" in his book *The Uneasy State*. It was "a liberal reform crusade that was finally defeated by a conservative minority and it stands somewhere in the wings, waiting to reenter the stage. . . ." Karl argues eloquently that "an efficient centralization of political and economic power in the U.S." similar to the vision of the New Deal is incompatible with our commitment to democracy: "Our historical experience suggests both the dangers of such a centralization and the practical difficulties that stand in its way."

These "practical difficulties" have indeed caused Americans to abandon their confidence in the nation's institutions. The trouble was caused by two decades of unfulfilled promises, of hopes lifted and then dashed by a national government incapable of exercising the very power it so zealously coveted. Now Americans are ignoring national elections and beginning to treat the federal government with a flippancy that borders on disdain.

A new form of intolerance, "survivalism," is infecting the professional classes. While popular culture depicts the survivalist as a redneck toting an M–14 and a cluster of stolen grenades around his neck somewhere in the mountains of Tennessee or Idaho, we see a kind of unarmed, upper-middle-class survivalism emerging in Vermont. It is not paramilitarist like the blue-collar variety, but it does exhibit striking overtones of raw individualism. A four-wheel-drive vehicle, a satellite dish, plenty of fencing, and financial, social, and cultural linkages to some network far away allow for a planned estrangement from the human community – and not just the immediate community.

273

What Robert Pranger's thesis suggests, we believe, is that Americans are not taking to the hills or to their condos (or away from the ballot box) to avoid contact with locals. Rather they have lost faith in the things they have always expected from the *nation*: security and a sense of wholeness with the fundamentals of public life. They have turned away because the national government has grown too weak, not too strong. They miss the sense of national *well-being*.

In a review of *Habits of the Heart*, Dennis Hale borrows from de Tocqueville in an argument against pure individualism, claiming that: "The republican ethic is strained by the scale of modern politics, which has reduced the city and town – the natural loci of republican virtue – to subordinate roles within a huge, managerial society." Hale agrees that the "private economy is a source of liberty." But he continues: "Tocqueville also pointed out that the private and public economics of the West were moving in a centralizing direction. Huge centralized economic institutions would be a threat to liberty especially among an atomized, mass population that had lost the arts and manners of democratic life. Industrialism, individualism and anomie – this was the prescription for tyranny ... the *longing for community is natural, after all, and takes pathological forms only when frustrated* [italics ours]."

With only a minimal dose of imagination one can look upon the protected enclaves of young professionals, guarded by electronic moats in their high-rise apartments, and see the campfires of backwoods survivalists. Both groups have lost community memory and their loyalty to America is as fragile as an October milkweed. What would happen, one wonders, if the affluent young were forced to really *do* something useful to their local communities, or to the nation? Will they graciously yield a way of life (as indeed someday they well may have to do) that with every passing season convinces them still more thoroughly that luxury is necessity? To ask them to think in civic-humanist terms in regard to *America* will require a healthy sense of national citizenship. They will not likely respond if they feel "uneasy" about their country.

Americans no longer feel at ease because Washington has become fascinated with the techniques of governance. It is too busy worrying about how many people die on the highways, or whether or not teachers do their job well, or about the details of pothole filling, or public-welfare programs. As the nation has lost faith in the localities' abilities to handle such matters, so too have individuals lost faith in the nation's capacity to provide for the *general* welfare. We say again: there is enough work for everyone. If the national government does not entrust domestic functions to the states and communities, it will fail at its most important task, the maintenance of the *context* for a democratic civil order. And in heart and mind Americans will continue to drift away from the center.

During the next century America must emulate the Vermont shire federation: it must radically decentralize people-based policy while it redefines the general welfare in terms of safety and liberty. That includes protecting the planet's environmental integrity, defending liberal principles of civil rights and liberties, protecting against foreign attack, and promoting the conditions that will help ensure a prosperous economic system. It does *not* mean the elimination of life's natural risks. It does *not* promise a long life, or a good education, or cavity-free teeth. It means that while these things are provided at the local level, the basic stuff of civilization is furnished by America the nation. Providing for the general welfare means ensuring that Americans can go to bed at night knowing that there is a sense of order to things, one that is protected by their country.

If the central government could do *that* well and let us worry about the rest, it would be a profound improvement on the current condition. What would be the result, we ask, if Washington turned some of the genius it squanders every year doing things for others that they would rather do for themselves toward the study of world peace and the conduct of efforts to that end? The nation doesn't fail to work hard at peace because it doesn't care. It fails because it is too involved with those things that, when compared to nuclear holocaust, can only be labeled trivia.

Beyond the Twenty-First Century

Let us peer into the future. If our Vermont experiment succeeds and illuminates the world, what sort of world would we see?

We would see in that distant era not two or three or four giant superpowers battling for dominance but a planet of a thousand flags, Leopold Kohr's vision of a world of ministates, from Tonkin to Punjab to Estonia to Slovenia to Scotland to Costa Rica to, yes, Vermont. We would see agreements, treaties, councils, federations, every form of multipolity cooperation in pursuit of common ends. There may be wars, yes, because barring some radical change in human nature, conflicts will always arise among peoples. But those wars would be small wars, not wars which threaten human life on the planet. Perhaps those thousand polities will have the sense to create a peacekeeping organization which will make even those little wars unlikely. Clearly it is the case that the present world system, which features a pair of superflags waving over all the others, is incapable of keeping the peace. It is too easy to blame the United Nations. When the United Nations fails, it fails not because it has too many member nations. It fails because it has too few and because the difference between megastates and small ones destroys the logic of its charter and, indeed, renders the very name of this most hopeful institution a bitter oxymoron.

If such a world of a thousand flags is to develop, America must continue to demonstrate its great patience and fundamental morality in world affairs. Over the two or three hundred years it may take a new world to evolve, America will have to see to it that such a world system is capable of preserving basic human rights. It will have to provide for the protection of America's citizens and the citizens of other democratic societies from rogue nations and imperialistic empires. It will have to do more to help the truly poor populations of the world. By this we do not mean that we must still our capacity for the application of genius to the cause of human progress. But we do mean that we must learn to define progress in terms other than the accumulation of things that simply make life easier for Americans. We are squandering a good share of the world's resources on playthings. At the very least we will have to do much more to help the poor countries of the world learn how to achieve greater prosperity for their people, for there will be no peace in a world of a thousand flags when some are so very rich and others are so very poor.

No ordinary civilization could pull this off. No ordinary nation, no ordinary government would have the wisdom and the will to preside over the fashioning of a world that is dominated by its principles and not its power. It would take a nation much like a farmer we knew in South Newbury, Vermont, named Charlie Cole, who late in life continued to graft apple trees, full in the knowledge that he would never see them bear fruit. He died of a heart attack he knew was impending while helping build a stable on his son's farm. No nation has ever demonstrated the moral capacity of persons like Charlie Cole. It would take a near-perfect democracy to do so. It is only because America is still, at its core and despite its troubles, a democracy – a land governed by Charlie Coles – that there is any hope at all.

To provide space for the coming of such a new world of a thousand flags, we will need the commitment of the greatest nation in the history of the planet. That nation is called America. To prepare itself for this kind of world leadership perhaps America should return in its mind's eye to the pasture spring of its governance, its most perfect democracy. That democracy is called Vermont. And perhaps Vermont, in its quest to keep and improve its own democracy, will entrust itself more completely than ever to those who care for the apple trees, the common people in their communities assembled.

Chapter 16

Getting from Here to There

I hold it, that a little rebellion, now and then, is a good thing, and as necessary in the political world as storms in the physical.

—Thomas Jefferson

A T the very time America's democracy seems most endangered, one of its small quiet states is positioned to demonstrate how it can be rescued. For the first time since it became apparent that only radical change would save Vermont's democracy, it is clear that radical change is possible.

Vermont's politics is bubbling like early sap over a new-fired arch. Conventional two-party politics has become obsolete in our state. The success of Democrats at the polls in modern Vermont has been wrongly identified as a "realignment" of the party system. We are in an advanced state of party *dealignment*. Candidates of either party can win, but the parties themselves are rootless. For perhaps the first time in Vermont's history the largest body of voters are self-styled independents. The state is full of nonparty political organizations: the Vermont Greens, the American Freedom Coalition, the Rainbow Coalition, the Vermont Republican Assembly. Over the past two decades the state has been a seedbed of third-party and independent movements.

In this chaos there is hope for fundamental change, but now is no time for the faint of heart. A leading scholar of American democracy, Hanna Pitkin, has said it, and it's true: "governing and privileged strata" everywhere seek "to suppress the least sign of a genuinely democratic movement." Vermonters must recapture the legacy of progressivism bequeathed them by ancestors who fashioned the most liberal government in the New World in 1777. In it they will find the courage to act boldly.

The conditions for change in Vermont are ripe.

The key event was the election of 1952, when Democrats made a dramatic breakthrough in what has been called an "aftershock" of the New Deal earthquake. They vaulted onto a plateau far above the 20- to 30 percent of the two-party vote where they had been mired for a hundred years. Then they began to climb. In 1958 the Democrats won (briefly) Vermont's only seat in the House of Representatives. In 1962 they took the governorship. Neither event had happened since before the Civil War. In 1964 Lyndon Johnson carried Vermont, the first Democratic candidate for president ever to do so. In the next decade the Democrats captured the governorship again, a U.S. Senate seat, and the speakership of the Vermont House of Representatives. In 1984 the victor in the gubernatorial race was a Democrat, the Vermont Senate went from 17–13 Republican to 18–12 Democratic, and the House of Representatives elected another Democratic speaker. No other state in this century has changed its political complexion so completely, so swiftly.

But change has not been limited to the distribution of the two-party vote. Vermont ranked second in the nation in supporting the independent presidential candidacy of John Anderson in 1980. Burlington has the only socialist mayor in the country, Bernard Sanders. In 1988 Vermont, the whitest state in America, sent more delegates to the Democratic National Convention committed to Jesse Jackson than to any other candidate. Later that same year Mayor Sanders came within a whisker of winning Vermont's only seat in Congress. Given another week or two in the campaign, he might well have won. Walter Shapiro, a senior editor of *Newsweek* magazine, has written that Vermont is "arguably the most liberal state in America." Wrong. What he sees is that Vermont is clearly different and that what makes it different is not conservatism. The only word left is liberal, and it leaves images that are dead wrong.

The willingness to change is not limited to the new immigrants to Vermont. Many observers attribute the end of Republicanism to the arrival of new Democratic voters. Most of these observers, however, are wrong. The most important year for the Democrats in Vermont was

1952, before the newcomers arrived. Nor can one statistically stitch population increase in Vermont to improving Democratic fortunes. Newcomers to Vermont were not a displaced economic wave seeking new opportunity like the ethnics who came to American cities to fuel the New Deal Democratic breakthrough. Vermont's immigrants, rather, were generally quite well heeled and were as apt to vote Republican as Democratic. When Philip Hoff, Vermont's modern symbol of political change, won the governorship, the greatest increase in his votes over past Democratic totals came in the outback towns of the Northeast Kingdom. Vermonters liked this young Democrat that was "from away" (Hoff was from Massachusetts) and they voted for him.

There is a subtle intellectual snobbery among those who claim that it took outsiders to change Vermont politics. It is the kind of sniff rural people are used to from those who always have a better way and believe they have been ordained to bring enlightenment to the boondocks. Fox Butterfield, writing for the *New York Times* in 1986, came to Vermont, arched his eyebrows, and decided that without the influx of outsiders, Vermont would still be conservative and Republican. Many newcomers themselves are also only too happy to claim credit for Vermont's renaissance in partisan politics. Even close observers take the easy way out, accept the linkage between correlation and causation, and simply assert that political change was not indigenous to Vermont but was brought to the state by outsiders.

The most telling proof they are wrong is found in the work of Dartmouth's Richard Winters, one of the nation's leading scholars of comparative state politics. Interested in the vast policy differences between New Hampshire and Vermont, he observes: "Despite the similarity of region, ethnic composition, size and economy, the differences in the public choices of the two states are striking." For instance: "In 1974, after controlling for population, size and wealth, Vermont was the fourth highest and New Hampshire forty-fourth in total state expenditures among the fifty states." Among an extensive list of policy differences he notes that "Vermont has the third most progressive tax system, while New Hampshire's ranks forty-second." And "Vermont is a nationally recognized leader in environmental planning, pollution controls, land-use planning, bottle deposit laws, welfare rights and programs, social rehabilitation, and correctional programs."

And where does all this come from? From the progressive and elastic tax system in Vermont. While Winters credits (as do we) institutional forces and the presence of important personalities like Philip

Hoff, his essential point is that the genesis of Vermont's very progressive reputation can be traced back to the early 1930s. Vermont's "malapportioned legislatures passed an early income tax in 1931, changed it to a graduated income tax in 1947, and increased the graduated or 'progressive' quality of the tax three more times in the next ten years," notes Winters. All this occurred long before Fox Butterfield's agents of social change trooped northward into the hill country armed with their pocket calculators and rototillers. Winters concludes: ". . . current policies were shaped decades ago with the adoption of a state income tax." Understanding that native Vermonters themselves are perfectly willing to accept change is critical to an understanding of the new coalition that can be built to sponsor a new revolution in Vermont politics.

A New Coalition

There is in Vermont a powerful majoritarian agreement on human-scale governance, but it is split by partisanship, class background, and by one issue area, foreign policy. The populist "Right" combines believers in agrarian decentralism in the tradition of George Aiken, small-town working people, and a scattering of professional people who come to it ideologically. The progressive "Left" is epitomized by socialist Bernard Sanders, mayor of Burlington. No one knows for sure how his politics might run should he win statewide office. But to this point, by word and deed, Sanders has been the strongest supporter of local democracy among Vermont's leading politicians over the past decade. The Vermont Greens, who often have serious disagreements with Sanders, are also active. A growing number of decentralists call themselves Democrats. They are professionals, artisans, and intellectuals. It was this coalition that nearly elected Sanders in 1988.

Between the populists and the progressives are centrist "moderate" Republicans and liberals in the Democratic Party. The question is how to educate them while fashioning a strong, majoritarian coalition between the populist agrarians and progressive communitarians. Using one of the major parties would be difficult. Winning seats is their motive for being, and their perspectives are often controlled by policy differences manufactured outside Vermont. Republicans, for instance, take positions on foreign policy that the communitarian left will not abide. The Democratic Party presents another problem. It is too relentlessly centralist to accept democracy.

Democrat Madeleine Kunin, elected governor in 1984, is a case in point. On every single critical issue to come before the state in the last several years, she has favored authority over democracy, law over liberty, and control over empowerment. She is, simply stated, an elitist centralist – even more elitist and centralist than her predecessor, millionaire Republican industrialist Richard Snelling.

Using a third party to push a human-scale agenda has the appeal that third parties always have. They are fresh and free of historical baggage. Even their weak track record in Vermont might be discounted because, with the important exception of the Vermont Greens, who have built their global interests from local roots, third parties have been energized by national and international agendas. A new party formed on behalf of a *Vermont* agenda that sustains itself on the application of democratic principles at the local level and seeks local office first and statewide office second would be unique.

Another option might be a combination of third-party strategy with the principles of networking. This approach could be modeled after progressive and populist movements in Wisconsin, Minnesota, and especially the Non-Partisan League in North Dakota during the 1920s. Perhaps it is time to try this approach: apply modern state-of-the-art organizational concepts based on information exchange, and draw together a working coalition for one specific purpose – the radical democratization of the state. This would eliminate the necessity to agree on everything. The populist right and communitarian left will simply agree to disagree on the rest and work together for democracy.

•

Witness: During the summer of 1987 the governor of Vermont, with the support of business leaders, the Department of Education and its board, and other powerful forces for centralism tried to consolidate over three hundred locally elected school boards in a superstructure of about sixty-five boards.

But the commission named to develop the proposal ran into a hornet's nest during the public-hearing process. Not within memory has a proposed public policy met with more hostility. Nine different well-attended public hearings were held around the state, each lasting from two to three hours. Not one citizen rose to support the proposal, even after the commission had watered it down considerably. While there was some support for this or that part of the plan, one overwhelming message was heard, and only one: hands off our school boards. So vociferous was the opposition that the governor, who had named the commission, pulled the rug out from under it and its prestigious chairman, former governor Philip Hoff, even before the last public hearing, running for cover by announcing at a news conference that the consolidation plan was dead.

What is important in the controversy is that this most unanimous expression of grassroots public outrage came from the very left/right coalition we are talking about. People like Hoff, who had been fighting with courage and candor for the centralization of local government in Vermont ever since the 1960s, had taken on the traditional populist right before.* He and his allies knew Vermonters treasured their town meetings. They knew they would fight hard to protect their democracy.

But what Hoff and the rest of the committee had not expected was the appearance of people like T. Hunter Wilson and Dan MacArthur, members of the school board in Marlboro, or Nancy Cornell, school board member in Starksboro. They knew about democracy from the ground up. Their neighbors had entrusted them with the governance of their schools by election. Between the time Hoff was first elected governor in 1962 and 1987 something very important had happened. All over Vermont clusters of newcomers, "leftists," the bright young progressives who had flocked to Vermont in the 1960s and 1970s, had worked their way into the culture. They had become, well, like the natives. They were serving on school boards along with the woodchucks—the flatlander's term for native Vermonters. These people are the antithesis of the systems-axiom newcomers discussed earlier. They are the people who, aligned with large portions of the native population, form the core of the new coalition that can tip the balance of power in Vermont toward real democracy.

Standing before a large audience in a high-school auditorium in Bristol, her long hair and determination reflecting the 1960s, Nancy Cornell talked about how local school boards maintained the link between community and schools, how they worked to fashion communal enterprise. She struck an old chord—but one that rang true. She looked the commission straight in the eye and said, "What we do is good and," there came a pause, "honorable." "Honorable." The word hit the audience like a distant thunderclap. The word generally

---

*Those fair to Hoff must agree, however, that his abiding concern was not so much state control as it was regional control.

associated with patriotism, soldiers, flags, and nation had at last been used to describe what is truly good about America – its democracy. As Mickey Kaus of *Newsweek* has reminded us, "It's easy to forget that for the radicals of the '60s *liberals* were enemy."

Several weeks later T. Hunter Wilson and Dan MacArthur, of Marlboro, looking strangely like Butch Cassidy and the Sundance Kid, made similar points. Marlboro is a town of 695 people in the liberal southeastern corner of the state. Wilson, who lives on the land of his great-grandparents and teaches poetry at Marlboro College, has three children in the ninety-six-student Marlboro grade school. "There is a sense of community built around the functions of a local school," he informed the commission to consolidate school boards at one of its hearings. "It gives your children a sense of security, a sense of their own worth. That comes from having a really local school." Dan MacArthur followed. He is a builder who specializes in alternative technologies. There is a difference between a builder and a developer in Vermont. Said MacArthur: "The one thing that concerns me more than education is the erosion of the democratic principles of town meeting. Once you lose town meeting and your taxing power, you're through." His words, carried in the *New York Times*, marked the hinge between left and right in Vermont: the recognition that democracy is as important to education as education is to itself.

Both Wilson and MacArthur are quintessential Vermont communitarians. In conversations with one of the authors after the hearing, they proved to be strongly anti-Reagan and articulate advocates of U.S. disengagement in Central America. In economics they are for government redistribution of wealth. In civil liberties they are strongly individualistic and against the government's interference with personal decisions on moral questions. Like Nancy Cornell they speak for the new immigrants who have kept their eye on the Vermont dream – who *live* its potentials and have not taken the wrong road toward the technocentrist, systems way of life. People like Wilson and MacArthur showed up all over Vermont to stand shoulder to shoulder with Reagan Republicans and beat down a proposal to extinguish a good chunk of their democracy.

The reaction to the 1987 school-board-consolidation plan proved that a left-right coalition can be dominant in Vermont politics. It has taken awhile to form, but in a land like Vermont, political alignments, like the springtime, come slowly. Yankee politics is like Yankee friendship, cautious at first, growing deeper over time.

Going for It

A final meeting of the commission to consolidate Vermont school boards was called by the governor to thank its members for their effort and to talk about the future. The governor proposed what the defeated in politics often propose: if the people turn down a policy offered up front, sneak it in the back door, under cover of darkness, a step at a time when no one is looking. Members of the commission suggested a first step might be to strengthen the office of superintendent of schools. The governor liked that idea. It was "a good start in what would be a long process." There it was, incrementalism – the politics of deception.

Incremental change often seems the only way to achieve progress, but it often is the best way to achieve mischief. We believe it is no way to accomplish a democratic revolution. The best way is openness and honesty in governmental reform. We found such a model under the big sky of a state that exudes these qualities by nature.

In 1972 the state of Montana approved a new constitution. It contained perhaps the most radical call for change in local government in the history of the American states. Article XI, Section 9 said flatly: "The legislature shall within four years of the ratification of this Constitution, provide procedures *requiring* [italics ours] each local government unit or combination of units to review its structure and submit one alternative form of government to the qualified electors of the next general or special election." The legislature acted to establish in law the procedures for the "local government review process" as it was called. It also funded the 184 Montana counties and municipalities that took part, and it passed laws outlining: (1) optional forms they might choose (there were six described by statute, including town meeting and an option for a locality to write its own charter); (2) means whereby municipalities could merge, consolidate, confederate, transfer services, or disincorporate; and (3) processes allowing local governments to adopt self-governing powers if they so desired.

What Montana did was to *constitutionally mandate* the consideration of real change and empower the state legislature to guide events and create enabling legislation. The process took five years (1972–77). It was overwhelmingly successful in terms of the review process itself. Montanans really did take the time to assess their situation. Even though few actual changes took place, the process was a success, for its purpose was not to mandate change but to mandate the opportunity for it. Subsequently Montana amended a provision in the constitution that ordered every unit of local government to consider a change every ten years but left intact a mechanism whereby any county or municipality might do so, at any time, if it wished. A process of governmental self-review like Montana's might be used for Vermont.

Yet we feel even Montana's bold quest for creative localism is too conservative. Here's why. To begin with, unlike Montana's Constitutional Convention, we are calling for a basic restructuring of *state government* as well as local government. The Montana incremental approach will not work, since the agent of change, the Vermont legislature, will itself be undergoing fundamental restructuring. Secondly, in an across-the-board revolution such as we propose the complexities of implementation will overburden the circuits of public comprehension if the process is attempted bit by bit. Thirdly, revolutions cannot sustain themselves for long periods of time. Finally, Vermont must consider its future in holistic terms. To establish the shires without giving them real *power* would be worse than no change at all. To destroy the towns to create the shires would be likewise horrendous. The state's new role in external activities must be understood in *the context* of its reduced role in the shires' internal activities. With each component of the system tied to every other component, any attempt to change everything must be planned, coordinated, and synchronized. It must be done in one fell swoop. The trick is to plunge into it, satisfied that the theoretical underpinning is sound and sustained by the belief that we have the energy and brains to debug the system once it is in place.

You Can Get There from Here

The steps we propose to create a Vermont federation of shires are as follows:

Early 1990: The Vermont legislature will begin the process by appropriating funds for a study commission like Montana's to develop an amendment to the Vermont Constitution that would call for a constitutional convention to be convened in 1993 for the purpose of considering a new constitution for the state. Vermont currently has no method of amendment by convention, and its constitution is protected by a "time lock" – constitutional language that only allows amendments to the constitution to be proposed at four-year intervals. The time lock is set to open again in the 1991–92 session of the legislature. If an amendment is passed in this two-year session, it must then be approved by the "next elected legislature" – the 1993–94 session. Following that it must be approved by a popular vote of the citizens. The earliest an amendment to call for a convention to consider the shire system could be established would be the summer of 1993. The proposed amendment would describe the structure of the convention to be called, outline the process of electing delegates to it, and call for an appropriation from the legislature to fund it. The convention itself could convene in the summer of 1993.

The Vermont legislature will appropriate a sum of money to each town and city in Vermont to fund study and discussion until the convention meets in the summer of 1993. Bear in mind that the first debate would be about whether or not to approve the calling of a constitutional convention. This process would serve as a means of generating the intellectual resources needed to put a new state government in place. It would also help to mobilize people interested in running as delegates to the convention. It might of course stimulate enough negative reaction to elect anti-convention legislators to the 1991–92 session where they could kill the entire proposal. Obviously the question of what kind of government might emerge from the convention, if called, would be the primary focus of the discussion of whether or not to call a convention in the first place. The length of Vermont's amending process would thus be turned to good advantage, for if a convention is called, it will have been preceded by four years of thought. This will allow in-depth treatment of the question in a risk-free environment, since no decisions need be made until the convention meets. In this way the benefits of both the incremental approach to reform and the "damn-the-torpedoes-approach" may be had.

The Vermont legislature will establish a State Office of Constitutional Revision (again, after the Montana model) to provide technical staffing and research capacity for the review process. This office would mobilize civic organizations, coordinate and publicize the process through the publication of a newsletter, manage a speaker's bureau, activate and inform the educational establishment, and conduct debates and symposiums on the review process at the state level. This agency would also become the staff agency for the convention.

1991–92: The legislature approves the Constitutional Convention Amendment.

Early 1993: The legislature again approves the Constitutional Convention Amendment and puts the question to the voters.

May 1993: The people of Vermont go to the polls to decide whether or not to meet in convention to consider the creation of a new Chapter II of the Vermont Constitution, which will fundamentally alter their form of government. (We would leave Chapter I, declaring the rights and principles of free government, out of the revision process.)

July 1993: Election of convention delegates takes place. Some notion of geographical representation should be built into the process, and a residency requirement should be included. Vermont requires that a person survive a few winters before he or she can hope to understand the place. While any number of years is arbitrary, perhaps five would be acceptable.

Our recommendation is that every town and city choose one representative in an at-large election. This will ensure a rural voice at the convention. Also, every legislative district should elect a number of delegates equal to the number they now send to the House of Representatives. In this way 150 more delegates will be added from districts reflecting one person, one vote. The result will be a convention of 396 delegates.

August 1, 1993: The convention is held, perhaps in Randolph's Chandler Music Hall, in the geographical center of the state. The proceedings could be brought to the people via cable television.

The Remainder of 1993–March 1994: Debate over ratification of the new constitution takes place. The State Office of Constitutional Change is disbanded so that discussion of the final document may be as free of elite influence as possible.

Town Meeting Day, March 1994: The ratification vote takes place. Our recommendation is that the convention require a statewide majority vote to ratify (as is the current practice for amendments) but that it also require a majority vote to occur in three quarters of Vermont's towns and cities to ensure widespread geographical support.

January 1995–December 1996: The period of proto-shire realignment takes place, and the state government prepares to devolve many of its functions to the shires.

January 1997: Vermont's new federation of shires opens for business.

In one brilliant blaze Vermont will light the firmament of American governance and become a civic model for the rest of the world to envy and emulate. It will demonstrate how a politics of human scale can give expression to humankind's longed-for ideals of liberty and community, freedom and unity.

CHAPTER REFERENCES

1: Viewing the Pasture Spring

Hannah Arendt, *On Revolution* (New York: Viking, 1963).

Carl Becker, *Progress and Power* (Stanford: Stanford Univ. Press, 1935).

Wendell Berry, *The Unsettling of America* (New York: Avon Books, 1977).

Harry C. Boyte, *The Backyard Revolution* (Philadelphia: Temple Univ. Press, 1980).

Robert Frost, *North of Boston* (New York: Henry Holt, 1915).

Curtis B. Gans, "The Empty Ballot Box: Reflections on Non Voting in America," *Public Opinion* (September-October 1987).

Barry D. Karl, *The Uneasy State* (Chicago: Univ. of Chicago Press, 1983).

John McClaughry, "Populism for the '80s Gaining Momentum," *Human Events* (April 16, 1983).

Daniel Moynihan, *Maximum Feasible Misunderstanding* (New York: Free Press, 1969).

2: The Gods of the Hills

George Aiken, *Speaking from Vermont* (New York: Frederick A. Stokes, 1938).

Lord Bolingbroke, "The Patriot King," in David Mallet, ed., *Works of Lord Bolingbroke* (London: 1754).

Thomas Jefferson, Letter to Joseph Cabell, (February 2, 1816), in Adrienne Koch and William Peden, eds., *The Life and Selected Writings of Thomas Jefferson* (New York: Random House, 1944).

Richard Carlson, "Vermont's Heritage of Independence," in Peter Jennison, ed., *The 1976-77 Official Vermont Bicentennial Guide,* (Taftsville, VT: Countryman, 1976).

Walter Crockett, *History of Vermont* (New York: Century History Co., 1921).

George E. Howard, *An Introduction to the Local Constitutional History of the U.S.* (Baltimore: Johns Hopkins Univ. Press, 1889).

John F. Kennedy, Remarks to the Italian American Club of Boston, *Boston Post* (April 12, 1950).

Ronald Reagan, Speech to the Executive Club of Chicago, September 26, 1975.

3: The Leapfrog Theory

Ira Allen, *The Natural and Political History of the State of Vermont* (London: J. W. Myers, 1798).

Hal S. Barron, *Those Who Stayed Behind* (New York: Cambridge Univ. Press, 1984).

Murray Bookchin, *The Limits of the City* (New York: Harper & Row, 1974).

Judson Hale, *Inside New England* (New York: Harper & Row, 1982).

Ralph Nading Hill, *Yankee Kingdom: Vermont and New Hampshire* (New York: Harper & Row, 1960).

Charles A. Jellison, *Ethan Allen: Frontier Rebel* (Syracuse: Syracuse Univ. Press, 1969).

Harold A. Meeks, *Time and Change in Vermont: A Human Geography* (Chester, CT: Globe Pequot, 1986).

H. Nicholas Muller, III, and John Duffy, *An Anxious Democracy: Aspects of the 1830's* (Westport, CT: Greenwood, 1982).

Earle Newton, *The Vermont Story* (Montpelier: Vermont Historical Society, 1949).

L. S. Stavrianos, *The Promise of the Coming Dark Age* (San Francisco: W. H. Freeman, 1976).

Frederick F. Van de Water, *The Reluctant Republic* (Taftsville, VT: Countryman, 1974).

Harold Fisher Wilson, *The Hill Country of Northern New England* (New York: AMS Press, 1967).

4: The Promise of Democracy Denied

Wendell Berry, *The Unsettling of America* (New York: Avon Books, 1977).

Murray Bookchin, *The Limits of the City* (New York: Harper & Row, 1974).

Frank M. Bryan, "Town Meeting at Wounded Knee," *Window of Vermont* (Fall 1985).

Hanna Fenichel Pitkin and Sara M. Shumer, "On Participation," *Democracy* (Fall 1982).

Joshua Toulmin Smith, *The Parish* (London: H. Sweet, 1851).

E. B. White, *The Wild Flag* (Boston: Houghton Mifflin, 1946).

5: The Promise of Democracy Restored

F. Christopher Arterton, *Teledemocracy* (Newbury Park, CA: Sage Publications, 1987).

Benjamin R. Barber, *Strong Democracy* (Berkeley: Univ. of California Press, 1984).

Harvey Brooks, "A Critique of the Concept of Appropriate Technology," in Franklin A. Long and Alexandra Oleson, eds., *Appropriate Technology and Social Values—A Critical Appraisal* (Cambridge, MA: Ballinger, 1980).

Frank M. Bryan, "Hill Farm with Computer," *North By Northeast* (June 1988).

David Burnham, *The Rise of the Computer State* (New York: Random House, 1983).

Paul Ekins, ed., *The Living Economy* (New York: Routledge & Kegan Paul, 1986).

Amitai Etzioni, Kenneth Landon, and Sara Lipion, "Participating Technology: The Minerva Communications Tree," *Journal of Communications* (Spring 1975).

Jane Jacobs, *Cities and the Wealth of Nations* (New York: Random House, 1984).

J. C. R. Licklider, "Computers and Government," in Michael L. Dertouzos and Joel Moses, eds., *The Computer Age: A Twenty-Year View* (Cambridge: MIT Press, 1980).

Michael Malbin, "Teledemocracy and Its Discontents," *Public Opinion* (June-July 1982).

Jane J. Mansbridge, *Beyond Adversary Democracy* (New York: Basic Books, 1980).

John Naisbitt, *Megatrends* (New York: Warner Books, 1982).

Robert A. Nisbet, *The Quest for Community* (New York: Oxford Univ. Press, 1971).

Langdon Winner, *Autonomous Technology* (Cambridge: MIT Press, 1977).

_____, *The Whale and the Reactor* (Chicago: Univ. of Chicago Press, 1986).

6: The Shires: Goverment with a Human Face

Christopher Alexander, Sara Ishikawa, and Murray Silverstein, *A Pattern Language* (New York: Oxford Univ. Press, 1977).

Benjamin R. Barber, *Strong Democracy,* (Berkeley: Univ. of California Press, 1984).

Robert A. Dahl, *Dilemmas of Pluralist Democracy* (New Haven: Yale Univ. Press, 1982).

Robert A. Dahl and Edward R. Tufte, *Size and Democracy* (Stanford: Stanford Univ. Press, 1973).

Warren Johnson, *The Future Is Not What It Used to Be* (New York: Dodd, Mead, 1985).

Leopold Kohr, "Critical Size," in Michael North, ed., *Time Running Out? Best of Resurgence* (Dorchester, Dorset: Prism Press, 1976).

James Madison, "Federalist No. 14," in Alexander Hamilton, James Madison, and John Jay *The Federalist Papers* (New York: New American Library, 1961).

Virgil McCarty, "The Evolution of Vermont Counties," unpublished paper (Montpelier: Vermont Historical Society, 1941).

Kirkpatrick Sale, *Human Scale* (New York: Coward, McCann & Geoghegan, 1980).

G. Ross Stephens, "State Centralism and the Erosion of Local Autonomy," *Journal of Politics* (February 1974).

Douglas Yates, *Neighborhood Democracy* (Lexington, MA: D. C. Heath, 1973).

7: The Shires: Architecture for a New Democracy

Steven J. Brams and Peter C. Fishburn, *Approval Voting* (Boston: Berkhauser, 1984).

Jane J. Mansbridge, *Beyond Adversary Democracy* (New York: Basic Books, 1980).

Robert E. Pike, *Tall Trees, Tough Men* (New York: W. W. Norton, 1967).

8: Celebrating Shire Identity

Carl Bode, *The American Lyceum* (New York: Oxford Univ. Press, 1956).

Charles E. Merriam, *The Making of Citizens* (Chicago: Univ. of Chicago Press, 1931).

Harold F. Wilson, *The Hill Country of Northern New England* (New York: AMS Press, 1967).

9: The State Government: Doing Much Less, Much Better

John Lukacs, *Outgrowing Democracy: The History of the United States in the Twentieth Century* (New York: Doubleday, 1984).

Clinton Rossiter, *The American Presidency*, rev. ed. (New York: Harcourt, Brace, Jovanovich, 1960).

David Schmidt and Martin Peretz, Exchange of letters, *New Options* (October 1986).

10: Financing Shire Democracy

Advisory Commission on Intergovernmental Relations, *The Organization of Local Public Economies* (Washington: ACIR, 1987).

11: Education on a Human Scale

Roger G. Barker and P. V. Gump, eds., *Big School, Small School* (Stanford: Stanford Univ. Press, 1964).

Denis P. Doyle and Chester E. Finn, Jr.,

"American Schools and the Future of Local Control," *The Public Interest* (Fall 1984).

Faith Dunn, "Good Government vs. Self-Government: Educational Control in Rural America," *Phi Delta Kappan* (December 1983).

Stuart Rosenfeld, "Centralization Versus Decentralization: A Case Study of Rural Education in Vermont," in Jonathan P. Sher, ed., *Education in Rural America: A Reassessment of Conventional Wisdom* (Boulder: Westview, 1977).

Kirkpatrick Sale, *Human Scale* (New York: Coward, McCann, & Geoghegan, 1980).

Jonathan P. Sher and Rachel B. Tompkins, *Heavy Meddle* (Raleigh, NC: The North Carolina School Board Association, 1986).

Theodore Sizer, *Horace's Compromise: The Dilemma of the American High School* (Boston: Houghton Mifflin, 1984).

12: The Compassionate Community

"Community Care," brochure (Rochester, VT: Community Care, 1987).

Ralph Segalman, "Welfare and Dependency in Switzerland," *The Public Interest* (Winter 1986).

Gerald D. Suttler and David Street, "Aid to the Poor and Social Exchange," *Working Paper No. 110* (Chicago: Center for Organization Studies, University of Chicago, 1969).

13: People and the Land

George Aiken, *Speaking from Vermont* (New York: Frederick A. Stokes, 1938).

R. D. Benedict, "Ethan Allen's Use of Language," Address to the Vermont Historical Society (October 30, 1902).

Robert C. Ellickson, "Alternatives to Zoning: Covenants, Nuisance Rules, and Fines as Land Use Controls," *University of Chicago Law Review* (40; 1973).

Dorothy Canfield Fisher, *Vermont Tradition* (Boston: Little Brown, 1953).

Jan Z. Krasnowiecki and James C. N. Paul,

"The Preservation of Open Space in Metropolitan Areas," *University of Pennsylvania Law Review* (110; 1961).

Robert LaFollette, Address to the Farmer's Institute (March 19, 1902), in Ellen Porelle, ed., *The Political Philosophy of Robert M. LaFollette* (Madison, WI: Robert M. LaFollette Co., 1920).

John McClaughry, "A Model State Land Trust Act," *Harvard Journal of Legislation* (12; 1975).

_____, "The New Feudalism," *Environmental Law* (5; 1975).

Donald P. Nagel, "Half-Threats, Half-Promises," *North By Northeast* (June 1988).

Richard Tarlov, *The Vermont Food Systems: Toward Regional Self-Reliance* (Emmaus, PA: Rodale, 1984).

14: Vermont's Agricultural Future

George Aiken, *Speaking from Vermont* (New York: Frederick A. Stokes, 1938).

Robert LaFollette, Address to the Farmer's Institute (March 19, 1902), in Ellen Porelle, ed., *The Political Philosophy of Robert M. LaFollette* (Madison, WI: Robert M. LaFollette Co., 1920).

15: No State Is an Island

Ralph Nading Hill, *Contrary Country* (New York: Rinehart, 1950).

Ralph Nading Hill, *Yankee Kingdom: Vermont and New Hampshire* (New York: Harper & Row, 1960).

Charles A. Jellison, *Ethan Allen: Frontier Rebel* (Syracuse: Syracuse Univ. Press, 1969).

Barry D. Karl, *The Uneasy State* (Chicago: Univ. of Chicago Press, 1983).

Howard Frank Mosher, *Where the Rivers Flow North* (New York: Viking, 1971).

Earle Newton, *The Vermont Story* (Montpelier: Vermont Historical Society, 1949).

"1,000 Local State Departments?" *New Options* (December 23, 1985).

Robert J. Pranger, "The Decline of the American National Government," *Publius* (Fall 1973).

Richard Sennett, *The Fall of Public Man* (New York: Knopf, 1977).

16: Getting from Here to There

Mickey Kaus, "Confessions of an Ex-Radical," *Newsweek* (September 5, 1988).

Hanna Fenichel Pitkin and Sara M. Shumer, "On Participation," *Democracy* (Fall 1982).

Richard Winters, "Political Choice and Expenditure Changes in New Hampshire and Vermont," *Polity* (Summer 1980).

BIBLIOGRAPHY

Note: In a book of this nature, which necessarily covers two lifetimes of experience and scholarship, it is almost impossible to prepare a selected bibliography. Nevertheless, our intellectual debt is enormous so we have taken a stab at it. The following includes many sources cited in the chapter references plus those sources that have influenced our thinking in more general ways.

GENERAL REFERENCES

Advisory Commission on Intergovernmental Relations. *The Organization of Local Public Economies*. Washington: AICR, December 1987.

Agar, Herbert. *Land of the Free*. Boston: Houghton Mifflin, 1935.

Alexander, Christopher, Sara Ishikawa, and Murray Silverstein. *A Pattern Language*. New York: Oxford University Press, 1977.

Arendt, Hannah. *On Revolution*. New York: Viking Books, 1963.

Arterton, F. Christopher. *Teledemocracy*. Newbury Park, CA: Sage Publications, 1987.

Baldacchino, Joseph. *The Moral Foundation of Economics*. Washington: National Humanities Institute, 1985.

Banning, Lance. *The Jeffersonian Persuasion: Evolution of a Party Ideology*. Ithaca: Cornell University Press, 1978.

Barber, Benjamin R. *Strong Democracy*. Berkeley: University of California Press, 1984.

Barker, Roger G. and P. V. Gump, eds. *Big School, Small School*. Stanford: Stanford University Press, 1964.

Becker, Carl. *Progress and Power*. Stanford: Stanford University Press, 1935.

Bellah, Robert N., Richard Madsen, William M. Sullivan, Ann Swidler, and Steven Tipton. *Habits of the Heart*. New York: Harper & Row, 1985.

Berger, Lawrence. "A Policy Analysis of the Taking Problem." 49 *New York University Law Review* 165, 1974.

Berkowitz, Bill. *Community Dreams*. San Luis Obispo: Impact Publishers, 1984.

Berry, Wendell. *The Unsettling of America*. New York: Avon Books, 1977.

Bernstein, Blanche. *The Politics of Welfare: The New York City Experience*. Cambridge, MA: Abt Books, 1982.

Bode, Carl. *The American Lyceum*. New York: Oxford University Press, 1956.

Boles, Janet K. and Dorothy K. Dean. "Communities of Interest in Legislative Redistricting." *State Government*, Fall 1985.

Bolingbroke, Lord. "The Patriot King." In David Mallet, ed. *Works of Lord Bolingbroke*. London: 1754.

Bookchin, Murray. *Post Scarcity Anarchism*. Berkeley: Ramparts Press, 1971.

_____. *The Ecology of Freedom*. Palo Alto: Cheshire Books, 1982.

_____. *The Limits of the City*. New York: Harper & Row, 1974.

_____. *The Rise of Urbanization and the Decline of Citizenship*. San Francisco: Sierra Club Books, 1987.

Borgmann, Albert. *Technology and the Character of Contemporary Life*. Chicago: University of Chicago Press, 1984.

Boyte, Harry C. *The Backyard Revolution*. Philadelphia: Temple University Press, 1980.

Brams, Steven J. and Peter C. Fishburn. *Approval Voting*. Boston: Berkhauser, 1984.

Brooks, Harvey. "A Critique of the Concept of Appropriate Technology." In Franklin A. Long and Alexandra Oleson, eds. *Appropriate Technology and Social Values – A Critical Appraisal*. Cambridge, MA: Ballinger, 1980.

Brownell, Baker. *The Human Community*. New York: Harper & Row, 1950.

Bryan, Frank. *Politics in the Rural States.* Boulder: Westview, 1981.

_____. "Rural Renaissance: Is America on the Move Again?" *Public Opinion,* June–July 1982.

_____. "Town Meeting: A Rural Option for Urban America?" *National Civic Review,* December 1978.

_____. "Trouble in the Vermont Hills." *Newsweek,* March 13, 1984.

Burnham, David. *The Rise of the Computer State.* New York: Random House, 1983.

Calder, Nigel. *Technopolis: Social Control of the Uses of Science.* New York: Simon & Schuster, 1970.

Campbell, William F. and Andrew W. Foshee. "Communism, Statism: Is There a Third Way?" *Southern Partisan,* Winter 1985.

Carroll, James D. "The New Judicial Federalism and the Alienation of Public Policy and Administration." *American Journal of Public Administration,* August 1982.

Chapman, M. Perry. "The Mature Region: Building a Practical Model for the Transition to the Sustainable Society." *Technological Forecasting and Social Change,* February 1982.

Clark, Douglas H. "Canadian Experience with the Representative Tax System." *Intergovernmental Perspective,* Winter 1986.

Coe, Benjamin P. "The Circuit Rider Concept: Meeting the Need of Rural Communities Government by Part-time Public Officials." *Small Town,* January–February 1987.

Cousins, Norman. *Human Options.* New York: W. W. Norton, 1981.

Cunningham, Ann Marie, and Sharon Begley. *The Techno/Peasant Survival Manual.* New York: Bantam Books, 1980.

Dahl, Robert A. *Dilemmas of Pluralist Democracy.* New Haven: Yale University Press, 1982.

_____ and Edward R. Tufte. *Size and Democracy.* Stanford: Stanford University Press, 1973.

DeTocqueville, Alexis. *Democracy in America.* New York: Harper & Row, 1966.

Dillman, Don A. "The Social Impacts of Information Technologies in Rural North America." *Rural Sociology,* Spring 1985.

Doyle, Denis P. and Chester E. Finn, Jr. "American Schools and the Future of Local Control." *The Public Interest,* Fall 1984.

Duncombe, Sidney and Tony Stewart. "Idaho's Unique Approach to State Legislative Appointment: Statewide Floterial Districts." *State Government,* Fall 1985.

Dunn, Faith. "Good Government vs. Self-Government: Educational Control in Rural America." *Phi Delta Kappan,* December 1983.

Dunphy, Paul. "The Pastoral Paradox." *Harrowsmith,* May–June 1988.

Ekins, Paul, ed. *The Living Economy.* London: Routledge & Kegan Paul, 1986.

Ellickson, Robert C. "Alternatives to Zoning: Covenants, Nuisance Rules, and Fines as Land Use Controls." 40 *University of Chicago Law Review* 681, 1973.

Ellul, Jacques. *The Technological Society.* New York: Random House, 1967.

Etzioni, Amitai, Kenneth Landon, and Sara Lipion. "Participating Technology: The Minerva Communications Tree." *Journal of Communications,* Spring 1975.

Fiske, John. *American Political Ideas.* New York: Harper and Brothers, 1885.

_____. *Civil Government in the U.S.* Cambridge, MA: The Riverside Press, 1890.

French, William C. "Local Control Under Attack." *Government in the Classroom.* New York: Academy of Political Science, 1979.

Gans, Curtis B. "The Empty Ballot Box: Reflections on Non Voting in America," *Public Opinion,* September–October 1987.

Goodman, Paul and Percival Goodman. *Communitas.* New York: Random House, 1960.

Gould, Carol C. *Rethinking Democracy.* New York: Cambridge University Press, 1988.

Greeley, Andrew. *No Bigger Than Necessary.* New York: Meridian, 1977.

Hale, Judson. *Inside New England.* New York: Harper & Row, 1982.

Hatfield, Mark O. "Bringing Political Power Back Home: The Case for Neighborhood Government." 1 *Ripon Quarterly,* 1974.

Hawkins, Robert B. Jr., *Self Government by District: Myth and Reality.* Stanford: Hoover Institution Press, 1976.

Held, David. *Models of Democracy.* Stanford: Stanford University Press, 1987.

Himmelfarb, Gertrude. *The Idea of Poverty.* New York: Knopf, 1984.

Hobbs, Daryl. "Rural School Improvement: Bigger or Better?" *Journal of State Government,* January–February 1988.

Howard, George E. *An Introduction to the Local Constitutional History of the U.S.* Baltimore: Johns Hopkins University Press, 1889.

Institute for Contemporary Studies. *No Land is an Island.* San Francisco: Institute for Contemporary Studies, 1976.

Jacobs, Jane. *Cities and the Wealth of Nations.* New York: Random House, 1984.

Janowitz, Morris. *The Reconstruction of Patriotism: Education for Civic Consciousness.* Chicago: University of Chicago Press, 1983.

Jefferson, Thomas. Letter to Joseph Cabell, February 2, 1816. In Adrienne Koch and William Peden, eds. *The Life and Selected Writings of Thomas Jefferson.* New York: Random House, 1944.

Jencks, C. S. *Inequality: A Reassessment of the Effects of Family and Schooling in America.* New York: Basic Books, 1972.

Johnson, Warren. *The Future is Not What It Used to Be.* New York: Dodd, Mead, 1985.

Karl, Barry D. *The Uneasy State.* Chicago: University of Chicago Press, 1983.

Kaus, Mickey. "Confessions of an Ex-Radical." *Newsweek,* September 5, 1988.

_____. "The Work Ethic State." *New Republic,* July 7, 1986.

Kennedy, John F. Remarks to the Italian American Club of Boston. *Boston Post,* April 12, 1950.

Kindley, Mark M. "Little Schools on the Prairie Still Teach a Big Lesson." *Smithsonian,* October 1985.

Kingsley, James F. "Decentralization of Planning Power: A Giant Step Toward Excellence." *Management Review,* March 1984.

Kirst, Michael W. "The State Role in Regulating Local Schools." *Government in the Classroom.* New York: Academy of Political Science, 1979.

Koch, Adrienne. *The Philosophy of Thomas Jefferson.* Chicago: Quadrangle Books, 1964.

Kohr, Leopold. "Critical Size" In Michael North, ed. *Time Running Out? Best of Resurgence.* Dorchester, Dorset: Prism Press, 1976.

_____. *The Breakdown of Nations.* New York: E. P. Dutton, 1978.

Kotler, Milton. *Neighborhood Government.* New York: Bobbs–Merrill, 1969.

Krasnowiecki, Jan Z. and James C. N. Paul. "The Preservation of Open Space in Metropolitan Areas." 110 *University of Pennsylvania Law Review* 179, 1961.

Kropotkin, Peter. *Fields, Factories and Workshops Tomorrow.* London: Allen & Unwin, 1974.

LaFollette, Robert. Address to the Farmer's Institute. Oconomowoc, Wisconsin, March 19, 1902. In Ellen Porelle, ed. *The Political Philosophy of Robert M. LaFollette.* Madison, WI: Robert M. LaFollette Co., 1920.

Laumann, Edward O., Paul M. Siegel and Robert N. Hodge. *The Logic of Social Hierarchies.* Chicago: Markham, 1970.

Lessinger, Leon. *Every Kid a Winner: Accountability in Education.* New York: Simon & Schuster, 1970.

Levin, Henry, ed. *Community Control of Schools.* New York: Simon & Schuster, 1970.

Levine, Andrew. *Liberal Democracy.* New York: Columbia University Press, 1981.

Licklider, J. C. R. "Computers and Government." In Michael L. Dertouzos and Joel Moses, eds. *The Computer Age: A Twenty-Year View.* Cambridge: MIT Press, 1980.

Long, Franklin A. and Alexandra Oleson. *Appropriate Technology and Social Values – A Critical Appraisal.* Cambridge, MA: Ballinger, 1980.

Lowi, Theodore J. *The End of Liberalism.* New York: W. W. Norton, 1969.

Lukacs, John. *Outgrowing Democracy: The History of the United States in the Twentieth Century.* New York: Doubleday, 1984.

MacLeod, Roy M. *Technology and the Human Prospect.* London: Frances Pinter, 1986.

Macpherson, C. B. *The Life and Times of Liberal Democracy.* New York: Oxford University Press, 1977.

Magleby, David B. *Direct Legislation: Voting on Ballot Propositions in the United States.* Baltimore: Johns Hopkins University Press, 1984.

Malbin, Michael. "Teledemocracy and Its Discontents." *Public Opinion,* June–July 1982.

Mandelker, Daniel J. "Municipal Incorporation on the Urban Fringe: Procedure for Determination and Review." 18 *Louisiana Law Review* 628, 1958.

Mansbridge, Jane J. *Beyond Adversary*

Democracy. New York: Basic Books, 1980.

Margolis, Michael. *Viable Democracy.* New York: St. Martins, 1979.

McClaughry, John. "A Community Based Welfare System." *Congressional Record,* May 9, 1973 (S 8720).

_____. "A Model State Land Trust Act." 12 *Harvard Journal on Legislation* 563, 1975.

_____. "Farmers, Freedom and Federalism: How to Avoid the Coming Serfdom." 21 *South Dakota Law Review* 486, 1976.

_____. "Populism for the '80s Gaining Momentum," *Human Events,* April 16, 1983.

_____. "Where is the Mob? I am Its Leader." *Vital Speeches,* November 1, 1981.

_____. "Who Says Vouchers Wouldn't Work?" *Reason,* January 1984.

McRobie, George. *Small is Possible.* New York: Harper & Row, 1981.

Mead, Lawrence M. *Beyond Entitlement: The Social Obligations of Citizenship.* New York: Free Press, 1986.

Merriam, Charles E. *The Making of Citizens.* Chicago: University of Chicago Press, 1931.

Michelman, Frank and Terence Sandalow. *Government in Urban Areas.* St. Paul: West, 1970.

Miles, Rufus E. Jr. "Miles' Six Other Maxims of Management." *Organizational Dynamics,* Summer 1979.

Miller, Arthur R. *The Assault on Privacy: Computers, Data Banks and Dossiers.* Ann Arbor: University of Michigan Press, 1971.

Morgan, Arthur. *The Small Community: Foundation of Democratic Life.* Yellow Springs, OH: Community Service, 1942.

Morgan, Philip. "The Problems of Rural New England." *The Atlantic Monthly,* May 1897.

Morris, David and Karl Hess. *Neighborhood Power: The New Localism.* Boston: Beacon Press, 1975.

Moynihan, Daniel. *Maximum Feasible Misunderstanding.* New York: Free Press, 1969.

Murray, Charles. *In Pursuit of Happiness and Good Government.* New York: Simon & Schuster, 1988.

_____. *Losing Ground: American Social Policy, 1950-80.* New York: Basic Books, 1984.

Naisbitt, John. *Megatrends.* New York: Warner Books, 1982.

National League of Cities. "Adjusting Municipal Boundaries: Law and Practice." Washington: NLC, 1966.

Nisbet, Robert A. *The Quest for Community.* New York: Oxford University Press, 1971.

_____. *Twilight of Authority.* New York: Oxford University Press, 1975.

Nock, Albert J. *Our Enemy the State.* New York: William Morrow, 1935.

Norman, Colin. *The God That Limps.* New York: W. W. Norton, 1981.

"1,000 Local State Departments?" *New Options,* December 23, 1985.

Ophuls, William. *Ecology and the Politics of Scarcity.* San Francisco: W. H. Freeman, 1977.

Pascarella, Perry. *Technology: Fire in a Dark World.* New York: Van Nostrand Reinhold, 1979.

Pateman, Carole. *Participation and Democratic Theory.* London: Cambridge University Press, 1970.

Peters, Thomas J. and Robert H. Waterman, Jr. *In Search of Excellence.* New York: Harper & Row, 1982.

Pitkin, Hanna Fenichel. *The Concept of Representation.* Berkeley: University of California Press, 1967.

_____ and Sara M. Shumer. "On Participation." *Democracy,* Fall 1982.

Piven, Frances Fox and Richard A. Cloward. *Regulating the Poor.* New York: Vintage Books, 1971.

Pocock, J. G. A. "Machiavelli, Harrington, and English Political Ideologies in the Eighteenth Century." *William & Mary Quarterly,* October 1965.

_____. *The Machiavellian Moment.* Princeton: Princeton University Press, 1975.

_____, ed. *The Political Works of James Harrington.* London: Cambridge University Press, 1977.

Popper, Frank J. *The Politics of Land Use Reform.* Madison: University of Wisconsin Press, 1981.

Pranger, Robert J. "The Decline of the American National Government." *Publius,* Fall 1973.

_____. *The Eclipse of Citizenship.*

New York: Holt, Rinehart & Winston, 1968.

Proudhon, P. J. *The Principle of Federation.* Toronto: University of Toronto Press, 1979.

Prude, Jonathan. *The Coming of Industrial Order: Town and Factory Life in Rural Massachusetts.* New York: Cambridge University Press, 1983.

Quinn, Patrick F. "Agrarianism and the Jeffersonian Philosophy." 2 *Review of Politics* 87, 1940.

Reagan, Ronald. Speech to Executive Club of Chicago. September 26, 1975.

Ropke, Wilhelm. *A Humane Economy.* Chicago: Henry Regnery, 1960.

Rosenfeld, Stuart. "Centralization Versus Decentralization: A Case Study of Rural Education in Vermont." In Jonathan P. Sher, ed. *Education in Rural America: A Reassessment of Conventional Wisdom.* Boulder: Westview, 1977.

Rossiter, Clinton. *The American Presidency.* Rev. ed. New York: Harcourt, Brace, Jovanovich, 1960.

Sale, Kirkpatrick. *Dwellers in the Land: The Bioregional Union.* San Francisco: Sierra Club Books, 1985.

_____. *Human Scale.* New York: Coward, McCann & Geoghegan, 1980.

Schmidt, David and Martin Peretz. Exchange of letters in *New Options,* October 1986.

Schumacher, E. F. *Small Is Beautiful.* New York: Harper & Row, 1973.

Scott, William B. *In Pursuit of Happiness: American Conceptions of Property.* Bloomington: Indiana University Press, 1977.

Segalman, Ralph. *The Swiss Way of Welfare: Lessons for the Western World.* New York: Praeger, 1986.

Segalman, Ralph. "Welfare and Dependency in Switzerland." *The Public Interest,* Winter 1986.

Sennett, Richard. *The Fall of Public Man.* New York: Knopf, 1977.

Sher, Jonathan P. *Education in Rural America: A Reassessment of Conventional Wisdom.* Boulder: Westview, 1977.

_____ and Rachael B. Tompkins. *Heavy Meddle.* Raleigh: North Carolina School Board Association, 1986.

Sizer, Theodore. *Horace's Compromise: The Dilemma of the American High School.* Boston: Houghton Mifflin, 1984.

Smith, Joshua Toulmin. *Local Self-Government.* London: J. Chapman, 1851.

_____. *The Parish.* London: H. Sweet, 1851.

Smith, Page. *A City Upon a Hill: The Town in American History.* New York: Knopf, 1966.

Stavrianos, L. S. *The Promise of the Coming Dark Age.* San Francisco: W. H. Freeman, 1976.

Stephens, G. Ross. "State Centralism and the Erosion of Local Autonomy." *Journal of Politics,* February 1974.

Suttler, Gerald D. and David Street. "Aid to the Poor and Social Exchange." *Working Paper No. 110.* Chicago: Center for Organization Studies, University of Chicago, 1969.

Thayer, Frederick C. *An End to Hierarchy and Competition.* New York: New Viewpoints, 1973.

Thompson, William Irwin. *Darkness and Scattered Light: Speculation on the Future.* New York: Doubleday, 1978.

Tomasic, Roman and Malcolm M. Feeley. *Neighborhood Justice.* New York: Longman, 1982.

Van Alstyne, Arvo. "Taking or Damaging by the Police Power: The Search of Inverse Condemnation Criteria." 44 *Southern California Law Review* 1, 1970.

Van der Ryn, Sim and Peter Calthorpe. *Sustainable Communities: A New Design Synthesis for Cities, Suburbs and Towns.* San Francisco: Sierra Club Books, 1986.

White, E. B. "Editorial." *The New Yorker,* July 3, 1944. Reprinted in E.B. White, *The Wild Flag.* Boston: Houghton Mifflin, 1946.

Whyte, William F. and Damon Boynton, eds. *Higher Yielding Human Systems for Agriculture.* Ithaca: Cornell University Press, 1983.

Winner, Langdon. *Autonomous Technology.* Cambridge: MIT Press, 1977.

_____. *The Whale and the Reactor.* Chicago: University of Chicago Press, 1986.

Winters, Richard. "Political Choice and Expenditure Changes in New Hampshire and Vermont." *Polity,* Summer 1980.

Yates, Douglas. *Neighborhood Democracy.* Lexington, MA: D. C. Heath, 1973.

Zimmerman, Joseph F. "Local Discretionary Authority in New England." *Suffolk University Law Review,* December 1981.

Zuckerman, Michael. *Peaceable Kingdoms.* New York: Random House, 1970.

VERMONT REFERENCES

Aiken, George D. *Speaking from Vermont.* New York: Frederick A. Stokes, 1938.

Allen, Ira. *The Natural and Political History of the State of Vermont.* London: J. W. Myers, 1798.

Barron, Hal S. *Those Who Stayed Behind.* New York: Cambridge University Press, 1984.

Benedict, R. D. "Ethan Allen's Use of Language." Address to the Vermont Historical Society, October 30, 1902.

Bookchin, Murray. "Can Democracy Survive in Vermont?" *Vermont Affairs,* Winter 1988.

Bryan, Frank. "Hill Farm with Computer." *North By Northeast,* June 1988.

_____. "Pivot Point for Democracy." *Window of Vermont,* February 1987.

_____. "The Lonely Villagers: Vermont in the Post Modern World." *Vermont,* Fall 1982.

_____. "Town Meeting at Wounded Knee." *Window of Vermont,* Fall 1985.

_____. *Yankee Politics in Rural Vermont.* Hanover, NH: University Press of New England, 1974.

_____ and Clark Bensen. "The 1986 Election in Vermont." *Vermont History,* Fall 1988.

Bush, G. G. *History of Education in Vermont.* Washington: U.S. Goverment Printing Office, 1900.

"Can We Manage Growth?" Symposium. *Vermont Affairs,* Summer–Fall, 1988.

Carlson, Richard. "Vermont's Heritage of Independence." In Peter S. Jennison, ed. *The 1976-77 Official Vermont Bicentennial Guide.* Taftsville, VT: The Countryman Press, 1976.

"Community Care." Brochure. Rochester, VT: Community Care, 1987.

Crockett, Walter. *History of Vermont.* New York: Century History Co., 1921.

D'Agostino, Lorenzo. *The History of Public Welfare in Vermont.* Washington: Catholic University of America Press, 1948.

Doyle, William. *The Vermont Political Tradition.* Montpelier: William Doyle, 1984.

Fisher, Dorothy Canfield. *Vermont Tradition.* Boston: Little Brown, 1953.

Graffagnino, J. Kevin. *Vermont in the Victorian Age: Continuity and Change in the Green Mountain State 1850-1900.* Bennington, VT: Heritage Press and The Shelburne Museum, 1985.

Hamlet, Penny Elizabeth. "Pre-Progressive Farm Activism in Vermont." Master's thesis, University of Vermont, 1982.

Hand, Sam, Jeffrey D. Marshall, and D. Gregory Sanford. " 'Little Republics' The Structure of State Politics in Vermont, 1854-1920." *Vermont History,* Summer 1985.

Hill, Ralph Nading. *Contrary Country.* New York: Rinehart, 1950.

_____. *Yankee Kingdom: Vermont and New Hampshire.* New York: Harper & Row, 1960.

Holbrook, Stewart H. *The Yankee Exodus: An Account of Migration from New England.* New York: Macmillan, 1950.

Jellison, Charles A. *Ethan Allen: Frontier Rebel.* Syracuse: Syracuse University Press, 1969.

Judd, Richard M. *The New Deal in Vermont: Its Impact and Aftermath.* New York: Garland, 1979.

Kunstler, James Howard. "Vermont." *New York Times Magazine,* April 10, 1988.

Ludlum, David M. *Social Ferment in Vermont 1791-1850.* New York: Columbia University Press, 1939.

Mathis, William J. "Uncontrolled Reform: The Strip Development of Vermont Education." *Vermont Affairs,* August 1988.

McClaughry, John. *Educational Choice in Vermont.* Concord, VT: Institute for Liberty and Community, 1987.

_____. "The New Feudalism." 5 *Environmental Law* 675, 1975.

Meeks, Harold A. *Time and Change in Vermont: A Human Geography.* Chester, CT: Globe Pequot Press, 1986.

Morrissey, Charles T. *Vermont: A History.* New York: W. W. Norton, 1981.

Mosher, Howard Frank. *Where the Rivers Flow North.* New York: Viking, 1971.

Muller, H. Nicholas, III. *From Ferment to*

Fatigue? 1870-1900: A New Look at the Neglected Winter of Vermont. Occasional Paper No. 7. Burlington: The Center for Research on Vermont, 1984.

_____ and John Duffy. *An Anxious Democracy: Aspects of the 1830's.* Westport, CT: Greenwood Press, 1982.

_____ and Samuel B. Hand. *In a State of Nature: Readings on Vermont History.* Montpelier: Vermont Historical Society, 1982.

Nagel, Donald P. "Half-Threats, Half-Promises." *North By Northeast.* June 1988.

Nuquist, Andrew. *Town Government in Vermont.* Burlington: University of Vermont, 1964.

Pike, Robert E. *Tall Trees, Tough Men.* New York: W. W. Norton, 1967.

Potash, P. Jeffrey, ed. *Health Care in Vermont: Then and Now.* Occasional Paper No. 20, Vermont Academy of Arts and Sciences, 1985.

Schmidt, Fred. "Vermont Trends and New Directions: Who Are We Becoming?" Address given at the Windham Foundation, Grafton, VT, July 19, 1987.

Smallwood, Frank. *Free and Independent.* Brattleboro, VT: Stephen Greene Press, 1976.

Stillwell, Lewis D. *Migration from Vermont.* Montpelier: Vermont Historical Society, 1948.

Stone, Mason S. *History of Education, State of Vermont.* Montpelier: Capital City Press, 1934.

Tarlov, Richard. *The Vermont Food System: Toward Regional Self-Reliance.* Emmaus, PA: Rodale Press, 1984.

Two Hundred Vermonters. *Rural Vermont: A Program for the Future.* Burlington: The Vermont Commission on Country Life, 1931.

Van de Water, Frederick F. *The Reluctant Republic.* Taftsville, VT: The Countryman Press, 1974.

Vermont Legislative Council. *Social Welfare Problems in Vermont.* Montpelier: VLC, 1966.

Wilson, Harold Fisher. *The Hill Country of Northern New England.* New York: AMS Press, 1967.

INDEX

Canada, 30, 32, 34, 114, 159, 165, 168, 238, 262-63
cantons, Swiss, 87, 126, 210-11
Carlson, Richard, 13
Carnegie Foundation for the Advancement of Teaching, 179
Carpenter, Josiah, 12
Carter, Harvey, 230
Champlain, Lake, 31, 113, 116, 119, 241, 246, 263, 270
Chandler Music Hall, 288
Charlotte, town of, 115, 121
checks and balances, 101
Chelsea, town of, 39, 66, 121
Chittenden, Thomas, 30
Chômeurs Createurs, 218
Church of the Brethren, 112
civic humanism, 20-26
Civil War, 36
classical republicanism, 20
Clinton, Sir Henry, 261
Colchester, town of, 115, 121
Cole, Charlie, 276
College of the Ozarks, 196
Commission on Vermont's Future, 230
community
    axiom, 46
    education, 196
    human-scale, 23, 64-66
    mediation centers, 112
Community Improvement Corporation, 214-15
Community Self-Reliance Center, 132
compensated regulation, 236
Concord, town of, 121, 127, 190
Congregationalism, 30
Connecticut, 19
Connecticut River Basin Commission, 263
Consensor, 75
conservatives, 6, 94
constables, 112
Constitution
    Canadian, 165
    Montana, 286
    Vermont, 21-24, 28-29, 102-3, 118-20, 137-38, 175, 223, 284-88
Constitutional Revision, Office of, 287-88
Continental Congress, 29, 261
Coolidge, Calvin, 136
Cooperative Fund of New England, 252
Corinth, town of, 121, 122
Cornell, Nancy, 283
court
    district, 109-11
    magistrate, 111-12

probate, 109, 111
shire, 110, 112, 234
shire family, 110-11
state supreme, 109-10, 112, 137, 139, 141, 234
superior, 109-11
U.S. Supreme, 150
Craftsbury, town of, 66, 121, 197, 229
creationist curriculum, 97
Crockett, Walter, 13

D
Dahl, Robert, 88, 89
dairy
    cooperatives, 249-51
    farming, 37-39, 68-69, 240, 240-46
    price support program, 243-44
Danby, town of, 14, 121, 130
Danish folk school, 196
Danville, town of, 121, 190, 195
Davenport, Thomas, 33-34
Davis, Deane, 182, 225
Dayton Mutual Exchange, Ohio, 217
de Tocqueville, Alexis, 274
decentralism, 67, 84-86
delegated powers, 103, 137-39
democracy
    direct, 82, 83-84, 89
    representative, 82, 83-84, 88, 148, 151-52
Democracy Day, 107
Deseret Industries, 213
development rights, 237, 257-59
Dewey, John, 62, 175
Dorrelites, 35
Dorset, town of, 86, 121
Douglas, Stephen, 35
Dover, town of, 121, 225
Dummerston, town of, 117, 121
Dunn, Faith, 174-75

E
East Hill School, 195, 196
Easton, John, 269
education, 54, 58-60, 97-98, 156, 174-201
    kindergarten, 58-60, 177-78
    minimum school standards, 180
Education, Board of, 142-43, 147, 184-86
Education, Department of, 142, 169, 179, 183-86, 191-93, 282
Education with Production, 196-97
EHV Weidmann, 69, 263
Ellickson, Robert, 236
Embargo Act of 1807, 262
emigration, 40
Employment and Training, Department of, 205

302

The Vermont Papers
was designed by The Laughing Bear Associates in Montpelier, Vermont.
It was typeset in Berkley Medium by Accura Type & Design in Barre, Vermont,
and printed on Rivertone, an acid-free paper, by The Book Press, Inc., in Brattleboro, Vermont.
Part opening illustrations are by Ed Epstein.